SELECTED
DIALOGUES OF
PLATO

SELECTED
DIALOGUES OF
PLATO

The Benjamin Jowett Translation

REVISED AND WITH AN INTRODUCTION BY

HAYDEN PELLICCIA

THE MODERN LIBRARY

NEW YORK

2001 Modern Library Paperback Edition

Copyright © 2000 by Hayden Pelliccia

This work was originally published in 2000 by Modern Library,
a division of Random House, Inc.

LIBRARY OF CONGRESS CATALOGING-IN-PUBLICATION DATA
Plato.
[Dialogues. English. Selections]
Selected dialogues of Plato: the Benjamin Jowett translation/revised
and with an introduction by Hayden Pelliccia.
p. cm.
ISBN 978-0-375-75840-9
1. Philosophy. I. Jowett, Benjamin, 1817–1893. II. Pelliccia, Hayden.
III. Title.
B358.J82   2000
184—dc21   00-30552

Modern Library website address: www.modernlibrary.com

Printed in the United States of America

PLATO

Plato was born in Athens c. 429 B.C. His father and mother, Ariston and Perictione, were both members of notably illustrious and aristocratic families. His stepfather, Pyrilampes, was an associate of the great democratic statesman Pericles (c. 495–429). His cousins Critias and Charmides, on the other hand, were heavily involved in antidemocratic activities, and both participated in the violent, unscrupulous, and thankfully short-lived oligarchical regime ("The Thirty") that came into power after Athens' final defeat by Sparta in the Peloponnesian War (431–404). The conflicts that wracked Athenian society during this entire period were thus embodied in Plato's own family life, a circumstance that undoubtedly contributed to his fascinated disillusionment with politics and political systems.

As a young man Plato became a follower of the philosopher Socrates. After the latter was put to death by the Athenian state for the crime of impiety (399 B.C.), Plato withdrew from Athens for a time, and from any form of civic career forever. Upon his return to Athens he established, in a grove outside the city walls, a philosophical school that took its name from that of the grove in which it was located, the Academy. Plato's teaching here, about which we know little, was combined with prolific writing, about which we know a great deal: his written works have formed the foundation of Western philosophy for the twenty-odd centuries since their composition.

Plato's teaching must have been similarly compelling: among the pupils who came from all over the Greek world to study at the Academy was Aristotle (384–322 B.C.), the only philosopher who can claim to have exerted an influence upon subsequent thought comparable to that of his master's.

Plato died in Athens in 347 B.C.

INTRODUCTION

Hayden Pelliccia

Having the task behind me, I can propose with some seriousness what I did not begin to guess when it still lay ahead of me: namely, that revising someone else's translations of works of Plato is not much less demanding than translating them afresh. That raises the question, Why stick with Jowett's old versions at all—why not simply produce new ones? I have consulted many of the translations produced since Jowett's, many of them up to date in every possible sense, and Jowett's, in my judgment, remain superior, in the most important respects, to them all. Jowett has a better command not just of English prose style, but of English prose styles, and that gives him a great advantage in rendering the language of a master of variation like Plato. In a work like the *Symposium,* to take a notable example, Plato puts on display his version of the idiosyncratic speaking styles of a group containing two dramatists of genius, plus a less original third who was ranked in antiquity as the greatest tragic poet after Aeschylus, Sophocles, and Euripides; of the remaining four speakers, one, the drunken Alcibiades, was reckoned by his contemporaries to be the most all-around brilliant member of his generation. (The longest speech is by Socrates, on whom see below.)

Jowett's successors, especially the more recent ones, are hampered by the contemporary abhorrence of any style other than the spontaneously informal and colloquial (which is not the same thing as the plain style)—though Jowett may sometimes have erred too much in the other directions. Modern tastes seem to coerce modern translators into adopting one or the other of two approaches only: the uniformly casual and colloquial, or the uniformly, and dryly, literal—neither approach likely to produce a particularly happy version of Plato's more literary works, which are those preeminently on display in this edition. Jowett, in comparison, had much greater freedom than we do—when Plato's speakers soar, Jowett often succeeds remarkably well in soaring with them—and we can follow along without too much embarrassment: after all, we expect such flights in nineteenth-century writers. Furthermore, I suspect that there are many besides me who actually prefer to think and find that the speech of such personages as Plato depicts might be more stylish, subtler, richer, and more accomplished than what we are used to hearing from our own friends and selves.

The revisions I have attempted are of two kinds: first, I have incorporated scholarly advances made in the establishment and interpretation of the Greek text since Jowett's time, in which category I include changes imposed where I disagree with Jowett's interpretation or think he made a mistake (sometimes Jowett changed the order of sentences, for example; I have tended to restore the order of the original). Second, I have removed archaisms or affectations of or in Jowett's English—those that strike me as likely to strike my contemporaries as ridiculous or, at best, off-puttingly quaint. For example, I change Jowett's "the tale of love was on this wise" to "the tale of love was like this." "What say you to going?" becomes "What do you say to going?" "Please to see to this" becomes "Please see to this." Adjustments of this basic tendency have been made widely and deeply. For example, the opening sentence of the *Symposium* is rendered by Jowett "Concerning the things about which you ask to be informed I believe that I am not ill-prepared with an answer"—which manages to be both stilted and a little arch in the high Victorian Oxford manner. The Greek, on the other hand, is somewhat informal and quite intimate; we are clearly overhearing a conversation that is already in progress, and is conducted among friends; the speaker, Apollodorus, uses an idiom that, while not quite diffident, is urbanely removed from the self-assertive: "Actually, it turns out that I am quite well up on the matter you are asking about." That is a fairly radical departure from Jowett's text. It must be emphasized, however, that I have not found the need for such significant tampering to be spread evenly through the works translated here: some passages have been subjected to extensive adjustment, others have been barely touched.

At this point, a word about sex would be appropriate, or at least about sex as it connects in a translator's mind to questions of language and style. Many of the changes I have made in revising Jowett comply with changes in taste that have occurred between Jowett's time and our own, and the public discussion of sex is a matter about which tastes have changed rather dramatically. Since readers can be assumed to have an interest in this subject, it seems worth getting it out in the open.

Contemporary readers may automatically assume that since Jowett was a Victorian, his translation of ancient Greek works largely devoted, as, for example, the *Phaedrus* and the *Symposium* are, to the joys (or at least the theoretical joys) of male homosexual love must be full of puritanical euphemisms and bowdlerizations of the frank and uninhibited original texts. Jowett is in fact not so prudish, and, more important, the originals do not even approach the lewd. When a speaker is referring unambiguously to physical sex acts—for example, a young boy's complying with the sexual initiatives of an older male suitor—Jowett says things like "the boy grants his lover this favour," which may strike us as coy. The fact of the matter is, however, that "grant a favor" is not a bad literal translation of the most characteristic Greek verb used in such contexts, *charizesthai* (cognate with the word from which our "charity" derives). Jowett's version, as it turns out, is misleading, but not because of any lack of literal accuracy—his infidelity to the original is rather a result of situating his literal rendition into an alien cultural context: in Greek, the association of *charizesthai* with sexual compliance is so common and consistent that the word is completely clear and hence completely uneuphemistic; in the cultures of both Victorian and present-day English, to refer to sexual submission as "granting a favor" is coy. In such instances as this I have nudged the renderings in the direction of a greater frankness, without, I hope, descending into the inaccurately vulgar. I have, for example, permitted *paederastia* to emerge as either "pederasty" or "boy-love" instead of "the love of youths," which is too sanitized. The essential fact guiding my efforts is that those people in Plato who speak of such matters are not as a rule leering, or coy, or indecent, but consistently urbane and, in many instances, amusedly detached.

The translation of passages that treat sexual matters invites discussion of the sexual matters themselves. Many readers of the *Symposium* and the *Phaedrus* in particular may be taken aback by some of the assumptions revealed in the characters' talk. Such readers might guess that the persons there depicted by Plato constituted an isolated, specifically homosexual group, or might generalize to the conclusion that pederasty was a much more open and widespread practice in Classical Greece than in the Western world of today. Both conclusions would be largely wrong, though each contains an element of truth. The evidence certainly does suggest that the average Greek male of the Classical period would be comparatively unsurprised and unimpressed if he detected bisexual impulses in his male acquaintance or even in himself (there are very few mentions of female homosexuality in the early periods—Aristophanes' speech in the *Symposium* contains one of the first—while references to male homosexuality, especially with insulting intent in the writings of comic poets such as, again, Aristophanes, are innumerable). On the other hand, however common it might have been thought to be, the homosexual impulse certainly does not seem to have been accorded blanket approval or admiration by the preponderance of Athenian citizens (to confine ourselves to the best documented community): for example, we often see the imputation of such impulses or activities deployed as a way of ridiculing or insulting a person. In sum, it seems about right to say that the culture of the period, if it did not *accept* homosexuality to quite the warmhearted degree that some modern advocates have hoped, it nonetheless did *expect* homosexual impulses and acts to exist and occur more routinely than present-day Western cultures have tended to. (Some of the characters in the *Symposium* and *Phaedrus* appear, in the aggregate, to go even further, and to exhibit an even greater receptivity, to the point of avidity in several cases.)

———

The five works assembled here have been chosen to serve as an introduction to Plato, and in particular to the more literary side of his genius. The volume also forms a good introduction to Plato's representation of his teacher Socrates, the figure who takes the dominant role in the majority of Plato's works.

Socrates was born in Athens in 469 B.C. and lived there until 399, when he was put to death by the Athenian state for the crime of impiety. He wrote nothing, but was so devoted to philosophical conversation that he neglected all other pursuits in its favor, eventually reducing his family to poverty as a result. He is quite rightly regarded as one of the chief founders of the Western philosophical tradition, and in antiquity the philosophical schools of Platonism, Cynicism, and Stoicism, among others, proclaimed their descent from him. Almost everything we know of him derives from the depictions of Plato, the historian and essayist Xenophon, and the comic poet Aristophanes, all fellow Athenians.

This evidence (especially that of Plato) indicates that Socrates was the originator of a distinctive method of philosophical inquiry: the *elenchus*, which can be characterized as a form of cross-examination aimed at revealing inconsistency of argumentation. Socrates persistently denies possessing any positive knowledge himself, except for the knowledge that he is ignorant, and his relentless application of the *elenchus* most often serves the entirely negative purpose of demonstrating the ignorance and errors of others—people who *do* claim to possess positive knowledge. Of course, such relentless and, it can be added in Socrates' case, utterly fearless questioning is likely to act as an irritant upon those vested interests that are often its most gratifying victims.

Socrates seems to have regarded himself as a pious man. In the *Apology* he represents his life of ceaseless interrogation as a mission on behalf of the god Apollo, and the one primary question underlying all of his inquiries is the ethical one, *What is the proper manner of our living?* Nonetheless, it is easy to understand how his determined skepticism toward all supposed wisdom, both traditional and newfangled, could be taken to imply also religious skepticism, and, even, as his prosecutors claimed, outright atheism. For the ancient Greeks did not isolate religion into one central institution, but rather assumed and felt the presence of a religious dimension in every activity and phenomenon. Thus they had, for example, no canon of sacred or scriptural texts that embodied the word of god, but rather conceived of all poetry as deriving from the communications of divine beings (the Muses) to poets. Was poetry then sacred, or profane? Both, and neither. It was, like almost everything else, a mixture of divine and nondivine, in proportions usually concealed to the perception of mere humans. Caution and respect were therefore always called for, and that was a great part of piety.

Impiety, on the other hand, was a public crime, because the provocations of a single person could bring divine wrath down upon his entire community (a principle well illustrated in the opening of the *Oedipus Rex* of Sophocles, Socrates' older contemporary). It was on this basis that Socrates was successfully prosecuted, as represented in the

Apology. In that work, which purports to record the speeches he made at his trial, Socrates defends himself by the perhaps risky, but to us informative, tack of explaining the history of his philosophical mission, that unending examination of his fellow citizens by means of the *elenchus,* his characteristic and, it would appear, purely destructive mode of inquiry.

My use of the word "purports" in the last sentence brings us to a central question, one that every reader of Plato must give some thought to: What is the relationship of the Socrates represented in Plato's writings to the historical Socrates, the flesh-and-blood man who died at age seventy in 399, when Plato, who lived to 347, was perhaps thirty? No wholly satisfactory answer is available. We can feel some confidence, however, that Plato, who in the *Apology* represents himself as having been present in support of Socrates at the latter's trial, was profoundly affected and disillusioned by the decision of his fellow citizens to put him to death—to take the life of a man whom Plato elsewhere characterized as "the most intelligent and most just of the people of his time."[1] We might accordingly conjecture that Plato's decision to represent the conversation of this admired friend was initially motivated by a desire to commemorate and do honor to him, and even to rectify the wrong done by his condemnation.

In several of Plato's works, Socrates' inquiries are purely negative: some other person advances a claim, and Socrates subjects it to rigorous testing; the ultimate outcome is either completely negative (the claim, in whatever form it is cast, is shown to be self-contradictory) or at best inconclusive (the claim leads to paradox, for example,

[1] *Phaedo* 118.

which is to say that it conflicts with some other claim). Since this procedure conforms to what is believed to be known of the historical Socrates' method, scholars have concluded that these negative or inconclusive works represent Plato's most faithful renditions of the historical Socrates, and probably belong to the earliest stage of his writing career.

The greater number of Plato's works, however, present large amounts of positive doctrine—systematic theories on an astonishingly wide range of subjects. And still the favorite lead character is Socrates, in whose mouth these doctrines are typically placed. It follows from the earlier premise—that the historical Socrates professed ignorance and propounded no positive doctrine—that the representation of Socrates in these other works significantly departs from what we know as the actual figure. Thus, within Plato's works themselves, we find on the one side an approximately historical Socrates whose characteristic mode of inquiry is the rapid-fire sequence of briefly answered questions, leading inexorably to the exposure of fallacy in his conversation-partner's position. On the other side, a rather different Socrates is able to tease out of his negative inquiries positive conclusions, sometimes expounded in speeches of impressive eloquence and length. This speechifying Socrates, then, is often regarded as an unhistorical version, contrived by Plato to be the spokesman for his own ideas.

We might wonder why, when Plato decided that he no longer wanted to do philosophy in the Socratic manner, he didn't drop the character of Socrates altogether (as he eventually did in some of his last works), instead of putting in his mouth doctrines that the real Socrates undoubtedly had never heard of, much less propounded. In fact, Plato does not rigorously uphold the divide between the two Socrateses delineated above. Many of his works give us both the cross-examining and the speech-making Socrates—the negative and the positive—side by side. And the reason for this is that Plato could never bring himself to abandon completely the essence of Socrates' approach. This essence can be summed up in the word "dialectic."

Plato's writings are traditionally called "dialogues": they report or directly represent conversations (that is, dialogues) between two or more persons (sometimes with an audience of mostly nonspeaking figures in the background). The use of this conversational form would have been dictated initially by the choice of Socrates as philosophical model, since conversation was the means by which Socrates engaged in philosophy. We might reflect that, given his initial assumptions, Socrates really had no choice about how to engage in philosophy: he knew that he knew nothing; knowledge, if it could be acquired at all, would have to come from without; his mission was an effort to discover knowledge in someone professing to possess it.

Plato agreed with his master that the most satisfactory way to examine claims to knowledge was through the give-and-take of conversation, to which process as a whole the name "dialectic" was given (from the same stem as "dialogue"). The ground rules for dialectic are spelled out at length in the *Protagoras* (included in this volume): one partner asks questions, the other answers; the latter is the defender of the given proposition, the former the cross-examining attorney, the agent of the *elenchus.* Unlike a courtroom cross-examination, however, dialectic requires that both partners give sincere assent to every step along the way; for, otherwise, where truth, not victory, is the goal, what is the point? So both partners must be willing to accept at any given moment that they are wrong, to find that their positions have reversed, or simply that they are left with no tenable position at all. What counts is the underlying loyalty and devotion to the quest for truth; this quest constitutes the closest approximation to truth or knowledge that we can hope for.

This cooperative inquiry, dialectic, then, is the ideal vehicle for philosophical inquiry. The writing of books, to take a relevant example, is necessarily inferior, for both sides of the discussion; since books cannot hear and respond to questions, the reader is cheated and the author is too: no matter how intensely you query a written text, it just keeps saying the same thing over and over again. Or so says Socrates in the *Phaedrus*—a book.

That point brings us to the paradox at the heart of Plato's project as a writer: he attempts to capture the living spirit of dialectic in a fixed text. Why did he depart from his master on this all-important point—why did he come to think that philosophy could be written? Or, perhaps more accurately, "sort of" written: for what he writes comes across as a transcript of the spoken, of the living dialectic. Still, the paradox remains, which may be the point: the effect is to force us to accept what is set down in the text, including the positive doctrines of the speechifying Socrates, as only provisional: the cross-examination can always start over again, the premises can always be reattacked. But written down it is, for us to read, and perhaps to try to glimpse through the spirit of the Socratic inquiry and Socrates himself. In almost all of Plato's works, Socrates is always there, in the marketplace, heading off to the Lyceum, returning to Athens from Peiraeus, always ready to rejoin the debate, to reopen the discussion, to drop all the old assumptions and to start again from scratch, to tire the sun with talk, and, as in the *Symposium*, the moon as well; and then, as the others stagger off to bed, to head back to his haunts and start, with the new day, yet again. It is not surprising that, through the fifty years he survived his master, Plato found it difficult to expel this inspiring and reproachful figure from his thinking, no matter how far it extended beyond the limits this extraordinary mentor had set down.

———

The dialogues presented in this volume give a good sample of the modes of philosophical inquiry as Plato explored and experimented with them. The *Ion* displays the *elenchus* in all its destructive, if amusing, force; the work's conclusions are completely negative, even derisive. The *Protagoras*, a much longer and more important work, is compounded of a mixture of set-speeches and dialectic. The *Phaedrus* is an inquiry into the nature of speech-making, and writing, that initially proceeds by the presentation of three independent speeches of increasing length; it then turns conversational, with some real excursions into dialectic. The *Symposium* comprises a sequence of seven speeches delivered over the course of a dinner party; Socrates manages to work a small bout of question-and-answer into it, but all in all, dialectic is kept to a bare minimum. Finally, the *Apology* reports Socrates' defense speech at his trial (with two briefer speeches forming a pendant); Socrates briefly cross-examines his prosecutor Meletus, but the sincerity requirement for true dialectic seems to be lacking on at least one side, and so the episode serves to remind us forcefully of the great gap between philosophical and courtroom cross-examination. It is in the *Apology* that Socrates gives an account of his lifelong mission of cross-examination, which brings us back to the method of the *Ion*.

The dialogue form is inherently dramatic. The works included here are perhaps the most entertaining dramas Plato ever wrote. They are often extremely funny, a quality not closely associated with philosophy in most people's minds. Socrates is of course famous for his irony, but perhaps not so well known is his exuberant, if often malicious and rhetorically devastating, sense of humor. He can be appallingly rude, as the *Protagoras* vividly shows.

More important, the works are united by their subject matter in ways that may be surprising for those unfamiliar with Platonic thought. Education—love and sex—poetry—What is the nature of virtue and can it be taught?—Is a true rhetoric possible?—What is the examined life?—these may not seem at first to be an organic grouping of topics. But if one can accept that virtue is knowledge, and that knowledge is approached through philosophical inquiry (dialectic), and if it is also true that the yearning for beauty (i.e., for love and sex) is in fact a yearning for knowledge, and if poetry and rhetoric are false but alluring paths to the same, then the coherence may begin to emerge.

In the first work, Socrates converses with Ion, a highly successful rhapsode, or performer of epic poetry, who insists that he is a supreme authority on Homer. This claim may sound fairly harmless to us, but it strikes to the heart of the contemporary Athenian debate over education. The Homeric poems were traditionally regarded by the Greeks as the most authoritative repository of knowledge and wisdom, in somewhat the same way that the Bible has been regarded in later traditions. As such, Homer formed the centerpiece of traditional Greek education. Plato, for one, was intensely dissatisfied with this state of affairs, and this brief dialogue as a whole puts into dramatic form a paradox stated directly elsewhere, in one of Xenophon's Socratic works: If knowledge of Homer is a sound basis for wisdom, then why are rhapsodes, those who know Homer best, so unutterably stupid?[2] And Ion *is* stupid, left at the end stubbornly protesting that he is in fact a superlative military leader (thanks to his knowledge of Homer). The more important question raised in the work is, What is the source and nature of poetic knowledge, if there is such a thing?

The *Protagoras* again broaches the subject of education. The sophist Protagoras presents himself as a teacher for hire. A teacher of what? Socrates wants to know. Of virtue, it finally appears. But can virtue be taught? One of the great advantages conferred by the dramatic form, at least in the hands of a genius like Plato, is that the debate over education—over how knowledge is to be gained and imparted—can itself be made to dramatize the available modes of seeking knowledge, with Protagoras expounding set texts and Socrates dragging him against his will into the dialectical process.

The *Phaedrus* tackles head-on the question of whether it is possible to embody truth in a speech in which the primary purpose is to persuade. The question is approached by way of that ultimate form of personal persuasion, sexual seduction. Three model speeches are delivered, all of them spoken in the role of an older man aiming at the seduction of the young boy he is (supposedly) addressing. It is in the third and longest of these that Plato's idiosyncratic, but enormously durable and influential, ideas about

[2]Xenophon, *Symposium* 3.5–6.

the relationship between eros and the pursuit of knowledge (or education) are first met with. The *Phaedrus* serves
in the volume as a kind of pivot between the dialectic dra-
matized in the first two works and the speech-making of
the last two.

With the *Symposium* we return to the subject of eros. As
we noted earlier, dialectic is at a minimum here, but the sequence of speeches forms a kind of conversation, presenting different views of love, and with the longest speech, by
Socrates, superceding the doctrines propounded in those
preceding it. Finally, Alcibiades bursts in and gives a
drunken but magnificent speech confirming what has already been made clear: that in the conduct of his own life,
Socrates is the supremely erotic man, in the sense of the
true eros the philosopher described in his own speech. As
the dinner party winds down, we catch a glimpse of
Socrates forcing the two dramatists, Agathon and Aristophanes, into a dialectical inquiry into the nature of drama
itself.

Finally, the tone shifts profoundly with the *Apology*.
Here is Socrates fighting for his life, unsuccessfully. It is a
painful irony that the philosopher whom we have earlier
seen (in the *Protagoras*) reject set-speeches as a legitimate
form of inquiry should in this climactic moment of his life
be forced to represent and defend his life's mission of dialectical inquiry in what the law requires to be a set-
speech. It is perhaps unsurprising that Socrates, who has
devoted his life to the pursuit of truth, as opposed to culti-
vating persuasiveness, should have failed to persuade his
judges. We return, with this speech, to the question with
which we began, namely that concerning the relation between the historical Socrates and the Platonic: Is the
speech of the *Apology* a transcript of what Socrates really

said, or is it Plato's version of what he *should have said*? Or some mixture of both?

Such, then, is the principle of organization that structures this volume and this selection. The most natural alternative, which obviously readers may follow if they wish, is to start with the *Apology*, and thus get to know the figure of Socrates through his own account of his life. Following the order given here, however, will have the reader end at the end, with the inspiring sounds of Socrates' defiant refusal to take fright at the prospect of death.

At any rate, that is enough of a preface. Regardless of what order they are read in, these works are more than able to speak for themselves, and they should be allowed to do so, without too much foreground chatter from their commentators.

The marginal numbers accompanying the text correspond to the page numbers and subsections (represented by the letters a through e) of the complete edition of Plato published in Paris by Henri Étienne (= Stephanus) in 1578. This pagination, known as the "Stephanus numbers," is universally used for referring to specific passages in Plato's works; thus, for example, Socrates' major speech in the *Symposium* ends in 212c.

HAYDEN PELLICCIA is associate professor and chair of classics at Cornell University.

CONTENTS

ION

DRAMATIS PERSONAE

Socrates
Ion

SOCRATES: Well hello, Ion. Are you here from home— 530
from Ephesus?

ION: No, Socrates; from Epidaurus, from the festival of
Asclepius there.

SOCRATES: Do the Epidaurians have a contest in his
honor that includes rhapsodes?[1]

ION: Oh yes; and of other kinds of music.

SOCRATES: And were you competing? How did you fare?

ION: I won first prize, Socrates.   b

SOCRATES: Bravo! Now we must win another victory, at
the Panathenaea.[2]

ION: It shall be so, god willing.

SOCRATES: I must say that I have often envied you rhapsodes your craft, Ion; for it is always appropriate to your
profession to wear gorgeous clothes and to look as beautiful as you can.[3] At the same time you necessarily spend
your lives in the company of many good poets, Homer

---

[1]In ancient Greece, poetry was performed before an audience, not read in
silent isolation. Rhapsodes were the performers of epic poetry, which meant primarily the poems of Homer. Rhapsodic contests were held regularly around the
Greek world, and the winners were awarded prizes, often of great value.

[2]The Panathenaea was one of the chief religious festivals of Athens. Socrates
must be referring here to the quadrennial version of it, called the Greater Panathenaea, which included a famous rhapsodic contest.

[3]Rhapsodes traditionally dressed flamboyantly, wearing such things as purple
robes and gold crowns.

above all, who is the best and most divine of them. What is more, you have to get to know his thought thoroughly, and not merely learn his words by rote. All this is certainly very enviable. I assume that no one could become a good rhapsode without understanding the meaning of the poet? So the rhapsode has to become an interpreter of the thought of the poet for his audience; but how can he interpret him well unless he knows what he means? All this deserves to be envied, I repeat.

ION: Very true, Socrates; to limit ourselves to my case—interpretation has certainly been the most time-consuming part of the profession for me. I believe that I can speak about Homer better than anyone else can. For neither Metrodorus of Lampsacus, nor Stesimbrotus of Thasos, nor Glaucon—nor indeed anyone who has ever lived has had as good ideas to put forward about Homer as I have, nor as many.[4]

SOCRATES: Bravo again, Ion. For obviously you will not begrudge me a display of them.

ION: Oh, certainly not, Socrates; and really, it is worthwhile to hear how elegant I have made Homer. In fact, I think the Homeridae should give me a golden crown.[5]

SOCRATES: I shall certainly make the time someday to attend one of your performances; but for now, just answer this question for me: Are you good at only Homer, or at Hesiod and Archilochus also?[6]

[4]Metrodorus and Stesimbrotus were contemporary intellectuals who interested themselves in, among other matters, the interpretation of Homer; little of their work survives. Glaucon has not been identified.

[5]The Homeridae were a famous and influential guild of rhapsodes, centered on the island of Chios, who at least in their early days claimed descent from Homer.

[6]Hesiod was the other great epic poet of early Greece besides Homer, and, like Homer, is hard to date. His chief surviving works, the *Theogony* and the *Works*

ION: Only Homer; he is quite enough.

SOCRATES: Are there any things about which Homer and Hesiod agree?

ION: Yes; in my opinion there are a lot.

SOCRATES: Could you interpret what Homer says about these matters better than what Hesiod says?

ION: I can interpret them equally well, Socrates, where b they agree.

SOCRATES: But what about issues they don't agree on? For example, about prophecy, on which both Homer and Hesiod have something to say.

ION: Yes, they have.

SOCRATES: Well then, would you or a good prophet be a better interpreter of what they say about prophecy— what they agree on, and what they disagree on?

ION: A prophet.

SOCRATES: And if you were a prophet, and could interpret them where they agree, wouldn't you also know how to interpret them where they disagree?

ION: Clearly.

SOCRATES: But then how on earth did you ever come to c have this skill about Homer only, and not about Hesiod or the other poets? Or doesn't Homer talk about the same things all the other poets do? Isn't he for the most part concerned with war? And with the relationships of people with one another—good men and bad men, both

---

and Days, are not, like Homer's poems, narratives (except incidentally), but rather didactic works, the former giving an account of the origins of the universe and the establishment of the Olympian order of gods, the latter in effect a farmer's guide for living. Archilochus, of the island of Paros, lived in the seventh century B.C. and composed poetry, now mostly lost, in a variety of nonlyric meters, and often of strikingly obscene and abusive character. His poetry has been aptly compared to that of John Wilmot, Earl of Rochester. The Greeks revered him, and his memory was honored with a hero-cult.

at home and at work—and with the interactions of the gods with one another and with humans, and with what happens in the heavens and in Hades, and with the
d   births of gods and heroes? Isn't it this that Homer has composed his poetry about?

ION: That's right, Socrates.

SOCRATES: And what about other poets? Don't they treat the same subjects?

ION: Yes, Socrates; but not in the same way as Homer.

SOCRATES: What, in an inferior way?

ION: Yes, far inferior.

SOCRATES: And Homer does it in a better way?

ION: Incomparably better, by god.

SOCRATES: And yet surely, my dear friend Ion, if a group of people have a discussion about arithmetic, and one of them speaks more intelligently than the rest, there has to be somebody who can recognize which of them is the good speaker, doesn't there?

e ION: Yes.

SOCRATES: And isn't this same person also going to be able to tell which ones are talking stupidly? Or will someone else?

ION: The same.

SOCRATES: That is, the one who knows the science of arithmetic?

ION: Yes.

SOCRATES: Or again, if a group of people are discussing which foods are healthful, and one speaks more intelligently than the rest, will the person who recognizes the better speaker be anyone other than the one who also recognizes the worse, or will it be the same?

ION: Clearly the same.

SOCRATES: And who is he, and what is he called?

ION: He's a doctor.

SOCRATES: And speaking generally, in all discussions in which the subject is the same and a group of people are speaking, won't the person who can identify the good speakers also know the bad? For obviously, if he doesn't 532 know the bad, then neither will he know the good, when the same topic is being discussed.

ION: True.

SOCRATES: We find, in fact, that the same person is qualified to do both?

ION: Yes.

SOCRATES: And you say that Homer and the other poets, such as Hesiod and Archilochus, all talk about the same things, but not in the same way; rather, the one, Homer, does it well, and the others not so well?

ION: Yes; and I am right in saying so.

SOCRATES: And if you can recognize the good speaker, then you must also be able to recognize the worse b speakers, to see that they speak worse.

ION: It would seem so.

SOCRATES: Then, my dear friend, can I be mistaken in saying that Ion is equally skilled in Homer and in other poets, since he himself acknowledges that the same person will be a good judge of all those who talk about the same things, and that just about all poets talk about the same things?

ION: But if that's true, Socrates, then why do I lose attention and have absolutely no ideas of any value at all and c practically fall asleep when anyone talks about any other poet? But as soon as Homer is mentioned, I wake up at once and am all attention and have plenty to say?

SOCRATES: The reason, my friend, is not hard to guess. It is perfectly clear that it is not thanks to any scientific knowledge of Homer that you are able to talk about him—for if it were, then you would be able to talk about *all* poets, since poetry is the whole business—good and bad—isn't it?

ION: Yes.

d SOCRATES: And if you take any other art as a whole, there will turn out to be the same method of inquiry for all of them, won't there?

Would you like me to explain my meaning, Ion?

ION: Yes, by god, Socrates, I would; for I love to hear you clever people talk.

SOCRATES: Oh, I wish that I *were* clever, Ion, and that you could call me that truthfully; but you rhapsodes and actors, and the poets whose verses you sing, are the ones who are clever. I, on the other hand, do no more than

e speak the truth, as befits a layman and amateur. For consider what a worthless and amateurish thing I said just now—a thing that anybody might observe—namely, that if you take an art as a whole, the inquiry into its good and bad realizations is one and the same. Let's pursue this point with our argument. Isn't there such a thing as an "art of painting in its entirety"?

ION: Yes.

SOCRATES: And there are and have been many good and bad painters?

ION: Yes.

SOCRATES: And did you ever know anyone who was good at pointing out the good parts and the bad in the paintings of Polygnotus the son of Aglaophon, but couldn't

533   do so with other painters?[7] So that, for example, when

---

[7]Polygnotus, of the island of Thasos, was active in the mid-fifth century B.C. He was regarded by subsequent generations as the first great painter.

somebody showed him the work of another painter, he went to sleep and was at a loss, and had no ideas to contribute? But as soon as he was called upon to give his opinion about Polygnotus, or whoever the painter might be, and about him only, he woke up and was alert and had plenty to say?

ION: No indeed, I have never known of such a person.

SOCRATES: Or take sculpture—did you ever know of anyone who was skillful in expounding the merits of Daedalus the son of Metion,[8] or of Epeius the son of Panopeus,[9] or of Theodorus the Samian,[10] or of any individual sculptor; but, when the works of sculptors in general were produced, was at a loss and went to sleep and had nothing to say?

ION: No; no more than I've ever known of the other.

SOCRATES: And I'd imagine that you have never encountered a pipe player or harp player or singer-to-the-harp or rhapsode who was able to talk about Olympus or Thamyras or Orpheus, or Phemius the rhapsode of Ithaca,[11] but was at a loss when he came to speak of Ion

---

[8]This is indeed the mythical quasi-magician associated with King Minos of Crete, and whose son was Icarus, who flew too close to the sun. The Athenians seemed to feel that a figure of such manifest intelligence and ingenuity must be Athenian, and so they contrived a genealogy whereby Daedalus was the son of Metion, son of Erechtheus, legendary founder of Athens. Daedalus served as something like the patron saint of sculptors.

[9]Another figure of myth—the builder of the Trojan Horse.

[10]Finally, a historical personage, of the sixth century B.C., not only a sculptor but architect, jeweler, and innovator of building techniques.

[11]Again, figures drawn from myth and legend, the first three of which served something of the patron-saint function in their respective departments of music and poetry: Olympus was said to have been taught pipe-playing by that Marsyas the satyr who was eventually flayed by Apollo, as memorably depicted by Titian; Thamyras of Thrace is reported in *Iliad* 2. 595–600 as having challenged the Muses themselves to a contest of harp-playing, for which impudence he was

of Ephesus, and had no idea of his merits or defects?

ION: I cannot deny what you say, Socrates. Nevertheless, I *know* this about myself, and the world agrees with me, namely, that I *do* speak better and have more to say about Homer than anyone else does; but I don't speak equally well about others. There must be some reason for this; what could it be?

SOCRATES: I see the reason, Ion, and I am going to explain
d to you what I imagine it to be. The gift which you possess of speaking excellently about Homer is not an art, but, as I was just saying, an inspiration; there is a divinity moving you, just as in the stone which Euripides calls a magnet, but which is commonly known as the stone of Heraclea. This stone not only attracts iron rings, but it also imparts to them the same power of attracting other rings; and sometimes you will see a number of pieces of iron and rings suspended from one
e another so that they form a very long chain: and all of them derive their power of suspension from the original stone. Similarly, the Muse herself first makes some men inspired; then from these inspired people a chain is suspended as still other people receive the inspiration. For

---

deprived of both his sight and his art; Orpheus, another Thracian, is of course the singer-cum-harp player whose music could charm the trees to follow him, and was also the devoted husband of Eurydice, whom he almost succeeded in returning from the underworld. Phemius is mentioned here as a representative bard, or singer of epic, because he is one of the two bards depicted in the *Odyssey*, in his case the virtuous singer who is compelled against his will to entertain the despicable suitors of Penelope. It is curious that Socrates' examples of artists are largely mythical or literary; what formed the basis of discussion of the artistry of Phemius, for example, whom we hear in the *Odyssey* sing not one word? The discussion of Phemius', or Thamyras', art resembles the inquiries of later Alexandrian scholarship into such whimsical questions as "What was the song that the Sirens sang?"

all good poets, epic as well as lyric, compose their beautiful poems not by art, but because they are inspired and
possessed. And just as the Corybantic revelers when
they dance are not in their right mind,[12] so also the lyric   534
poets are not in their right mind when they compose
their beautiful songs: as soon as they get into step with
the music and the rhythm, they are inspired and possessed, like Bacchic maidens who draw milk and honey
from the rivers when they are under the influence of
Dionysus, but not when they are in their right mind.[13]
The soul of the lyric poet does the same thing, as they
themselves report; for they tell us that, after culling
their songs from rivers of honey that flow out of the
Muses' gardens and glens, they bring them to us, as if   b
they were bees, and they are themselves wingéd like
bees. All of which is true. For the poet is a light and
wingéd and holy thing, and he has no ability to create
until he has been inspired and is out of his senses, and
reason is no longer in him (for absolutely no man, while
he retains that faculty, can make poetry or prophesy).

Now because it is not by any rules of art that poets,
like yourself when speaking about Homer, compose and   c
say many beautiful things about their subjects, but by
divine dispensation, it follows that each of them is able
to do well only that to which the Muse impels him—
this one to dithyrambs,[14] another to songs of praise, another to dance songs, and another to epic or iambic

[12]Worshipers of the Phrygian goddess Cybele; the rites involved frenzied and
ecstatic dancing. The idea that poets and, in particular, musicians are possessed
by ecstatic frenzy seems perfectly banal to us, but Plato, in this work, was apparently the first to propose it.

[13]The worship of Dionysus (Bacchus) is vividly depicted in Euripides' play
The Bacchae.

[14]The dithyramb is a song sung in honor of Dionysus.

verses; but each of them is worthless when it comes to other genres. For it is not by art that the poets make their utterances, but by divine power; for if their ability to speak about any one subject were based upon systematic knowledge, then their ability would extend to all the rest. It is for a purpose, therefore, that the god takes reason away from poets, and uses them as his servants, as he also uses the pronouncers of oracles and holy prophets, namely, in order that we who hear them can know that it is not these men who, bereft of reason, utter these words, but it is the god himself who speaks them, and that through them he is addressing us. Tynnichus the Chalcidian[15] affords a striking proof of what I am saying: he wrote no other poem that anyone would want to remember, but he did write the famous paean[16] that everybody knows, one of the finest lyric poems ever written; literally, as he himself says, "an invention of the Muses." In this instance above all, the god seems to show to us, in order that we not be in doubt, that these beautiful poems are not human, nor the work of humans, but divine and the work of gods, and that the poets are only the interpreters of the gods, each one possessed by whichever god possesses him. Was this not the lesson which the god intended to teach when by the mouth of the worst of poets he sang the best of songs? Am I not right, Ion?

ION: Yes, indeed, Socrates, I feel that you are; for your words touch my soul, and I am persuaded that in these works the good poets, under divine inspiration, interpret for us the voice of the gods.

---

[15]Early fifth century B.C. Apart from the phrase "invention of the Muses," his poem does not survive.

[16]The paean is a song sung in honor of Apollo.

SOCRATES: And you rhapsodists are the interpreters of the poets?

ION: There again you are right.

SOCRATES: Then you are the interpreters of interpreters?

ION: Precisely.

SOCRATES: Hold on now, Ion, and tell me this, and don't b keep anything back: When you produce the greatest effect upon the audience in the recitation of some striking passage, such as the scene where Odysseus leaps to the doorway and, recognized by the suitors, pours out his arrows at his feet,[17] or the description of Achilles rushing upon Hector,[18] or the sad parts about Andromache, Hecuba, or Priam[19]—are you in your right mind? Aren't you carried outside of yourself, and doesn't your soul in c its inspired state think it is right there among the people or places you are singing about, either in Ithaca or in Troy or wherever the poem locates the scene?

ION: That point strikes home to me, Socrates. For I will speak without concealing anything from you: when what I sing is sad, my eyes fill up with tears, and when I tell of frightening events, my hair stands on end and my heart pounds in my chest.

SOCRATES: Well, Ion, and what are we to say of a man d who at a sacrifice or festival, when he is dressed in an embroidered robe, and has golden crowns upon his head, and though he has lost none of these things, yet he appears weeping or panic-stricken in the presence of

[17]*Odyssey* 22, opening.

[18]The final confrontation of Achilles and Hector occupies most of *Iliad* 22; the specific reference to Achilles' "rush" is presumably to line 312 and following, where the Greek hero at last kills the Trojan.

[19]Especially after the death of Hector, the son of Priam and Hecuba, and husband of Andromache, *Iliad* 22. 405 to end.

more than twenty thousand friendly faces, when there is no one trying to rob him or otherwise wrong him—is he in his right mind or not?

ION: No indeed, Socrates, I must say that, strictly speaking, he is not in his right mind.

SOCRATES: And are you aware that you produce similar effects on most of the spectators?

e ION: Only too well; for I look down upon them from the stage, and behold the various emotions of pity, wonder, or terror, stamped on their faces when I am speaking. You see, I have to pay very close attention to them, since if I make them cry I will be myself laughing when I get the prize money, and if I make them laugh I will myself be crying when I don't.

SOCRATES: Do you know that the spectator is the last of the rings which, as I was saying, receive the power of the original magnet from one another in a chain? A rhapsode like you, and an actor, are intermediate links, and the poet himself is the first of them. Through all these the god draws the souls of men in any direction which he pleases, causing each link to communicate the power to the next. Thus there is a vast chain of choral singers and dancers, and their trainers and subtrainers, who are suspended, as if from the magnet, at the side of the rings which hang down from the Muse. And every poet has some Muse from whom he is suspended, and by whom he is said to be "possessed," which is nearly the same thing; for he is taken hold of. And from these first rings, which are the poets, hang others, some deriving their inspiration from Orpheus, others from Musaeus;[20] but the greatest number are possessed and held by

536

b

---

[20]Another mythical singer; his name simply means "of the Muses."

Homer. And of these last, Ion, you are one, and you are possessed by Homer; and when anyone repeats the words of another poet you go to sleep, and do not know what to say; but when anyone recites something of Homer's you wake up instantly, and your soul cavorts within you, and you have plenty to say. For it is not by art or knowledge about Homer that you say what you say, but by divine inspiration and by possession. Just as the Corybantic revelers too are sensible only of that song which belongs to the god by whom they are possessed, and they have plenty of dances and words for that but are indifferent to any other, so also you, Ion, when the name of Homer is mentioned have plenty to say, and have nothing to say of others. You ask me, "Why is this?" and the answer is that your skill in the praise of Homer is based not on art but derives from divine inspiration.

ION: That's a good theory, Socrates. But I'd be amazed if you could ever have enough eloquence to persuade me that I praise Homer only when I am mad and possessed. If you could hear me speak about him I am sure you would never think this to be the case.

SOCRATES: And indeed I have every intention of going to hear one of your performances—but not until you answer this for me: On what part of Homer do you speak well? Surely not on every part?

ION: There is no part, Socrates, about which I do not speak well: of that I can assure you.

SOCRATES: Surely not about things in Homer of which you have no knowledge?

ION: And what is there in Homer of which I have no knowledge?

SOCRATES: Well, doesn't Homer speak in many passages 537

about various arts? For example, about chariot-driving; if I remember the lines I will repeat them.

ION: But I will repeat them; after all, I have it all committed to memory.

SOCRATES: Recite for me then, what Nestor says to his son Antilochus, when he's urging him to be careful making the turn at the horse race in honor of Patroclus.

ION: "Lean slightly," he says,

> *in your polished chariot,*
b > *to the left of your pair, and crying out to the horse on the right*
> *give him the whip, and slacken his rein.*
> *Now when you are hard on the turning-post, bring the left-hand*
> *horse right up against it,*
> *so that the hub of the wheel seems to graze its edge;*
> *but avoid actually touching the stone.*[21]

c SOCRATES: Enough. Now, Ion, will the charioteer or the doctor be the better judge of the validity of this advice?

ION: The charioteer, clearly.

SOCRATES: And will the reason be that this is his art, or will there be some other reason?

ION: No, that will be the reason.

SOCRATES: And the god allots to every art the capacity to know and understand a certain activity; for obviously the things we know by means of the art of the helmsman we won't also arrive at by the art of medicine.

ION: Certainly not.

SOCRATES: Nor what we know through medicine will we arrive at also by means of the builder's art.

ION: Certainly not.

d SOCRATES: And this is true of all the arts—that the things

---

[21] *Iliad* 23. 335–340.

we know through some one art we will not know
through some other? But let me ask a prior question: Do
you agree that the arts differ from one another?

ION: Yes.

SOCRATES: You would argue, then, as I would, that if
there are two kinds of knowledge, dealing with different
things, these can be called different arts?

ION: Yes.   e

SOCRATES: Yes, surely; for if the object of knowledge
were the same, there would be no meaning in saying
that the arts were different—since they both gave the
same knowledge. For example, I know that here are five
fingers, and you know it too. And if I were to ask
whether you and I became acquainted with this fact by
the help of the same art of arithmetic, you would acknowledge that we did?

ION: Yes.

SOCRATES: Tell me, then, what I was intending to ask you   538
just now—whether in your opinion this holds universally? If two arts are the same, mustn't they necessarily
have the same objects? And if one differs from another,
mustn't it be because the object is different?

ION: That is my opinion, Socrates.

SOCRATES: Then whoever has no knowledge of a particular art will not be able to judge correctly the precepts
and practice of that art?

ION: Very true.   b

SOCRATES: Then who will be the better judge of the lines
which you were reciting from Homer, you or the charioteer?

ION: The charioteer.

SOCRATES: Why, yes, because you are a rhapsode and not
a charioteer.

ION: Right.

SOCRATES: And the art of the rhapsode is different from that of the charioteer?

ION: Yes.

SOCRATES: And if a different art, then a knowledge of different matters?

ION: Yes.

SOCRATES: What about the passage in which Hecamede, the concubine of Nestor, is described as giving to the wounded Machaon a potion, as he says,

c

> *Made with Pramnian wine; and with a bronze grater*
> *she grated goat cheese into it,*
> *and placed by it an onion as a relish for the drink.*[22]

Now would you say that the art of the rhapsode or the art of medicine was better able to judge of the utility of this prescription?

ION: The art of medicine.

SOCRATES: And when Homer says,

d

> *And Iris descended to the depth of the sea like a lead weight,*
> *which, set in a hook made from the horn of a field-dwelling ox,*
> *rushes along bringing death to the ravenous fishes,*[23]

will the art of the fisherman or the rhapsode be better able to judge what these lines mean, and whether they are accurate or not?

ION: Clearly, Socrates, the art of the fisherman.

SOCRATES: Come now, suppose that you were to say to me: "Since you, Socrates, are able to assign different

[22] *Iliad* 11. 639–640, with 630.
[23] *Iliad* 24. 80–82.

passages in Homer to their corresponding arts, I want e you to tell me what are the passages whose value should be judged by the prophet and prophetic art," and you will see how easily and truthfully I will answer you. For there are many such passages, particularly in the *Odyssey*; as, for example, the passage in which Theoclymenus the prophet of the house of Melampus says to the suitors:

Wretched men! What is wrong with you?   539
Your heads and your faces and your limbs underneath are
   shrouded in night;
and voices of lamentation burst forth, and your cheeks are
   drenched with tears.
And the vestibule is full of ghosts, and the courtyard too,
all descending into the darkness of Erebus, and the sun
has perished out of heaven, and an evil mist is spread abroad.[24]   b

There are many such passages in the *Iliad* also; as for example in the description of the battle near the Greek wall, where he says:

As they were struggling to cross over the ditch, there came to them
   an omen:
a soaring eagle, skirting the people on his left,
bore a huge blood-red serpent in his talons,   c
still living and panting. But he had not yet lost his fighting spirit,
for he curled back and struck the bird carrying him
right on the breast below the neck,
and in anguish the eagle let him drop to the ground
into the middle of the crowd,
and, with a cry, flew off on the gusts of the wind.[25]   d

[24] *Odyssey* 20. 351–353, 355–357.
[25] *Iliad* 12. 200–207.

These are the sorts of things that I would say the prophet ought to consider and render judgment on.

ION: And you are quite right, Socrates, in saying so.

SOCRATES: Yes, Ion, and you are right also. And as I have found for you passages from the *Iliad* and *Odyssey* that describe the business of the prophet and the doctor and

e   the fisherman, so you, who know Homer so much better than I do, Ion, find for me passages that relate to the rhapsode and the rhapsode's art, and which the rhapsode is going to study and evaluate better than other men do.

ION: That would be all passages, Socrates.

SOCRATES: You can't mean that, can you? Are you really so forgetful? A rhapsode ought to have a better memory.

540 ION: Why, what am I forgetting?

SOCRATES: Don't you remember that you declared the art of the rhapsode to be different from the art of the charioteer?

ION: Yes, I remember.

SOCRATES: And you admitted that since they are different they will have different objects?

ION: Yes.

SOCRATES: Then, on your own showing, the rhapsode, and the art of the rhapsode, will not know everything?

ION: Well, I'm willing to exclude the kinds of things you are referring to, Socrates.

b   SOCRATES: Which is to say that you exclude pretty much all the subjects of the other arts. All right. But if the rhapsode doesn't know *all* of them, which ones *does* he know?

ION: He will know what it is appropriate for a man and for a woman to say, and a freeman and a slave, and a ruler and a subject.

SOCRATES: Do you mean that a rhapsode will know better

than a ship's captain what a person in charge of a ship in a storm ought to say?

ION: No. The captain will know better.

SOCRATES: Or will the rhapsode know better than the c doctor what a person in charge of a sick man ought to say?

ION: Again, no.

SOCRATES: But he will know what a slave ought to say?

ION: Yes.

SOCRATES: Suppose the slave is a cowherd; the rhapsode will know better than the cowherd what he ought to say in order to soothe infuriated cows?

ION: No, he will not.

SOCRATES: But he will know what is suitable for a spinning-woman to say about the working of wool?

ION: No.

SOCRATES: At any rate he will know what a general ought d to say when exhorting his soldiers?

ION: Yes, that is the sort of thing that the rhapsode will be sure to know.

SOCRATES: What? The art of the rhapsode is the art of the general?

ION: I am sure that I would know what a general ought to say.

SOCRATES: Well, maybe you would—but only if you happened to have the knowledge of a general as well as that of a rhapsode; and you might also have a knowledge of horsemanship as well as of the lyre, and then you would know when horses were well or badly managed. But suppose I were to ask you: By the help of which art, Ion, e do you know whether horses are well managed, by your skill as a horseman or as a performer on the lyre—what would you answer?

ION: I would reply, by my skill as a horseman.

SOCRATES: And if you judged lyre players, you would admit that you judged them by your skill at lyre-playing, and not by your horsemanship?

ION: Yes.

SOCRATES: And in judging the general's art, do you judge as a general, or as a good rhapsode?

ION: To me there appears to be no difference between them.

541 SOCRATES: What do you mean? Do you mean to say that the art of the rhapsode and of the general is the same?

ION: Yes, one and the same.

SOCRATES: Then whoever is a good rhapsode is also a good general?

ION: Certainly, Socrates.

SOCRATES: And whoever is a good general is also a good rhapsode?

ION: No, I can't agree to that.

SOCRATES: But you do agree that whoever is a good rhap-
b   sode is also a good general.

ION: Certainly.

SOCRATES: And you are the best of all the rhapsodes of Greece?

ION: By far the best, Socrates.

SOCRATES: And so you are also the best general, Ion?

ION: You can be sure of it, Socrates, and I learned it all from Homer.

SOCRATES: But then, Ion, why in heaven's name do you, who are the best of generals as well as the best of rhap-sodes in all Greece, go around reciting rhapsodies when you could be a general? Do you think that the Hellenes
c   are in grave need of a rhapsode with a golden crown, and have no need at all of a general?

ION: Why, Socrates, the reason is that my countrymen, the Ephesians, are the subjects and soldiers of you Athenians, and so we do not need a general.[26] And neither you nor the Spartans are likely to appoint me, since you think that you have enough generals of your own.

SOCRATES: My good Ion, have you never heard of Apollodorus of Cyzicus?[27]

ION: Who might he be?

SOCRATES: A man who, though a foreigner, has often been chosen to be their general by the Athenians. And there is Phanosthenes of Andros, and Heraclides of Clazom- d enae, whom they have also appointed to the command of their armies and to other offices, even though they are foreigners, after they had shown their merit.[28] And won't they choose Ion the Ephesian to be their general, and honor him, if they judge him to be qualified? Weren't the Ephesians originally Athenians, and isn't Ephesus an important city?

But the fact is, Ion, that if you are correct in saying e that it is by art and knowledge that you are able to praise Homer, then you are being unfair with me, and after all your claims of knowing many glorious things about Homer, and promises that you would display them to me, you only cheat me, and you are so far from exhibiting the art of which you are a master, that you will not, even after my repeated entreaties, explain to me the na-

[26]Ephesus, as a member of the Delian League, was a subject state of Athens for much of the fifth century B.C.

[27]Otherwise unknown.

[28]Phanosthenes took command of the Athenian fleet in 408–7, during the war with Sparta; Heraclides is mentioned elsewhere, but not in a specifically military capacity.

ture of it. You literally assume as many shapes as Proteus,[29] twisting and turning up and down, until at last you slip away from me in the disguise of a general, in

542 order that you may escape showing me your Homeric expertise. So, if your skill is based on art, as I was saying, and you are cheating me of your promise to expound Homer for me, then you are not being honest. But if, as I believe, you have no art, but speak all these beautiful words about Homer unconsciously under his inspiring influence, then I acquit you of dishonesty, and shall only say that you are inspired. Which do you prefer to be thought, dishonest or inspired?

b ION: There is a great difference, Socrates, between the two alternatives, and inspiration is by far the nobler.

SOCRATES: Then, Ion, I shall assume the nobler alternative, and attribute to you in your praises of Homer inspiration, and not art.

---

[29]The so-called Old Man of the Sea, a minor divinity; if seized, he would attempt to escape capture by rapidly assuming different shapes. See *Odyssey* 4. 351–570, especially 455–458.

PROTAGORAS

DRAMATIS PERSONAE

The external setting, or "frame," of the work is an encounter between Socrates and an unnamed friend, to whom Socrates reports a meeting earlier the same day, at the house of Callias, with the sophist Protagoras. Most of this report is devoted to the conversation of Socrates and Protagoras, but subsidiary roles are given to several others, listed below. The scene for the frame is unspecified, but it is clearly some public place, most likely either one of Athens' famous gymnasiums, which were not devoted exclusively to athletics, but were also places for the leisured classes of the city to gather and converse; another possibility for the locale would be one of the colonnades in or near the agora. Not far along into the opening conversation, Socrates' friend starts using "we" instead of "I," which suggests that the encounter took place somewhere where others were present who, when it emerged that Socrates had a good story to tell, were in a position to gather around for several hours and listen. This would suit a gymnasium or other popular place of leisure.

Socrates: *the narrator of the dialogue to his unnamed* **companion.**

Protagoras: *lived from about 490 to 420* B.C.; *from Abdera; the most famous of the sophists, perhaps the first to charge for instruction. Brief fragments of his writings survive; one work opened with the famous sentence "Man is the measure of all things, of the things that are, that they are, of the things that are not, that they are not." This line appears to have been part of a doctrine of radical relativism asserting that perception is reality for the perceiver.*

Hippias: *slightly younger contemporary of Protagoras; from Elis; a polymath, claiming expertise in virtually every branch of learning and the crafts; he would appear at the Olympic Games* *and challenge members of the crowd to ask him a question he could not answer, apparently with results that caused no serious harm to his reputation. He made his own clothing, jewelry, etc. Not an entirely frivolous figure, he did some important historical research, such as compiling a comprehensive list of victors in the Olympics; since many events in antiquity were dated by Olympiad, such a list is of more importance than might at first appear.*

Prodicus: *born about 470 B.C., date of death unknown; from Ceos; another sophist, one especially interested in clarifying the meaning of words, often to the point of implausibility, as suggested in the parodies found in the present work (see especially his speech beginning at 337a). He also appears to have been one of the first to give rationalistic accounts of religious phenomena. Socrates seems to have had some genuine association with Prodicus, although he tends, as here, to adopt an amused tone with him.*

Callias: *lived from about 450 to 370 B.C.; scion of one of the greatest and richest Athenian families, he is said to have exhausted his fortune paying tuition to various sophists, among other luxuries. Apart from this odd form of extravagance, he led a full and useful public life.*

Hippocrates: *Nothing is known of him outside of what appears here.*

Alcibiades: *lived from 451 or 450 to 404 or 403 B.C.; another scion of a great Athenian family, Alcibiades, though the son of the general Cleinias, was reared in the house of the great Pericles; an aristocrat to the bone, notoriously arrogant and good-looking, he was also one of the most talented people of his era, one not lacking in talented people. His political opportunism, his wealth and powerful connections, and his military brilliance combined to make him an extremely dangerous if indispensible man. The popular belief that he was a "disciple" of Socrates may well have* *contributed to the popular sentiment against the latter, as manifested ultimately in his trial and condemnation.*

Critias: *lived from about 460 to 403 B.C.; yet another scion of a great Athenian family, sharing much in common with his friend Alcibiades, but ultimately a more sinister figure, chiefly because Critias took a leading role in the vicious oligarchy ("The Thirty") that briefly and brutally ruled Athens after the defeat by Sparta in 404; he died in the fighting that overthrew the regime. Critias had intellectual interests and did some writing. He figures in several of the works of Plato, his cousin.*

Unlike many of Plato's dialogues, the Protagoras *is fairly easy to date: Alcibiades is just getting his beard, and the Peloponnesian War has not yet broken out. This suggests a date in the mid- to late 430s, possibly around 433. Socrates would have been in his mid- to late thirties.*

COMPANION: Where are you coming from, Socrates? But 309 I hardly need ask the question, since I can be sure that you have been on the hunt for the lovely Alcibiades. I saw him the day before yesterday, and he seemed to me still to be a very handsome man, but a man nonetheless, Socrates, and, between you and me, he's beginning to sprout a bit of beard.

SOCRATES: What of it? Don't you agree with Homer's view that "Youth is most charming when the beard first b appears"?[1] Which is the stage Alcibiades is now in.

COMPANION: Well, how is it going? Are you just coming from visiting him? How is the boy disposed toward you?

[1] *Iliad* 24. 348, *Odyssey* 10. 279.

SOCRATES: Very benevolently, I thought, especially today; for he came to my rescue repeatedly; and yes, I have just come from him. But let me tell you a strange thing: I paid no attention to him, and several times I completely forgot that he was even there.

c COMPANION: What could have brought *this* about? Has anything happened between you and him? For surely you can't have found anyone more beautiful, at least not in this city.

SOCRATES: Actually, much more beautiful.

COMPANION: What do you mean? A citizen or a foreigner?

SOCRATES: A foreigner.

COMPANION: From where?

SOCRATES: Abdera.

COMPANION: And this foreigner is really in your opinion better-looking than the son of Cleinias?

SOCRATES: Isn't it inevitable, my friend, that the wisest is always more beautiful?

COMPANION: But have you come here from a meeting with some wise man, Socrates?

d SOCRATES: Not at all—rather with the *wisest* man alive, assuming you grant that title to Protagoras.

COMPANION: What! What do you mean? Protagoras is in Athens?

SOCRATES: For two days now.

COMPANION: And you have come here now from a meeting with him?

310 SOCRATES: Yes; one in which I heard many things and said many things.

COMPANION: Then, unless something prevents you, why don't you move my slave here out of the way, and sit down and tell us about your meeting.

SOCRATES: Certainly; and I'll be grateful to all of you for listening.

COMPANION: And we to you for telling us.

SOCRATES: That will make a double dose of thanks. Listen then:

Last night, at the earliest stages of dawn, Hippocrates, son of Apollodorus and brother of Phason, came and started beating at my door with his stick; a slave opened b the door for him, and he came rushing in and yelled out: Socrates, are you awake or asleep?

I recognized his voice, and said: Oh, it's Hippocrates. You aren't bringing bad news, are you?

Good news, he said; nothing but good.

Wonderful, I said; but what is it? And why did you have to come at *this* hour?

He drew nearer to me, and reverently intoned: Protagoras is come.

Yes, I replied; two days ago: have you only just heard?

Yes, he said; only this past evening; at the same time he c felt around for the bed-stool, sat down near my feet, and said: Yesterday quite late in the evening, after I got back from Oenoe. My slave Satyrus had run away; I had meant to tell you that I was going off to track him down, but something put it out of my head; then when I got back, after we had finished supper and were about to turn in, my brother said to me: "Protagoras is come." I immediately set about to come right to you, but then it occurred to me that the night was too far along. But as soon as sleep released me from the bonds of fatigue,[2] I got up and came straight d over.

I, knowing his violent and excitable nature well, said:

---

[2]Hippocrates borrows from Homer a poetic locution for "I woke up."

How does it concern you? Has Protagoras wronged you in some way?

He replied, laughing: Yes, he certainly has, Socrates—he keeps his wisdom to himself, and does not share it with me.

But surely, I said, if you give him some money, and persuade him, he will make you as wise as he is himself.

I pray to god, he replied, that it should turn out to be so.

e I wouldn't leave any of my assets untouched, nor any of my friends'. But that is why I have come to you now, to get you to speak to him on my behalf; for I am young and have never seen or heard him; when he last visited Athens, I was a child. But as you know, all men praise him, and say that he is the finest of speakers. There's no reason we shouldn't

311 go at once, so that we find him at home. He is staying, I am told, with Callias the son of Hipponicus. Let's go.

I replied: Let's not go there now, my good friend—it's too early. But let's go out into the courtyard here and spend the time until sunrise strolling around out there; then we can go. Protagoras spends most of his time at home anyhow, and we can be pretty sure that we'll find him there. Don't worry.

At this we got up and walked around in the courtyard, b and I thought that I would test the strength of his resolve. So I examined and questioned him. Tell me, Hippocrates, I said, as you are going to Protagoras, and will be paying him a fee for teaching you, what is he to whom you are going? And what will he make you into? If, for example, you had thought of going to Hippocrates of Cos, the Asclepiad,[3] and were going to give him a fee for teaching you, and someone had said to you, "Hippocrates, you are pay-

---

[3] The great doctor, to whom is attributed the famous oath. He is called an Asclepiad because Asclepius, the son of Apollo, is regarded as the founder of medicine, and all doctors as his heirs.

ing money to your namesake Hippocrates; tell me, what is c
he?" how would you have answered?

I would say, he replied, a doctor.

And what will he make you into?

Another doctor, he said.

And if you had decided to go to Polyclitus the Argive, or
Phidias the Athenian,[4] and were intending to give them a
fee for teaching you, and someone had asked you, "What
are Polyclitus and Phidias? And why do you intend to give
them this money?" how would you have answered?

I would have answered that they were sculptors.

And what will they make you into?

A sculptor, of course.

Well now, I said, you and I are going to Protagoras, and d
we are ready to pay him money on your behalf. If our own
means are sufficient to procure his services, we will be
glad; but if not, then we are ready to spend the money of
your friends as well. Now suppose that, while we are en-
thusiastically pursuing our object in this way, someone
were to say to us, "Tell me, Socrates, and you, Hippocrates,
what is Protagoras, that you are going to pay him money?"
how should we answer? I know that Phidias is a sculptor, e
and that Homer is a poet; but what is Protagoras? What is
his title?

The name they call him, at any rate, Socrates, is sophist,
he replied.

Then we are going to pay our money to him in the capacity of a sophist?

Certainly.

---

[4]The two greatest sculptors of Classical Greece. Polyclitus is best known for
his Spearbearer, which survives only in copies; Phidias for his Athena, adorned in
more than a ton of gold, in the Parthenon at Athens, and his Zeus, in the Temple
of Zeus at Olympia; these too survive only in copies.

But suppose a person were to ask this further question: "And how about yourself? You are going to Protagoras in 312 order to become what?"

He answered, blushing (for the day was just beginning to dawn, so that I could see him), Well, if this case is at all like the earlier ones, then clearly to become a sophist, but . . .

Good heavens! I said. Wouldn't you be ashamed at presenting yourself to the Hellenes as a sophist?

Yes, Socrates, to be honest, I would be.

But perhaps you should not assume, Hippocrates, that Protagoras' teaching is of this kind, but is more like what b you learn from your grammar teacher, or music teacher, or athletic coach—that is, an art cultivated without a view to making any of them a profession, but only as a part of education, and because a gentleman of liberal culture ought to know them?

Yes, that's it, he said; that, in my opinion, is a much more accurate account of what Protagoras' teaching is.

I said: I wonder whether you know what you are about to do, or are still oblivious . . .

Of what?

You are about to entrust your soul to the care of a man c whom you call a sophist. Frankly, I would be very surprised if you could tell me what a sophist is. And yet, if you don't know, then you also don't know what it is you are entrusting your soul to, whether it's a good thing or bad.

I certainly think that I do know, he replied.

Then tell me: What do you imagine it is?

I take it to be someone who knows wise things, he replied, as the name implies.

Couldn't you also say this of the painter and of the carpenter? Don't they, too, know wise things? But suppose a d person were to ask us: "Painters know things that are wise in respect to what?" We would say: "In respect to the making of images," and likewise for the rest. But now if he were to ask further: "The wise things that a sophist has knowledge of—they are wise in respect to what?" what would we answer to him?

What other answer could there be but that he is the master of the art that makes men eloquent?

Yes, I replied, that is very likely true, but it's not enough; for this answer demands of us a further question: What does the sophist make a man talk eloquently *about*? For example, a lyre player may be supposed to make a man talk eloquently about the subject that he makes him under- e stand, that is, about playing the lyre. Isn't that so?

Yes.

Then what does a sophist make him eloquent about?

Evidently, about the subject that he makes him understand.

Yes, we can take that as read. But what *is* the subject that the sophist knows and makes his disciple know?

No, he said, I haven't reached an answer to that yet.

Then I proceeded to say: Well, but are you aware of the 313 danger you are going to expose your soul to? If you had to entrust the care of your body to someone who might do good or harm to it, wouldn't you carefully consider the question and get your friends' views, and your family's, and ponder for many days whether you should give this person the care of your body? But now your soul is in question, which you believe to be of far more value than your body; for good or evil, all that you have and are depends upon its virtue or vice; yet about this you never consulted either with your father, or with your brother, or with any one of us who are your friends, whether you should entrust it to b the care of this adventitious stranger or not. In the evening, you say, you hear of him, and in the morning you get up and go to him, giving it no thought, without getting the opinion of anyone whether you ought to entrust yourself to him or not. But you have made up your mind that you will at all costs be a pupil of Protagoras, and are prepared to expend all your own property and that of your friends in carrying out at any price this plan, although, as you admit, you do not know him, and have never spoken to him: and

c you call him a sophist, but are manifestly ignorant of what a sophist is; and yet you are going to commit yourself to his keeping.

He listened to me and replied: It looks like that, Socrates, the way you put it.

I continued: Isn't a sophist, Hippocrates, a person who deals wholesale or retail in goods that are supposed to nourish the soul? That's what he appears to me to be.

And what, Socrates, are "goods that nourish the soul"?

Surely, I said, knowledge is the food of the soul; and we must take care, my friend, that the sophist does not cheat us when he praises the goods he is hawking, like the whole-

d salers and retailers who sell the food for the body; for they praise indiscriminately all their goods, without knowing which are really beneficial or harmful; and neither do their customers know, with the exception of a trainer or doctor who may happen to buy some of them. Similarly, those traveling salesmen of knowledge, who make the round of the cities and sell or retail their wares to any customer who wants them, praise them all alike; though I wouldn't be surprised, my friend, if among them, also, some were really unaware which articles of their merchandise are good for

e the soul, and which bad; and their customers are equally unaware, except when the purchaser happens to be a doctor of the soul. If, therefore, you understand which among these articles is good and which evil, you may safely buy knowledge from Protagoras or anyone; but if not, then, O my friend, stop, and do not gamble with your dearest interests and put them at risk. For there is far greater peril in 314 buying knowledge than in buying food and drink: the latter you buy from the wholesale or retail dealer, and carry away in independent containers, and before you take them into your body as food or drink you can bring them home and call in any experienced friend who knows what is good to be eaten or drunk, and what not, and how much, and when; and then the danger of purchasing them is not so great. But you cannot buy the wares of knowledge and b carry them away in an independent container; when you have paid for them, you must receive them into your soul and go your way, either harmed or benefited; and therefore we should deliberate and get the advice of our elders; for we are still young—too young to decide such a matter. And now let us go, as we were intending, and hear Protagoras; and when we have heard what he has to say, we may get advice from others; for not only Protagoras is at Callias' house, but there is Hippias of Elis, and, if I am not mis- c taken, Prodicus of Ceos, and many other wise men.

To this we agreed, and proceeded on our way until we reached the front door of the house. We stopped there, before we went in, to finish a discussion we had started on the way; and we stood talking by the door until we had come to an understanding. And I think that the doorkeeper, a eunuch, who because of the great number of sophists at the house had taken a general disliking to visitors, must have d heard us talking. At any rate, when we knocked at the door, and he opened it and saw us, he grumbled: "Ugh! Sophists!

The master is busy," and he instantly slammed the door shut with both his hands. We knocked again, and he answered without opening: "Didn't you fellows hear me say that he is busy?" But, my friend, I said, don't be upset: we are not sophists, and we are not here to see Callias, but we
e want to see Protagoras; so please announce us. At last, after some further difficulty, the man was prevailed upon to open the door.

When we entered, we found Protagoras taking a walk in the cloister; and next to him, on one side, were walking Callias the son of Hipponicus, and Paralus, who is Callias'
315 maternal half-brother by Pericles, and Charmides the son of Glaucon.[5] On the other side of him were Xanthippus the other son of Pericles, and Philippides son of Philomelus; also Antimoerus of Mende, who of all the disciples of Protagoras is the most famous, and intends to make sophistry his profession.[6] A train of listeners followed him; the greater part of them appeared to be foreigners—the people Protagoras brings with him out of the various cities he visits on his journeys, he, like Orpheus,
b charming them with his voice, and they, following the voice, enchanted. There were also some Athenians in the procession.

I vastly enjoyed watching the choreography. They were beautifully careful never to get in Protagoras' way at all, and when he and those who were with him changed direction, then the band of listeners parted regularly on either side, wheeled around, and took their places behind him in perfect order.

[5]Charmides was Plato's uncle and was himself the nephew of Critias, with whom he was closely associated in the regime of The Thirty, and with whom he died defending it. A Platonic dialogue bears his name.
[6]Nothing more is known of Philippides and Antimoerus.

"After him," as Homer says, "I beheld"[7] Hippias of Elis enthroned in the opposite cloister, and around him, seated on benches, as if in school, were Eryximachus, the son of Acumenus,[8] and Phaedrus the Myrrhinusian, and Andron,[9] son of Androtion, and there were strangers whom he had brought with him from his native city of Elis, and some others: they appeared to be putting certain physical and astronomical questions to Hippias, and he was making his way through the questions and rendering judgments *ex cathedra* on each particular.

Also, "my eyes beheld Tantalus";[10] for it turns out that Prodicus the Cean is here in Athens: he had been lodged in a room which, in the days of Hipponicus, was a storeroom; but, as the house was full, Callias had cleared it out and made the room into a guest-chamber. Now Prodicus was still in bed, almost completey concealed under a vast abundance of sheepskins and bedclothes. And there was, sitting by him on an adjacent couch, Pausanias of the deme of Ce-

[7]Socrates gives this part of his narrative an amusing mock-heroic flavor by borrowing language from Homer, in particular from Odysseus' account (in *Odyssey* 11) of the heroes and heroines whose shades he saw down in the underworld. The formula "after him I beheld X" is used repeatedly in that passage, and the words with which Socrates introduces Prodicus (in the next paragraph), "my eyes beheld Tantalus," is an almost verbatim quotation of *Odyssey* 11. 582. At least one implication of all this would seem to be that a visit to a house full of sophists is like a descent into Hades.

[8]Both father and son were doctors; Eryximachus is also represented as Phaedrus' companion in the *Symposium*. Phaedrus is of course Socrates' interlocutor in the dialogue that bears his name.

[9]Referred to in Plato's *Gorgias* as an associate of the rather brutal Callicles, prominent in that work.

[10]Tantalus, who served his boy Pelops up to the gods as a stew, was one of the sinners who suffer spectacular punishments in Hades (Sisyphus being another): water and food are always within reach, except for the moment when reached for, whereupon they quickly recede. It has been supposed that Prodicus, who has a cold, is like Tantalus in respect to physical suffering.

rameis, and with Pausanias was a very young man, who is
e certainly remarkable for his good looks and, if I am not
mistaken, is also of a good and noble nature. I thought that
I heard him called Agathon, and my suspicion is that he is
the beloved of Pausanias.[11] There was this youth, and there
were also the two Adimantuses, one the son of Cepis and
the other of Leucolophides,[12] and some others. I was
primed and ready to hear what Prodicus was saying, for he
seems to me to be a supremely wise and godlike man; but I
316 was not able to get into the inner circle, and his fine deep
voice made a reverberative booming in the room which
rendered his words indistinct.

No sooner had we entered than there followed the
lovely Alcibiades, as you call him, not that I disagree with
you, and also Critias the son of Callaeschrus.

After we had gone in, there were some other distrac-
tions; after giving them our attention, we walked up to Pro-
b tagoras, and I said: Protagoras, I have come with my friend
Hippocrates, here, to see you.

Do you wish, he said, to speak with me alone, or in the
presence of the rest?

It doesn't matter to us, I said; but why don't you decide
yourself, after you've heard the purpose of our visit.

And what is your purpose? he said.

Hippocrates, here, is a native Athenian; he is the son of
Apollodorus, and belongs to a great and prosperous family.
As far as natural ability is concerned, he seems to me a

[11]Socrates' suspicion is correct. The eminent tragedian Agathon is the host of
the *Symposium*, at which Pausanias is also prominently present. See the notes at
the beginning of that work.

[12]The former Adimantus is not otherwise known; the latter was a political associate of Alcibiades, and was eventually charged with betraying the Athenian
fleet in the final disastrous naval battle of the Peloponnesian War.

match for anyone his age. I believe that he aspires to political eminence, and he thinks that he might best achieve c
this by becoming your protégé. So now please consider
whether you wish to speak to us about all this alone or in
the presence of others.

Very proper indeed is your consideration on my behalf,
Socrates. For certainly a stranger who makes his way into
great cities, and persuades the flower of the youth in them
to abandon all their other associations—those with family
and friends, with old and young—and rather to consort
with him because they will be improved by his company—
a man doing this really must be very cautious; great jeal- d
ousies are aroused by his activities, and he is the object of
much enmity and intrigue. Now the art of the sophist is, as
I believe, of great antiquity; but in ancient times, those
who practiced it, fearing this odium, veiled and disguised
themselves under various names, some under that of poets,
such as Homer, Hesiod, and Simonides,[13] some of hiero-
phants and prophets, such as Orpheus and Musaeus, and
some, as I observe, even under the name of gymnastic
trainers, like Iccus of Tarentum, or our contemporary
Herodicus,[14] now of Selymbria and formerly of Megara, e
who is more of a sophist than anyone. Your own fellow
countryman Agathocles pretended to be a musician, but
was really an eminent sophist; also Pythocleides the Cean;
and there were many others; and all of them, as I was saying, adopted these arts as veils or disguises because they
were afraid of the odium which they would incur. I, however, do not comply with their unanimity on this subject, 317

---

[13]Simonides of Ceos lived from the mid-sixth to early mid-fifth centuries
B.C.; lyric and epigrammatic poet.

[14]Iccus was a winner of the Olympic pentathlon and established himself as a
trainer on this basis. Herodicus is also mentioned in the opening of the *Phaedrus*.

for I do not believe that they achieved their purpose, which was to deceive those holding the power in their cities, who were not taken in by them; and as to the common people, to put it bluntly, they notice nothing anyhow, and only repeat whatever their rulers are pleased to tell them. Now to fail to escape, and yet to be caught running away, is the very

b height of folly, and also greatly increases the hostility of mankind; for they regard him who runs away as a rogue, in addition to any other objections which they have to him. I therefore take an entirely opposite course, and acknowledge myself to be a sophist and instructor of mankind; such an open acknowledgment appears to me to be a better sort of caution than concealment. Nor have I neglected other precautions, and therefore, with the favor of heaven, be it said, I suffer no great harm from the acknowledgment that

c I am a sophist. And I have been now many years in the profession—for all my years when added up are many: there is no one here present of whom I might not be the father. Wherefore I would much prefer conversing with you, if you want to speak with me, in the presence of the company.

And I—for I suspected that he wanted to preen himself in front of Prodicus and Hippias, and show off to them that

d we had come to the house as his besotted admirers—I said: But why don't we invite Prodicus and Hippias and their friends to hear us?

Excellent idea, he said.

Shall we arrange the furniture to make, as it were, a council-chamber, so that you can hold your discussion sitting down? asked Callias. This was agreed upon, and all of us felt great delight at the prospect of hearing wise men talk; we ourselves went and got the chairs and benches, and arranged them around Hippias, where other benches were already in place. Meanwhile, Callias and Alcibiades got

Prodicus out of bed and brought in him and his companions. e

When we were all seated, Protagoras said: Now that the company are assembled, Socrates, you might repeat what you said to me just now on behalf of this young man.

I replied: I will begin again at the same point, Protago- 318
ras, and tell you once more the purpose of my visit: this is my friend Hippocrates, who is desirous of becoming your protégé; he would like to know what will happen to him if he does so. That's all there is to it.

Protagoras answered: Young man, if you associate with me, on the very first day you will return home a better man than you came, and better on the second day than on the first, and better every day than you were on the day before.

When I heard this, I said: Protagoras, I don't see at all b
what is so impressive about that—it's entirely to be expected; even at your age, and with all your wisdom, if anyone were to teach you something you happened not to know before, you would become better: but please give a different kind of answer—I will explain by an example. Let's suppose that Hippocrates, instead of wanting to become your protégé, were suddenly to desire to become that of the young man Zeuxippus of Heraclea,[15] who has lately arrived on a visit to Athens, and let us suppose he had come to Zeuxippus as he has come to you, and had heard him say, as he has heard you say, that every day he c
would grow and become better if he associated with him: and then suppose that he were to ask him, "In what shall I become better, and in what shall I grow?"—Zeuxippus

---

[15]It is assumed that this Zeuxippus of Heraclea is the same as Zeuxis of the same, one of the most famous painters of the late fifth and early fourth centuries B.C. He was legendary for his realistic effects, birds supposedly having tried to eat the grapes in one of his paintings. He would have only begun establishing a reputation at the time at which this work is set.

would answer, "In painting." And suppose that he went to Orthagoras the Theban, and heard him say the same thing, and asked him, "In what shall I become better day by day?"—he would reply, "In flute-playing."[16] Now I want you to make the same sort of answer to this young man and
d to me, as I am asking questions on his account. When you say that on the first day on which he associates with you he will return home a better man, and on every day will grow in the same way—in what, Protagoras, will he be better? And about what?

When Protagoras heard me say this, he replied: You ask questions fairly, and I like to answer a question that is fairly put. If Hippocrates comes to me he will not have happen to him what would happen if he took up with any other sophist. For other sophists outrageously abuse their pupils, who, when they have just escaped from what is in effect vo-
e cational training, are taken against their will and driven back into it by these teachers, and made to learn calculation, and astronomy, and geometry, and music (as he said this, he riveted his gaze upon Hippias); but if he comes to me, he will learn that which he comes to learn. And this is prudence in affairs private as well as public; he will learn to order his own house in the best manner, and he will be
319 fully qualified to speak and act in the affairs of the state.

Am I following you and your claim? I asked. It appears to me that you are claiming to teach the art of politics, and that you promise to make men good citizens?

That, Socrates, is exactly the claim that I make.

Then, I said, this is a truly magnificent skill that you possess, if in fact you do possess it—for I will not say to you anything other than precisely what I think, Protagoras.

---

[16]Little more is known of Orthagoras the flute teacher.

I must admit that I used to be of the firm opinion that this was something incapable of being taught, and yet I do not know how I am to disbelieve your claim. But I ought to tell b you why I believe that this cannot be taught or communicated by person to person. I, like the rest of the Greeks, think that the Athenians are a clever people. Now I observe that when we meet together in the Assembly, and the matter in hand relates to building, the builders are called in as advisers; when the question has to do with shipbuilding, then the shipbuilders are consulted; and likewise with other skills and arts which they think capable of being taught and learned. And if some person whom they don't c suppose to have any expertise in the relevant profession tries to give them advice, even if he is terrifically good-looking and rich and blue-blooded, they still will not put up with it, but they laugh and hoot at him, until either he is shouted down and withdraws on his own, or the sergeants-at-arms drag him away or remove him at the command of the prytanes.[17] This is their way of behaving with regard to whatever they deem to be the subject of a professional skill. But when the question concerns state policy, then every- d body is free to have a say—carpenter, tinker, cobbler, merchant, sea captain; rich and poor, upper class and lower class—anyone who wants to gets up, and no one criticizes him, as in the previous case, for lack of expertise, or because he didn't go to school in the subject, and yet is trying to give advice—all of which shows that people don't believe that this sort of knowledge can be taught. And not only is this true of the state, but of individuals; the best and e wisest of our citizens are unable to impart that peculiar virtue in which they excel themselves to others: as for ex-

[17]The presiding magistrates (pronounced as three syllables). See further section 32 of the *Apology*, with the notes there.

ample, Pericles, the father of these young men here, who provided them with an excellent education in all those subjects that can be learned at school, but in his own area of 320 expertise, politics, he neither taught them himself, nor gave them other teachers. Instead, they were allowed, like sacred cows, to wander at their own free will, in some sort of hope that they would hit upon civic virtue of their own accord. Or take another example: there was Cleinias the younger brother of our friend Alcibiades here, of whom this very same Pericles was the guardian; and Pericles, being fearful that Cleinias would be corrupted, if you can imagine, by Alcibiades, snatched him away from the company of his brother, and deposited him at the house of Ariphron[18] to be educated; but before six months had elapsed, Pericles had b him brought back to Alcibiades, at a complete loss as to what to do with him. And I could mention countless other instances of persons who were good themselves, and yet never made anyone else good, either friend or stranger. Now I, Protagoras, when I reflect upon these examples, conclude that virtue cannot be taught. But then again, when I hear your words, I waver, and am tempted to think that there must be something in what you say, because I know that you have a great deal of experience, and have learned many things and on your own discovered others. So, if you are able to prove to us a little more clearly that c virtue can be taught, don't hold back, but prove it.

That I will, Socrates, and gladly. But what would you like? Shall I, as an older man to younger, give my proof in the form of a fable, or shall I argue out the question?

To this, several of the company answered that he should choose for himself.

[18]Pericles' brother.

Well, then, he said, I think that a fable will be more enjoyable:

Once upon a time there were gods only, and no mortal creatures. But when there came the appointed time of d birth for these also, the gods fashioned them out of earth and fire and various mixtures of both elements in the interior of the earth; and when they were about to bring them into the light of day, they ordered Prometheus and Epimetheus to equip them each with appropriate qualities. Epimetheus said to Prometheus: "Let me do the distributing, and you be the inspector." This was agreed to, and Epimetheus made the distribution. There were some to whom he gave strength without speed, which he in turn bestowed upon weaker ones; some he armed, and others he e left unarmed; for the latter he devised some other means of preservation: upon those whom he equipped with diminutive bodies, he bestowed winged flight or subterranean habitation. Those which he aggrandized with magnitude, he protected by their very size; and the rest he distributed similarly, always keeping things even. He followed this 321 procedure as a precaution that no race should be extinguished. And after he had provided them with means to elude mutual destruction, he also contrived protection against the seasons; clothing them with thick fur and tough hides sufficient to defend them against the winter cold, yet able to resist the summer heat, and serving also as a natural bed of their own when they wanted to rest; he also shod them, some with hooves, others with hard and callous skins b under their feet. Then he gave them various foods, herbs of the soil to some, to others fruits of trees, and to others roots, and to some again he gave other animals to eat. And some he made to have few young ones, while those who were their prey were very prolific; and in this manner the race was preserved. Now, since Epimetheus was not terribly clever, he failed to notice that he had distributed

c among the brute animals all the qualities which he had to give, and so when he came to man, who was still unequipped, he was terribly perplexed. And while he was in this perplexity, Prometheus came to inspect the distribution, and he found that the other animals were quite suitably furnished, but that man was naked and shoeless, and had neither a bed nor armor. The appointed hour was now approaching when man in his turn was to emerge from the earth into the light of day; and Prometheus, not knowing how he could devise his salvation, stole the mechanical arts

d of Hephaestus and Athene, and fire with them (they could have been neither acquired nor used without fire), and gave them to man. Thus man obtained the wisdom necessary to support life, but political wisdom he did not possess; for that was in the keeping of Zeus, and it was not possible for Prometheus to take the necessary next step of penetrating the citadel of heaven, where Zeus dwelt (there were, moreover, ferocious guards maintained there); but he did enter by stealth into the joint workshop of Athene and Hephaestus, where they practiced their fa-

e vorite arts, and carried off Hephaestus' art of working by fire, and also the art of Athene, and gave them to man. And in this way man was supplied with the means of life. But later, as the story is told, there overtook Prometheus a

322 reckoning for the theft that had been committed on account of Epimetheus.

Now man, having a share of the divine attributes, was, in the first place, the only one of the animals who worshiped gods, because he alone was of their kindred; and he undertook to raise altars and images of them. Second, he was not long in inventing articulate speech and words; and he also discovered the making of houses and clothes and shoes and beds, and how to draw sustenance from the earth. Thus provided, mankind at first lived dispersed, and there were no cities. But the consequence was that they b were destroyed by the wild beasts, for they were utterly weak in comparison to them, and their practical attainments were only sufficient to provide them with the means of life, and did not enable them to wage war against the animals: for they did not as yet possess the art of government, of which the art of war is a part. After a while the desire for self-preservation gathered them into cities; but when they were gathered together, having no art of government, they treated one another unjustly, and soon again were embarking on the cycle of dispersion and destruction. Zeus feared that the entire race would be exterminated, and so he sent c Hermes to them, bearing justice and the sense of shame to be the ordering principles of cities and the bonds of friendship and conciliation. Hermes asked Zeus how he should impart justice and shame among men: "Should I distribute them in the same way as technical skills are distributed? Which is as follows: if one man possesses medical skills, that is sufficient for the care of many laymen, and likewise for the rest of the professions and crafts. Am I to distribute justice and shame among men according to the same principle? Or shall I give them to them all?" "To all," d said Zeus. "Let them all have a share; for cities cannot exist if the virtues are shared by only a few, as the professional skills are. And furthermore, make a law on my authority that anyone who is unable to comply with justice and to feel shame shall be put to death as a blight on the state."

And this is the reason, Socrates, why the Athenians and mankind in general, when the question before them relates to carpentering or any other professional skill, allow only a

few to take part in their deliberations; and when anyone
outside of these few tries to give advice, then, as you say,
e they do not tolerate it; which, I say, is very natural. But
when it is on a question of civic virtue that they are debat-
ing—and such a debate must be characterized by pru-
323 dence and justice throughout—then they tolerate any man
who addresses them, as is also natural, because they think
that every man ought to share in this sort of virtue, and
that states could not exist if this were otherwise. Such,
Socrates, is the reason for this phenomenon.

And that you may not suppose yourself to be deceived
in thinking the belief that every man has a share of justice
or honesty and the rest of civic virtue to be universal, let
me give you a further proof. In other cases, as you are
aware, if a man says that he is a good flute player, or skillful in any other art in which he has no skill, people either
laugh at him or become angry with him, and his relations
b think that he is insane and go and admonish him; but when
honesty is in question, or some other civic virtue, even if
they *know* that he is dishonest, still, if the man comes forward publicly and tells the truth against himself, that he is
dishonest, then, what in the other case was held by them
to be good sense, that is, telling the truth, they now deem
to be utter lunacy. They say that all men ought at least to
claim to be honest, whether they are honest or they are not,
and that a man is out of his mind who makes no claim to
that virtue. Their assumption is that every man must pos-
c sess it to some degree, or else he ought not to be counted
human.

I have been arguing so far that people are right in ad-
mitting every man as a counselor about this sort of virtue,
as they are of the opinion that every man is a partaker of it.
I will next try to show that they do not conceive this virtue

to be given by nature, or to grow spontaneously, but to be a thing which can indeed be taught, and which comes to those to whom it does come through their own deliberate effort. No one corrects or rebukes or becomes angry with people whose ills they suppose to be due to nature or d chance; they do not try to punish or to prevent them from being what they are; rather, they pity them. Who is so foolish as to chastise or instruct the ugly, or the small, or the feeble? And this is because everyone knows that good and evil of this kind are the work of nature and of chance; whereas if a man lacks those good qualities which are held to be attainable by diligence and practice and teaching, and possesses only the contrary evil qualities, other men are e angry with him, and punish and reprove him. Of these evil qualities one is impiety, another injustice—to put it briefly, everything that is contrary to civic virtue. In such cases any 324 man will be angry with another, and reprimand him— clearly because he thinks that by study and learning the virtue can be acquired. If, Socrates, you are willing to consider what the punishment of wrongdoers signifies, the matter itself will show you that in the opinion of mankind virtue can be passed on to another: no one, unless he is seeking unreasoning revenge in the manner of a beast, ex- b acts punishment with his mind focused exclusively on the fact of the past misdeed. Anyone who wishes to inflict punishment *rationally* does not retaliate for the past wrong (since what has been done cannot be undone); rather, he punishes with a view to the future—to bring it about that the man who is punished, and any other man who sees him punished, will be deterred from doing wrong again. Now if this is the way he conceives punishment, then he also conceives that virtue can be taught—so much is implied, if punishment can deter. And this is the view held by all who

c seek the punishment of others in either private or public
affairs. And the Athenians, too, your own citizens, like
other men, punish and take vengeance on all whom they
regard as evildoers; and hence we may infer that they belong to the class of those who think that virtue can be acquired and taught. Thus far, Socrates, I have shown you
clearly enough, if I am not mistaken, that your countrymen are right in allowing the tinker and the cobbler to advise about politics, and also that they believe virtue to be
d capable of being taught and acquired.

There yet remains one difficulty which has been raised
by you about good men. What is the reason that good men
teach their sons the knowledge which can be gained from
teachers, and make them wise in that, but make them no
better than anyone else in the virtues which distinguish
themselves? And here, Socrates, I will no longer speak to
you in the form of a story, but in argument. Please consider: Is there or is there not some one thing in which all
citizens must partake, if there is to be a city at all? The only
e solution of your difficulty is contained in the answer to
this question or nowhere at all. For if there is any such
thing, and this one thing is not the art of the carpenter, or
325 the smith, or the potter, but justice and prudence and
piety, which taking them all together as one single thing I
designate humane virtue—if this is the thing in which it is
necessary that each man partake, and if he wishes to learn
or do anything else, he must do so in concert with this
thing, and if not in concert with this thing he must not act
at all, and if he who is lacking in this, whether he is a child
or a grown-up man or woman, he must be taught it and
punished, until by being punished he becomes better, and
whoever rebels against the instruction and punishment
b must be either exiled or condemned to death as incur-

able—if what I am saying is true, and yet good men have their sons taught other things and not this, consider how extraordinary and inexplicable their conduct is. For we have shown that they think virtue capable of being taught and cultivated both in private and public, and yet, though it is for them a given that this *can* be both cultivated and taught, they nonetheless have their sons taught *other* matters, in the case of which death is not the penalty for ignorance; but in the case of that one thing which their children, if they do not learn, and are not advanced to excellence in, they will suffer death and exile, and over and above death, confiscation of property, and, in a word, the total destruction of their families—this one thing, I say, we are to believe that they do not have their children taught, and do not take the utmost care that they should learn? I think not, Socrates!

Education and admonition begin in the first years of childhood and continue to the very end of life. Mother and nurse and father and tutor start competing with one another over the improvement of the child as soon as he is able to understand what is being said to him: he cannot say or do anything without their teaching him and setting forth to him that this is just and that is unjust; this is honorable, that is dishonorable; this is pious, that is impious; do this and don't do that. And if he obeys, well and good; if not, he is straightened out with threats and blows, like a piece of bent or warped wood. At a later stage they send him to teachers, and order them to see to his good behavior even more than to his reading and music; and the teachers do as they are told. And when the boy has learned his letters and is beginning to understand what is written, just as earlier he came to understand what was spoken, they put on his desk the works of great poets for him to read; in

326 these are contained many admonitions, and many stories and praises and encomia of famous men of old, which he is required to learn by heart, in order that he may imitate or emulate them and desire to become like them. Then, again, the lyre teachers[19] take similar care that their young pupil is prudent and gets into no trouble; furthermore, when they have taught him the use of the lyre, they introduce him to the poems of other excellent poets, the lyric poets;

b and they set these to music, and they make the harmonies and rhythms become permanent inhabitants of the children's souls, in order that they may learn to be more gentle, and harmonious, and rhythmical, and so more suited for speech and action; for every part of the life of man has need of harmony and rhythm. Then, in addition, they send them to the teacher of gymnastic skills, in order that the improvement of their bodies may better minister to the virtuous mind, and that they may not be compelled

c through bodily weakness to play the coward in war or on any other occasion.

All these things are done most by those who have the most means, and the people who have the most means are the rich; their children begin to go to school the soonest and leave it the latest. When they are finally delivered from their teachers, the state in turn compels them to learn the laws, and to live in accordance with them, in order that

d their behavior not be dictated by their own random impulses. And just as the writing teacher first traces outlines

---

[19]Music formed a much larger part of a child's education than it does today; if we bear in mind that literature formed the greatest part of the curriculum, and that literature consisted of poetry, and poetry was either sung or recited to musical accompaniment—in short, poetry, and therefore literature, was in effect song—then we may get an idea of the importance of, for example, the lyre teacher.

of the letters with a stylus for the use of the young begin-
ner who is not yet able to write, and then gives him the
tablet and makes him write within these guidelines, so the
city outlines the laws, which were the inventions of good
lawgivers of old, and compels us to exercise and to obey
authority in accordance with them; and anyone who trans-
gresses them the city corrects, or, in other words, calls to
account, which is a term used not only in your country, but
also in many others, seeing that justice calls men to ac-   e
count.[20] Now when there is all this effort made about virtue
both private and public, why, Socrates, are you amazed and
in doubt whether virtue can be taught? Stop being amazed,
for the opposite would be far more surprising.

But why then do the sons of good fathers often turn out
badly? This too I will explain. There is nothing very surprising in the phenomenon, if what I said before was true,
that the existence of a state implies that no man is not   327
competent in this matter, virtue. If this is so—and nothing
could be truer—then I will further ask you to take as an illustration some other pursuit or branch of knowledge, and
reflect upon that. Suppose that there could be no state unless we were all flute players, as far as each had the capacity, and everybody freely taught everybody else the art,
both in private and public, and reproved the bad player and
did not begrudge the art to him, just as no man now with-
holds the teaching of justice and the laws, or conceals them
as if they were trade secrets—for all of us have a mutual   b
interest in the justice and virtue of one another, and this is
the reason why everyone is so ready to propagate and teach

[20]Protagoras is making a feeble pun on the "straightening out, correcting"
(*euthynein*) done by justice, and the accounting rendered by magistrates at the end
of their term (*euthynae*). What makes the pun so weak is that the second word is
clearly just a specialized application of the first.

justice and the laws—supposing then, I say, that there were the same readiness and liberality among us in teaching one another flute-playing, do you imagine, Socrates, that the sons of good flute players would be more likely to be good flute players than the sons of bad ones? I don't think so. Wouldn't in fact their sons grow up to be distinguished or

c undistinguished according to their own natural capacities as flute players, and the son of a good player would often turn out to be a bad one, and the son of a bad player to be a good one? But at least they would all play the flute reasonably well in comparison to those who were ignorant and unacquainted with the art of flute-playing. Similarly, I ask you to reflect that the person who appears to you to be the worst of those who have been brought up in laws and human society would appear to be a just man and an artificer of justice if he were to be compared with men who had

d no education, or courts of justice, or laws, or any constraints forcing them constantly to the practice of virtue— with savages like those whom the poet Pherecrates exhibited on the stage at last year's Lenaean festival.[21] If you were living among people like the misanthropes of his chorus, you would be only too glad to meet with Euryates and Phrynondas,[22] and you would utter loud lamentations in your yearning to return to the depravity exhibited by the men of this part of the world. Now you, Socrates, are

e being overly fastidious: all men are teachers of virtue, each one according to his ability; but you look around and say, "Where are the teachers?" You might as well ask, "Who teaches Greek?" For of that too there will not be any

328 teachers found. Or you might ask, "Who is to teach the

---

[21]A contemporary Athenian comic poet; the play was indeed entitled *Savages.*
[22]Historical figures—bywords for moral depravity, treachery in particular.

sons of our craftsmen?"—teach them this very craft that they have learned from their fathers as well as he and his fellow craftsmen were able to teach them. It is not going to be easy, I don't think, Socrates, to find the teacher who could teach those who have already been taught; but there is no difficulty in finding a teacher for those who are ignorant. And this is true of virtue and of anything else. But if there is anyone better able than we are to advance virtue even just a little bit, we should be grateful. And I believe b myself to be one of these, excelling all other human beings in the power to raise a man toward nobility and goodness; and I give my pupils their money's worth, and even more, as they themselves confess. And therefore I have introduced the following method of payment: when a man is my pupil, if he likes, he pays my fee; if he does not, he has only to go into a temple and state under oath the value of c the instruction, and he pays no more than that.

Such is my fable, Socrates, and such is the argument by which I endeavor to show that virtue can be taught, and that this is the opinion of the Athenians. I have also attempted to show that you are not to wonder at good fathers having bad sons, or at good sons having bad fathers; thus the sons of Polyclitus, who are the companions of our friends here, Paralus and Xanthippus, are nothing in comparison with their father; and this is true of the sons of many other artists. As yet we ought not to bring the same charge against Paralus and Xanthippus themselves, for d they are young and there is still hope for them.

Such was the speech of Protagoras, who now left off speaking. For a long time I could not take my eyes off him, still spellbound, expecting him to speak further, and eager to hear him. At length, when the truth dawned upon me that he had really finished, then, not without difficulty, I pulled myself together, as it were, and, looking at Hippocrates, I said to him: O son of Apollodorus, how deeply grateful I am to you for having urged me to come here; I

e would not have missed the speech of Protagoras for a great deal. You see, in the past I used to imagine that it was not any human contrivance through which the good became good, but now I know better. Yet I have still one very small difficulty which I am sure that Protagoras will easily clear up, as he has already clarified so much: if a man were to go and consult Pericles or any of our great orators about these

329 matters, he might perhaps hear from them some such discourse as Protagoras' now; but if he should ask a question of any of them, then, like books, they can neither answer nor themselves ask questions; and if anyone challenges the least particular of their speech, then they spin out a long harangue in answer to a short question, like brass pots, which, when they are hit, ring loud and go on ringing un-

b less someone puts his hand on them; whereas our friend Protagoras can not only speak very well at length, as he has just shown, in fact, but when he is asked a question, he can answer briefly; and when he asks, he will wait and hear the answer; and this a very rare gift. Now I, Protagoras, have almost all I need, and would have everything if you should answer me this one question. You were saying that virtue can be taught—and if it is the case that I would believe any man who should claim this, then I believe you.[23] But I was

c perplexed by one thing in your speech, and I ask you now to make up this deficiency in my soul.[24] You said that Zeus

[23]Socrates' expression may be deliberately convoluted here: for it is *not* the case and he does *not* believe Protagoras.

[24]I.e., the deficiency in Socrates' soul will be filled if Protagoras answers the "one question" Socrates mentioned two sentences ago as all that he needed to "have everything."

sent justice and the sense of shame to men; and conversely, at several points in your speech it was stated by you that justice, and prudence, and piety, and all these qualities, taken together, constitute some one single thing, virtue. Now I want you to tell me definitely whether virtue is a single entity, of which justice and prudence and piety are parts; or whether all these that I just mentioned are names for the same one thing. This is the thing I still need to d know.

But it is easy to answer this question, Socrates: the things that you ask about are parts of virtue, which is one single thing.

And are they parts, I said, in the same way in which the mouth, nose, and eyes, and ears are the parts of a face? Or are they like the parts of gold, which differ from the whole and from one another only in being larger or smaller?

I would say that they differed, Socrates, in the first way; they are related to one another as the parts of a face are re- e lated to the whole face.

Then is it the case that some men acquire some one of these parts of virtue, and other men some other? Or is it that if a man acquires one part, he must have them all?

By no means, he said; for many a man is brave but unjust, or just but not wise.

Oh. Are these things, wisdom and courage, also parts of 330 virtue, then?

More than anything, he answered: wisdom is the *greatest* of the parts.

And they are all different from one another? I said.
Yes.

And each of them has its own distinct function? For example, with the parts of the face—the eye is not like the ear, and does not have the same functions; and the other

parts are none of them like one another, either in their functions, or in any other way. So then: I want to know if the comparison holds concerning the parts of virtue. Do they also differ from one another in themselves and in
b their functions? Obviously that *must* be so, *if* the comparison holds.

Yes, Socrates, it is so.

Then, I said, no other part of virtue is like knowledge, or like justice, or like courage, or like prudence, or like piety?

No, he answered.

Well, then, I said, suppose that you and I inquire into the nature of each of them. Let us start with a question like
c this: Is justice an actual thing, or is it not? My opinion is that it is; and yours?

That is mine also, he said.

Now then—if someone should ask us: "O Protagoras, and you, Socrates, tell me—this thing that you just mentioned, justice, is it itself just or is it unjust?" I for my part would answer that it is just. How would you place your vote, on my side or the other?

With you, he said.

So I would answer the man who asked, that justice has the property of being just; and you likewise?
d Yes, he said.

And suppose that he went on to ask us: "Well now, is there also such a thing as piety?"—we would answer "Yes," if I am not mistaken?

Yes, he said.

"Which you would also acknowledge to be a thing?"— wouldn't we say "Yes"?

He assented.

"And is this a sort of thing which has by nature the property of being pious, or of being impious?" I would be angry at his putting this question, and would say, "Mind your tongue, fellow; it is hardly likely that anything else would be pious if piety itself isn't going to be." What would you e say? Wouldn't you answer in the same way?

Certainly, he said.

And then after this, suppose that he came and asked us, "What were you saying just now? Did I not hear you correctly? I thought you said that the relationship of the parts of virtue was that none was like the other?" I would answer, "Your hearing was otherwise fine, but if you think that I'm the one who made that last claim, it went astray there; I just asked the question; it was Protagoras who gave the answer." 331 And suppose that he turned to you and said, "Is he telling the truth, Protagoras? Do you really maintain that one part of virtue is unlike another? Is this your position?"—how would you answer him?

I could not help acknowledging the truth of what he said, Socrates.

Well then, Protagoras, if we agree on that, then how will we answer if he asks us this: "Then piety doesn't have the quality of being just, nor justice that of being pious, but of being not pious; and piety has the quality of being not just, and therefore unjust, and the just is impious?" How shall we answer him? Speaking for myself, I would b certainly say that justice is pious, and that piety is just; and if you should allow me to speak for you, I would give the same answer, namely, that justice is either identical to piety, or as much like it as possible, and above all, that justice is the sort of thing piety is and piety the sort justice is. But tell me if I may be permitted to give this answer on your behalf, and if you agree with me.

He replied, It doesn't seem to me to be as simple as that,
c Socrates, that justice is pious and that piety is just; for there
appears to me to be a difference between them. But what
does it matter? If it pleases you, then let us grant that justice is pious, and that piety is just.

I'll have none of that, I replied; I didn't come here to
find out "if it pleases you" or "if that's your opinion," but to
test you and me and the validity of our beliefs—and I do
not think that an argument's validity can be successfully
d tested unless these "ifs" are removed from it.[25]

Well, he said, I do admit that justice resembles piety in
some way—for there is always some way in which one
thing can be found to resemble any other thing; for example, white is in a certain way like black, and hard is like soft,
and the most extreme opposites have some qualities in
common; and even the parts of the face, which, as we were
saying before, are distinct and have different functions, are
still from a certain point of view similar, and one of them
is like another of them. So in this sense you might prove, if
e you wanted to, that these things are all like one another.
But with things that just share some point of likeness—to
call them "alike," even though the point of likeness is utterly trivial, is illegitimate (as it is also to call things that
are unlike in some small particular "unlike").

Astonished, I said to him: Am I to take it, then, that in
your view justice and piety stand in such a relationship to
each other that they share only a small degree of likeness?

[25]Socrates believes that dialectic can succeed only if the interlocutors give
their sincere assent to every step of the argument; "these 'ifs'" therefore refers
not to all conditionals, which he would never consider banishing, but to the for-
mulas of insincere assent just mentioned ("if it pleases you," "if that's your
opinion").

Certainly not, but their relationship is not what you apparently think it is, either.

332

Well, I said, since this line of inquiry seems to annoy you, let's let it go, and take another of the examples you mentioned instead. Do you admit the existence of folly?

I do.

And isn't wisdom the exact opposite of folly?

I believe so, he said.

And when men act rightly and advantageously they seem to you to be prudent or the reverse?

Prudent, he said.

And prudence makes them prudent?

Certainly.

b

And those who do not act rightly act foolishly, and in acting thus are not prudent?

I agree, he said.

Then to act foolishly is the opposite of acting prudently?

He assented.

And foolish actions are done with folly, and prudent actions with prudence?

He agreed.

And that which is done with strength is done strongly, and that which is done with weakness, weakly?

He assented.

And that which is done with swiftness is done swiftly, and that which is done with slowness, slowly?

He assented again.

And that which is done in the same manner is done with c the same; and that which is done in an opposite manner with the opposite?

He agreed.

Come then, I said, is there such a thing as the beautiful?

Yes.

To which the only opposite is the ugly?

There is no other.

And is there such a thing as the good?

There is.

To which the only opposite is the evil?

There is no other.

And there is the high in tone?

Yes.

To which the only opposite is the low?

There is no other, he said, but that.

Then every opposite has one opposite only and no more?

He assented.

d   Then now, I said, let us recapitulate what we have agreed upon. First of all we have agreed that everything has one opposite and not more than one?

We have agreed on that.

And also that that which was done in opposite ways was done with opposite qualities?

Yes.

And that which was done foolishly, as we further agreed, was done in the opposite way to that which was done prudently?

Yes.

And that which was done prudently was done with prudence, and that which was done foolishly with folly?

He agreed.

e   So if things are done in an opposite way, they must be being done with opposite qualities?

Yes.

And one thing is done with prudence, and quite another thing with folly?

Yes.

And in opposite ways?

Certainly.

And therefore with qualities that are opposite?

Yes.

Then folly is the opposite of prudence?

Clearly.

And do you remember that folly has already been acknowledged by us to be the opposite of wisdom?

He assented.

And we said that everything has only one opposite?

Yes.

Then, Protagoras, which of the two assertions shall we renounce? One says that everything has only one opposite; the other that wisdom is distinct from prudence, and that each of them is a part of virtue; and that they are not only distinct, but dissimilar, both in themselves and in their functions, like the parts of a face. Which of them shall we renounce? Uttering the two of them together is very jarring to the ear; they do not agree or harmonize: for how could they harmonize, if it is truly necessary that each one thing have only one opposite and no more than one, and yet folly, which is one thing, clearly has two opposites—wisdom and prudence? Isn't that true, Protagoras, or not?

He assented, but with great reluctance.

Then prudence and wisdom must be one thing, just as earlier it became clear to us that justice and piety are nearly the same. And now, Protagoras, I said, we must finish the inquiry, and not give up from exhaustion. Do you think that a man doing wrong is exhibiting prudence in doing wrong?

I would be ashamed, Socrates, he said, to acknowledge this, which nevertheless many may be found to assert.

And shall I argue with them or with you? I replied.

If it is the same to you, he said, address first the argument of the many.

Whichever you please, provided only that you answer me, regardless of whether you are of their opinion or not.[26] My aim is to test the validity of the argument; and yet the result may be that I, in asking the questions, and you, in answering them, may both be put on trial.

d   At this Protagoras began to stand on his dignity, alleging that the format was awkward—inconvenient—not to his taste; but finally he consented to cooperate.

Now then, I said, let's start afresh, and you answer me. Do some men in your view exhibit prudence in doing wrong?

Let that be granted, he said.

And prudence is to use good sense?

Yes.

And to use good sense is for them to plan their wrongdoing well?

Let it be granted.

If their wrongdoing succeeds, I said, or if it does not?

If it succeeds.

And you would admit the existence of things that are good?

Yes.

And are they the things that are profitable to mankind?

e   Yes, indeed, he snapped; and even if they are unprofitable to mankind, I still call them good.

---

[26]This demand would appear to violate the requirement of sincere assent discussed in the previous note; apparently, in order to keep an inquiry going, Socrates is willing (here more than willing) to have his interlocutor play a part: answer as you sincerely would answer if you sincerely held this view, which you don't.

Protagoras seemed at this point to be getting exasperated and resentful; he looked as if he were marshaling himself to do battle against the answering of questions. Seeing this, I took care to question him gently, and said:

When you say, Protagoras, that unprofitable things are good, do you mean things that are not profitable to one 334 person, or not profitable at all? And do you call the latter good?

Certainly not the last, he replied; for I know of many things—meats, drinks, medicines, and ten thousand other things—that are unprofitable for man, and some that are profitable; and some that are neither profitable nor unprofitable for man, but are for horses; and some for oxen only, and some for dogs; and some for no animals, but only for trees; and some things are good for the roots of trees, but bad for their buds, as for example manure, which is a good thing when laid about the roots of a tree, b but utterly destructive if thrown upon the shoots and young branches; or I may cite olive oil, which is destructive to all plants, and generally highly injurious to the hair of every animal with the exception of man, but beneficial to human hair and to the human body generally. What the good is, is so various and complex a matter that here too what is good for a man's body externally is the very worst thing for his internal organs: for this reason c doctors always forbid their patients the use of oil in their food, except in very small quantities, just enough to extinguish a disagreeable sensation of smell in breads and relishes.

When he had given this answer, the company cheered him. And I said: Protagoras, I have a wretched memory, and when anyone makes a long speech to me I never remember what he is talking about. It is just as if I were deaf, d and you were going to converse with me; you would think it necessary to speak more loudly than you do to others. Likewise, now, having such a bad memory, I will ask you to cut your answers down and make them shorter, if you wish to take me with you.

What do you mean? he said. How am I to shorten my answers? Am I to make them too short?

Certainly not, I said.

But short enough?

e Yes, I said.

Am I to give answers that appear to me to be short enough, or that appear to you to be short enough?

I have heard, I said, that you can speak and teach others to speak about the same things at such length that the speech never ends, or with such concision that no one 335 could make it shorter. Please, therefore, if you talk with me, adopt the latter or more compendious method.

Socrates, he replied, many a battle of words have I fought, and if I followed the method of disputation that my adversaries desired, as you want me to do, I would be no better than anyone, and the name of Protagoras would not have become renowned in Greece.

I saw that he was not satisfied with his previous answers, b and that he would not play the part of answerer anymore if he could help it, and I realized that there was no point in my remaining in the company, so I said: But you should know, Protagoras, that I, too, do not want our discussion to proceed in a way that goes against your judgment; but when you are willing to argue with me in such a way that I can follow you, then I will argue with you. Now you, as is said of you by others and as you say of yourself, are able to have discussions in shorter forms of speech as well as in longer— c for you are an expert—but I cannot manage these long speeches; I only wish that I could.[27] You, on the other hand, are capable of either, and so ought to speak shorter as I beg you to, and then we might converse. But I see that you are disinclined, and as I have an engagement which will prevent my staying to hear you stretch out great long speeches (for I have to be someplace else), I will leave; although I would probably enjoy hearing you deliver these, too.

Thus I spoke, and was rising as if to depart when Callias seized me by the right hand, and with his left hand caught hold of this cloak of mine.[28] He said: We will not let you d go, Socrates, for your departure will have a terrible effect on the quality of our talk. So I beg you to stay, since there is nothing in the world that I would hear with greater pleasure than you and Protagoras conversing. Do not refuse us this favor.

Now I had already gotten up to leave, and I said: Son of Hipponicus, I have always admired your zeal to learn, and I do now heartily applaud and love your philosophical spirit, and I would gladly comply with your request, if I could. e But the truth is that I cannot do what you ask—it is as if you were to bid me to keep pace with Crison the runner of Himera,[29] when in his prime, or with someone of the long- or day-course runners.[30] To such a request I would reply 336 that, even more urgently than you beseech me, do I beseech

[27]Socrates' claim here that he cannot manage long speeches serves his present purpose of trying to compel Protagoras to accede to the question-and-answer format; its actual truth value, however, can be measured against the speeches Socrates is shown giving in, for example, the *Phaedrus* and the *Symposium*, or even later in this work, as for example in his explication of the poem of Simonides.

[28]Socrates habitually wore a short cloak in the austere Spartan style, different from the normal outfit of the Athenian male.

[29]Olympic victor in three successive Olympiads, so that his "prime" spanned at least eight years.

[30]"Day-course": what we would call a marathon.

my own legs to do just these things; but they refuse to comply. And therefore if you want to see Crison and me running together, you must induce him to slow his speed down to mine, for I cannot run quickly, and he can run slowly. And likewise if you want to hear me and Protagoras conversing, you must ask him to shorten his answers, and

b keep to the point, as he did at first; if not, what sort of thing is our discussion going to be? For discussion is one thing, and making an oration is quite another, in my humble opinion.

But don't you see, Socrates, said Callias, it seems fair for Protagoras to want to be allowed to speak in his own way, and you in yours.

Here Alcibiades interposed, and said: That, Callias, is not a true statement of the case. For Socrates here admits that he cannot make a long speech—in this he yields the palm to Protagoras: but I would be amazed if he yielded to

c any man in the power of conversing and in the give-and-take of argument. Now if Protagoras admits that he is inferior to Socrates in argumentative skill, that is enough for Socrates; but if he claims a superiority in argument as well, let him ask and answer—not returning a long-winded harangue to every question, impeding the argument and

d evading the point, and speaking at such length that most of his hearers forget the question at issue (not that Socrates is likely to forget—that I will bet on, although he may pretend for fun that he has a bad memory). Socrates appears to me to be more in the right than Protagoras; that is my view, and every man ought to say what he thinks.[31]

When Alcibiades had done speaking, someone—

---

[31]To appreciate the character of this last speech, and its speaker, it is important to bear in mind that Alcibiades is about fifteen years old, and Protagoras about sixty.

Critias, I believe—went on to say: Prodicus and Hippias, Callias appears to me to be a partisan of Protagoras, and Alcibiades is always eager to prevail in any matter in which he concerns himself. But we should not be partisans of either Socrates or Protagoras; let us rather unite in imploring both of them not to break up the discussion in the middle.

Prodicus added: That, Critias, seems to me to be well said, for those who are present at such discussions ought to be impartial hearers of both the speakers; remembering, however, that impartiality is not the same as equality, for both sides should be impartially heard, and yet an equal prize should not be assigned to both of them; but to the wiser a greater should be given, and a lower to the less learned. And I as well as Critias would beg you, Protagoras and Socrates, to grant our request, which is that you will argue with each other, but not quarrel; for friends argue with friends out of goodwill, but only adversaries and enemies quarrel. And then our meeting will be most successful; for in this way you, who are the speakers, will be most likely to win esteem rather than applause from us who are your audience; for esteem is a sincere conviction in the hearers' souls, whereas applause is often the insincere expression of men uttering falsehoods contrary to their conviction. And thus we who are the hearers will be delighted rather than pleasured; for delight is a product of the mind alone, when it receives wisdom and knowledge, but pleasure comes about when someone eats or enjoys some other pleasant thing with his body alone. Thus spoke Prodicus, and many of the company commended his words.

Hippias the wise spoke next. He said: All of you who are here present I consider to be kinsmen and friends and fellow citizens, by nature and not by law; for by nature, like is akin to like, whereas law is the tyrant of mankind, and often compels us to do many things which are against nature. How great would be the disgrace then, if we, who know the nature of things, and are the wisest of the Hellenes, and as such meet here in this city, which is the parliament of wisdom for all Greece, and, in this city, in the the greatest and most glorious house, should have nothing

e to show worthy of this height of dignity, but should only quarrel with one another like the most debased of mankind! I do beg and advise you, Protagoras, and you, Socrates, to agree upon a compromise. Let us be your

338 peacemakers. And do not you, Socrates, aim at this precise and extreme brevity in discourse, if it is disagreeable to Protagoras, but loosen and let go the reins of speech, offering us your thoughts in a diction statelier and more graceful. And you, Protagoras, do not commit yourself to the fair wind, and, with every sail set, fly out of sight of land into an ocean of words; but let both of you cut a middle course. Do as I say. And let me also persuade you to choose an arbiter or overseer or president; he will keep

b watch over your words and will prescribe their proper length.

This proposal was received by the company with universal approval; Callias said that he would not let me go, and they begged me to choose an arbiter. But I said that to choose an umpire for a conversation would be disgraceful; for if the person chosen was inferior to us, it would not be proper for the inferior to preside over his betters; or if he was the same as we are, that would not be proper, either; for a person who is the same will do the same as we do, and what will be the use of choosing him? And if you say, "Let's

c have someone who is better, then," I will answer that you

cannot have anyone who is wiser than Protagoras. And if you choose another who is not really better, and who you only say is better, that also would be to inflict a disgrace upon Protagoras, putting another in a position above him as though he were an inferior person; not that, as far as I am concerned, it makes any difference either way. But let me tell you what I would like to do in order that the conversation and discussion may go on as you desire. If Protagoras is not disposed to answer, let him ask the questions and I d will answer; and I will try to show him at the same time how, as I maintain, a person answering ought to answer; and when I have answered as many questions as he wants to ask, let him in the same manner answer me; and if he seems to be reluctant to answer the precise question asked of him, you and I will jointly entreat him, as you entreated me, not to ruin the discussion. And this will require no spe- e cial arbiter—all of you shall be arbiters.

This was approved by all, and Protagoras, though very much against his will, was obliged to agree that he would play the part of questioner; and when he had asked enough of them, that he would in turn answer those that he was asked, with short replies. He began to put his questions something as follows:

I am of the opinion, Socrates, he said, that skill in poetry is the principal part of education; and this I conceive to be the power of knowing what compositions of the 339 poets are good poetry, and what are not, and how they are to be distinguished, and of explaining, when asked, the reason for the difference. And now our question shall be concerned with the same subject that you and I discussed before, virtue, only transferred to the domain of poetry: this will be the only difference. Now, as you know, Simonides says in his poem for Scopas, son of Creon the Thessalian,[32] that

b   *While it is hard to become truly good,*
      Built foursquare in hands and feet and mind, with nothing to
          fault . . .

Do you know the poem? Or shall I go through the whole thing?

No need to, said I; I am perfectly well acquainted with the poem, and have in fact made a careful study of it.

Good, he said. And do you think it to have been well and properly composed?

Yes, I said, very well and properly composed.

But do you think a poem is well composed if the poet contradicts himself?

No, not well composed, I replied.

Then look at it more closely, he said.

c   But I have already studied it enough, my friend.

So then you know, he said, that as the poem continues he says:

      To me the adage of Pittacus sounds out of tune,[33]
      Though spoken by a mortal wise:
      It is hard, said he, to be good. . . .

Now you will observe that both this and the former sentiment proceed from the same poet.

[32]The Scopadae were a dynasty ruling the city of Crannon in central Thessaly (in the north of Greece) in the sixth century B.C.; the Cean poet Simonides was closely associated with the dynasty before its collapse around 515.

[33]Pittacus was tyrant of Mytilene on the island of Lesbos towards the end of the seventh century B.C.; his rule succeeded in moderating the extreme factions of the city, and he was traditionally reckoned one of the "Seven Sages" of archaic Greece.

Yes, I know.

And do you think, he said, that the two sayings are consistent?

Yes, I said, I think so (and at the same time I could not help fearing that there might be something to what he said). Do you think otherwise?

Why, he said, how could I think he was consistent when d he says both these things? First of all, he lays it down that "it is hard to become truly good," and then a little further on in the poem, he forgets, and criticizes Pittacus and refuses to agree with him when he says, "it is hard to be good"—the same thing that he had said himself. And yet when he criticizes a man who says the same things as he says, he criticizes himself; so that he must be wrong in either his first or his second assertion.

This speech ignited a burst of cheering and applause from most of the audience. I myself immediately started to e get dizzy and black out, as if I had been struck a blow by an expert boxer, when I heard his words and the sound of the cheering; and to tell the truth, I wanted to get time to think what the poet's meaning really was. So I turned to Prodicus and called out to him:

Prodicus, I said, Simonides is a countryman of yours,[34] and you ought to come to his aid. I must appeal to you, like 340 the River Scamander in Homer, who, when besieged by Achilles, summons the River Simois to aid him, saying:[35]

Brother dear, let us both together check the might of the hero.

And I summon you, for I am afraid that Protagoras will take Simonides by storm. The defense of Simonides

[34]Both being from the island of Ceos.
[35]*Iliad* 21. 308–309.

requires that special art of yours by means of which you
b distinguish "will" and "wish," and make other subtle distinctions like those you drew just now. I would like to know
if you agree with what I said; in my opinion there is no
contradiction in the words of Simonides. So you, Prodicus,
state your view plainly: do you think "being" is the same as
"becoming," or something different?

Something different, certainly, replied Prodicus.

Didn't Simonides first set forth, as his own view, that "it
is hard to become truly good"?

c Quite right, said Prodicus.

And then he criticizes Pittacus, not, as Protagoras
imagines, for saying the same thing as he himself says,
but for saying something different. Pittacus does not say
as Simonides says that it is hard for a person to *become*
good, but it is hard for a person to *be* good. But they are
not the same thing, being and becoming, as our friend
Prodicus avers, Protagoras; and if they are not the same,
then Simonides is not contradicting himself. Perhaps
d Prodicus here, and many others too, would say, as Hesiod
says, that on the one hand, it is hard for someone to become good,

> For the gods have set a barrier of sweat on the path to virtue;
> But when he has climbed the height,
> Then to retain virtue, however hard the acquisition, is easy.[36]

Prodicus heard and approved; but Protagoras said: Your
correction, Socrates, creates a greater error than the one it
is correcting.

That was badly done by me then, Protagoras, I said; I am

[36]Hesiod, *Works and Days* 289–291.

a laughably poor healer, aggravating a disorder I am seek- e
ing to cure.

But that's the way it is, he said.

How so? I asked.

The poet, he replied, never could have been so stupid as
to say that retaining virtue, which in the opinion of all men
is the hardest of all things, is a trifling matter.

Well then, I said, how opportune it is that Prodicus is
here among us; for he has a wisdom, Protagoras, which, as
I imagine, is more than human and of very ancient date, as   341
old as Simonides or even older. Learned as you are in many
things, you appear to know nothing of this; but I do, because I am a disciple of Prodicus'. And now, if I am not
mistaken, you do not understand the word "hard" in the
sense that Simonides intended. But it's just as when Prodicus here corrects me on each occasion that I use the word
"awful" as a term of praise. If I say that Protagoras or anyone else is an awfully wise man, he asks me if I am not
ashamed of calling that which is good awful; and then he   b
explains to me that the term "awful" means "bad" and is
applied only to bad things: no one speaks of being awfully
healthy or wealthy, or of awful peace, but rather of awful
disease, awful war, awful poverty, meaning, by the term
"awful," "evil." Perhaps similarly, then, Simonides and his
countrymen the Ceans, when they said "hard," meant evil,
or something that you do not understand. So let's ask Prodicus, for he ought to be able to answer questions about the
dialect of Simonides. What did he mean, Prodicus, by the
term "hard"?   c

Evil, said Prodicus.

And therefore, I said, Prodicus, he criticizes Pittacus for
saying "It is hard to be good," just as if that were equivalent
to saying "It is evil to be good."

Yes, he said, that was certainly his meaning; and he is twitting Pittacus with ignorance of the use of terms, which in a Lesbian, who has been brought up to speak a barbarous dialect, is natural.[37]

d Do you hear, Protagoras, I asked, what our friend Prodicus is saying? And do you have an answer for him?

You are entirely mistaken, Prodicus, said Protagoras; I know perfectly well that Simonides, in using the word "hard," meant what all of us mean—not evil, but whatever is not easy and takes a great deal of trouble.

I said: But I, too, think Simonides meant this, Protagoras, and that our friend Prodicus certainly knows it, but he thought that he would tease us, and see if he could make you defend your position; for that Simonides could never have

e meant "evil" when he said "hard" is clearly proved by the context, in which he says that "only a god could have this privilege." He surely cannot mean to say that to be good is evil, when he afterward proceeds to say that "only a god could have this," and accorded "this privilege" to a god only. For if this were his meaning, Prodicus would impute to Simonides a character of profligacy which is distinctly un-Cean.[38] But I would like to tell you, I said, what I imagine to be the real meaning of Simonides in this poem, if you would

342 like to test me in this matter you mention—that is, competence in poetry; or, if you would prefer, I will be the listener.

To this proposal Protagoras replied: Do as you please; and Hippias, Prodicus, and the others told me by all means to do as I proposed.

---

[37]The suggestion seems to be that the island of Lesbos, being close to Asia Minor, has been linguistically corrupted by the speech of the non–Greek speakers (which is what "barbarian" means in Greek) of Asia.

[38]There is evidence elsewhere that the Ceans were regarded as unusually rectitudinous.

Then now, I said, I will endeavor to expound to you my opinion about this poem of Simonides:

There is a very ancient philosophy which is more cultivated in Crete and Lacedaemon[39] than in any other part of Hellas, and there are more philosophers in those countries than anywhere else in the world.[40] This, however, is a secret b which the Lacedaemonians deny; and they pretend to be ignorant, just because they do not wish it to be known that they surpass all other Greeks in wisdom, like the sophists of whom Protagoras was speaking, and not in military skill and valor; considering that if the reason for their superiority were disclosed, all men would be practicing their wisdom. And this secret of theirs has never been found out by the imitators of Lacedaemonian fashions in other cities, who go around mimicking them, with their ears bruised, and they bind their hands with leather straps for boxing, c and are always in training, and wear short cloaks;[41] for they imagine that these are the practices that have given the Lacedaemonians their power over Greece. Now when the Lacedaemonians want to unbend and hold free conversation with their wise men, and become annoyed with having to consult them in private, they drive out all these laconizers,[42] and any other foreigners who may happen to be in their country, and they hold a philosophical conference unknown to strangers; and they themselves forbid their young men to go out into other cities—in this they are like d

---

[39]I.e., Sparta.

[40]This is a deliberate paradox, the region in question having a reputation for not only rustic conservativism, but for active and aggressive anti-intellectualism.

[41]These affectations were characteristic of the aristocratic elites of non-Spartan cities, not least of Athens; the Spartan cloak is that worn by Socrates himself (discussed in note 28).

[42]After Laconia (from which our "laconic"), the region of Sparta.

the Cretans—in order that they may not unlearn the lessons which they have taught them. And in Lacedaemon and Crete, not only men but also women pride themselves on their education and culture. You may know that I am right in attributing to the Lacedaemonians this excellence in philosophy and argument by the following: if somebody talks to the most insignificant of Lacedaemonians, he will

e find him seldom good for much in the way of general conversation, but at any point in the discussion he will suddenly flash out some notable saying, terse and full of meaning, with unerring aim, so that the person with whom he is talking seems no better than a child. And many men of our own era and of former ages have noted that to laconize is much more to love philosophy than to do gymnastics; they are conscious that only a perfectly educated

343 man is capable of uttering such apophthegms. Such were Thales of Miletus, and Pittacus of Mitylene, and Bias of Priene, and our own Solon, and Cleobulus the Lindian, and Myson the Chenian; and seventh in the catalog of wise men was the Lacedaemonian Chilon.[43] All these were lovers and emulators and disciples of the culture of the Lacedaemonians, and anyone may perceive that their wisdom was of this character, consisting of short memorable

b sentences. And they met together and dedicated to Apollo in his temple at Delphi, as the first-fruit offerings of their wisdom, the far-famed inscriptions, which are in all men's mouths—"Know thyself" and "Nothing in excess."

Why do I say all this? To show that a kind of Laconic brevity was the style of early philosophy. In particular, there was this saying of Pittacus' which was circulated

[43]The traditional "Seven Sages" of Greece (the list sometimes varies, from source to source).

from one to the other of the wise men and received their approbation: "It is hard to be good." And Simonides, whose ambition was to be famous for wisdom, recognized that if c he could overthrow this saying, then, as if he had won a victory over some famous athlete, he would carry off the palm among his contemporaries. And if I am not mistaken, he composed the entire poem in opposition to this saying and its author, scheming to discredit them.

Let us now join in examining his words, and see whether I am speaking the truth. Simonides must have been a lunatic, if, in the very first words of the poem, wanting to say only that to become good is hard, he inserted "while": the d introduction of this word is entirely pointless, except on the assumption that he is speaking with a polemical reference to the aphorism of Pittacus. Pittacus is saying "It is hard to be good," and Simonides, in refutation of this thesis, counters that the truly hard thing, Pittacus, is to *become* good, but not "truly good": "truly" here does not modify "good," as though there were some truly good men, and there were others who were good but not truly good (this e would be a rather fatuous thing to say, and completely unworthy of Simonides); no, you must make a trajection of the word "truly,"[44] and put the saying of Pittacus first, as if Pittacus were the first speaker and Simonides the respondent: "People," says Pittacus, "it is hard to be good," and then Simonides answers, "In that, Pittacus, you are mis- 344 taken; it is not difficult to *be* good, while, on the other hand, it *is* truly difficult to *become* good, foursquare in hands and feet and mind, with nothing to fault." This way of reading

[44]This "trajection" is not as preposterous as it will seem to speakers of English: Greek is a highly inflected language, and syntactical relationships (which are rigidly determined by word order in English) are indicated by the inflectional endings of words, the order of which therefore can be very free.

the passage accounts for the insertion of "while," and shows that the word "truly" should properly be taken with "hard," and all that follows shows this to be the meaning. A
b great deal might be said in praise of the details of the poem, which is a charming piece of workmanship, and very polished, but such minutiae would be tedious. I would like, however, to point out the general character and intention of the work, which is certainly designed in every part to be a refutation of the saying of Pittacus. For he says in what follows a little further on (it is almost as if he were making a speech) that although it is truly difficult to *become* good, yet this is possible for a time, and only for a time. But
c having become good, to *remain* in a good state and *be* good, as you, Pittacus, affirm, is not possible, and is not granted to man; only a god could have this privilege:

> It is not possible for a man to avoid being bad
> When the force of irresistible circumstances overpowers him.

Now whom does the force of irresistible circumstance overpower in the command of a ship? Not the layman, for he is always already overpowered; it is like a person who is already lying down—you couldn't *put* him down, since he *is* down; only a person who is standing upright can be put
d down. In the same way "the force of irresistible circumstances" can overpower him who is sometimes able to resist calamity, but not him who is always helpless anyhow. The onslaught of a great storm may make a helmsman helpless, or the severity of the weather a farmer; the same might be true of a doctor; for the good may become bad, as another poet[45] testifies:

45Unknown.

The good are sometimes good and sometimes bad.

But it is not open to the bad man to become bad; he is *al-* e *ways* bad. So that when the force of irresistible circumstances overpowers the man of resources and skill and virtue, then "it is not possible to avoid being bad." And you, Pittacus, are saying, "it is hard to be good." Now it is hard to become good, and yet it is possible; but to *be* good is an impossibility:

For success makes any man good, while failure makes him bad.

Now what is success in letters? And succeeding at what 345 makes a man good at letters? Clearly success at knowing of them. And what sort of success makes a man a good doctor? Clearly knowing the art of healing the sick. "While failure makes him bad": Who might become a bad doctor? Clearly a person who has it in him to be a doctor in the first place, and in the second place to be a *good* doctor—that person might also become a bad doctor. But none of us laymen can by any amount of unsuccessful medical practice become doctors, any more than we can by failed practice become carpenters or anything of that sort; and a person who b cannot by unsuccessful practice become a doctor at all clearly cannot become a *bad* doctor, either.[46] Likewise the good may deteriorate, and in that sense become bad, through passage of time, through toil or disease, or some other reversal of fortune (failure is only this: to be deprived of knowledge),[47] but the bad man will never be-

[46]Socrates' argument here seems particularly lame and forced.

[47]The parenthetical comment's place in the argument is not made very clear. You can lose knowledge only if you have it to begin with; age, illness, etc., might bring about a loss of knowledge; loss of knowledge is the only real failure; to

come bad, for he is always bad; and if he were to become
bad, he must first become good. Thus this part also of the
c poem seems to aim at showing that a man cannot be con-
tinuously good, but that he can become good and can also
become bad; and those whom the gods love are the best for
the longest time.

All this relates to Pittacus, as is further proved by the se-
quel. For Simonides says—

> *Therefore I will not throw away my span of life to no purpose*
> *In searching after the impossible, hoping in vain to find*
> *A perfectly blameless man among those who eat the fruits of the*
> *broad-seated earth:*
> *If I find one, I will send you word.*

d   —you see how vehemently throughout the whole poem
he pursues his attack against Pittacus' saying—

> *But everyone who does no evil voluntarily I praise and love;*
> *Not even the gods war against necessity.*

All this has a similar drift, for Simonides was not so un-
educated as to say that he praised those who did no evil
voluntarily, as though there were some who *did* do evil
voluntarily. For no wise man, as I believe, will allow that
e any human being does wrong voluntarily, or voluntarily
does evil and dishonorable actions; but they are very well
aware that all who do evil and dishonorable things do

---

fail—"failure" here—means becoming bad; success is to possess knowledge; success makes any man good. Thus a knowing > successful > good man can, by
being deprived of his knowledge (through age, illness, etc.), *become* a deprived of
knowledge > unsuccessful > (= failed) > bad man; but a bad man cannot *become*
a bad man: he already *is* one anyhow.

them against their will.[48] And Simonides never says that he praises him who does no evil voluntarily; the word "voluntarily" applies to himself. For he was of the opinion that a good man will often compel himself to love and praise another—for instance, it often befalls a man to have a father or mother of bad character, or a country, or the like. Now bad men, when anything of that sort befalls them, view it with malignant joy, and gleefully censure and expose and denounce the wickedness of their parents or their country, under the idea that the rest of mankind will be less likely to criticize themselves and accuse them of the neglect of which they are guilty; and in consequence they exaggerate their parents' (or country's) defects beyond what they deserve, and add optional animosities over and above the compulsary ones. But the good man in such circumstances conceals and suppresses his feelings, and is constrained to praise his parents or country; and if they have wronged him and he is angry, he pacifies his anger and is reconciled to them, compelling himself to love and praise them as his own flesh and blood. And Simonides, as is likely, believed that he himself had often praised and extolled a tyrant or the like,[49] much against his will. So he wants to tell Pittacus "I do not censure you just because I am censorious":

346

b

c

[48]The paradoxical claim that no one does wrong knowingly or intentionally is one of Socrates' most characteristic doctrines. The whimsical pretense here that it is a truth universally acknowledged by the wise is also characteristic. Nonetheless, it is clear that "voluntarily" in the first part of the couplet contrasts with "necessity" in the last part; for that contrast to make any sense, "voluntarily" must go with "does no evil" and not with "I praise and love."

[49]For example, the Scopas in whose honor this very poem was composed. Simonides was alleged to be very avaricious and mercenary, and was supposedly the first poet to write poems of praise on commission.

For I am satisfied when a man is neither bad
Nor a helpless weakling, and when he knows what is just (which
    is the health of states), and is of sound character,
I will find no fault with him—for I am not given to finding
    fault—
For the race of fools is without number. . . .

—implying that anyone who delighted in censure might have abundant opportunity of finding fault with them—

All things are good with which evil has not been mixed.

d   These last words are not to be taken as if he had said "All things are white which have no black in them," for that would be utterly ridiculous; but he means to say that he accepts and finds no fault with the moderate or intermediate state. "I do not hope," he says, "to find a perfectly blameless man among those who eat the fruits of the broad-seated earth, and if I find one, I will send you word." So that I will not praise anyone for that achievement; but whoever is moderately good, and does no evil, is good enough for me, who "praise and love everyone"—and here observe that because he is addressing Pittacus he uses the Lesbian di-

e alect,[50] when he says "everyone who does no evil, voluntarily I praise and love" (the comma should come, as here,

347 before "voluntarily") "who does no evil"; but there are some whom I involuntarily praise and love. And you, Pittacus, I would never have criticized, if you had spoken what was moderately good and true; but I do blame you because,

[50]Lyric poetry was written in an artificial language that incorporated features of several Greek dialects, one of them being Lesbian Aeolic, i.e., the dialect of Pittacus. As it happens, Simonides did in fact use an Aeolic version of the verb "praise" here, and Socrates exploits the accident.

putting on the appearance of truth, you speak gross false-hoods about the most important matters.—And this, Prodicus and Protagoras, I take to be the meaning of Simonides in this poem.

Hippias said: I think, Socrates, that you have provided a very good interpretation of the poem; but I also have an excellent one of my own which I will propound to you, if b you would like.

Yes, definitely, Hippias, said Alcibiades; but at some other time. For now we must adhere to the arrangement that was made between Socrates and Protagoras, to the effect that as long as Protagoras is willing to ask questions, Socrates should answer; or that if he would rather answer, then Socrates should question.

I said: I wish Protagoras either to ask or answer as he is inclined; but if it is all right with him I would like to drop these songs and poems, and return to the subject I first asked you about, Protagoras, an inquiry that I would c greatly enjoy seeing, with your help, to the end. Talking about the poets reminds me most of the after-dinner conversation of commonplace people—tradesmen and the like—who by reason of their stupidity and lack of education are not able to converse or amuse one another, while they are drinking, with the sound of their own voices and conversation. They cause the price of flute-girls in the market to go up by hiring for great sums the voice of a flute d to be the medium of intercourse among them; but where the company are gentlemen and men of education, you will see no flute-girls, nor dancing-girls, nor harp-girls; and they have no nonsense or silly games, but are contented with one another's conversation, of which their own voices are the medium, and which they carry on by turns and in an orderly manner even when they have been drink-e   ing wine in large quantities. And a company like this of ours, and men such as we profess to be, do not require the help of another's voice, or of the poets whom you cannot interrogate about the meaning of what they are saying; the common people cite them declaring, some, that the poet has one meaning, and others, that he has another, and the point which is in dispute can never be decided. This sort of entertainment the better sort curtly dismiss, and prefer to

348   rely on their own resources in conversing with one another, putting themselves and their companions to the test. These are the models that I think you and I should imitate. Laying the poets aside, let us converse with each other from our own resources, and put the truth, and ourselves, to the test. And if you want to continue doing the questioning, I am ready to answer; or if you would prefer, then you answer, and give me the opportunity of resuming and completing our unfinished argument.

b   I made these and some similar observations; but Protagoras would not distinctly say which he would do. Thereupon Alcibiades turned to Callias, and said: *Now* do you think, Callias, that Protagoras is being fair, refusing to say whether he will or will not answer? I certainly don't think he is; he ought either to proceed with the discussion, or explicitly refuse to, so that we can know this about him; and then Socrates will be able to converse with someone else, and the rest of us will be free to talk with one another.

c   I think that Protagoras was really made ashamed by these words of Alcibiades, and when the importunings of Callias and of almost the whole company were further added, he was at last induced to proceed with the discussion, and said that I might ask the questions and he would answer.

So I said: Don't imagine, Protagoras, that I have any interest in asking questions of you other than that of clearing up my own difficulties. For I think that Homer was very right in saying that[51]

When two go together, one sees before the other   d

for it is the human lot that we are all better prepared for action, speech, or thought if we have a partner or companion; but if a man

notices something when he is alone

he immediately runs around looking until he finds someone to show his discovery to, and who can confirm it for him. And I would rather have a discussion with you than with any other person, because I think that no one has a better understanding of most things which a good man may be expected to understand, and in particular of virtue. e For who is there but you? You who not only claim to be a good man and a gentleman yourself—for many are such, but they don't have the power of making others that way— whereas you are not only good yourself, but you are able to make others good as well. Moreover, you have such confidence in yourself that, although other sophists conceal their profession, you proclaim in the face of Hellas that 349 you are a sophist or teacher of culture and virtue, and are the first of them to demand pay in return. How then could it not be necessary to invite you to the examination of these subjects, and to ask questions and consult with you? There is no way. So with regard to those questions which I was asking you at first, I would like to go back and start again, and have my memory about some of them refreshed

[51]The quotations are from *Iliad* 10. 224–226.

by you, and also to have your help in considering the oth-
b ers. If I am not mistaken, the question was this: Are wisdom
and prudence and courage and justice and piety five names
for the same thing? Or does each of the names have a separate underlying reality, a definite thing having a peculiar
function, no one of them being like any other of them?
And you replied that the five names were not the names of
c the same thing, but that each of them covered a separate
object, and that all these objects were parts of virtue, not in
the same way that the parts of gold are like one another
and the whole of which they are parts, but in the way in
which the parts of the face are unlike the whole of which
they are parts and unlike one another, each of them having
a distinct function. I would like to know if this is still your
opinion; if not, please define your meaning, since I will not
hold it against you if you now take a different position. For
I wouldn't be surprised if you said what you did before
d only to test me.

But I have not changed my view, Socrates, he said, and I
say that all these qualities are parts of virtue; but four out of
the five are to some extent similar, while the fifth of them,
courage, is very different from the other four.[52] That I am
right will be seen as follows: you will find that many men
are utterly criminal, and impious, and licentious, and ignorant, but are nevertheless remarkable for their courage.

e   Hold on there, I said; what you say deserves a closer
look. When you speak of courageous men, do you mean
the confident, or something else?

Yes, he said; I mean the impetuous, ready to go headlong
into what others are afraid to approach.

Let me ask you next if you believe that virtue is a good

[52]Courage is also the only one Socrates has not already discussed.

thing, of which good thing you represent yourself to be a teacher.

Yes, he said; since I am not a madman, I say it is the best of all things.

And is it partly good and partly bad, I said, or wholly good?

Wholly good, and to the highest degree.

Tell me then: Who are the people who feel confidence when diving into a well?

350

I would say, divers.

And is this because they have knowledge, or is there some other reason?

Because they have knowledge.

And who feel confidence when fighting on horseback—skilled horseman or unskilled?

Skilled.

And who when fighting armed with peltae—the peltasts or the non-peltasts?[53]

The peltasts. And that is true of all other things, he said, if that is your point: those who have knowledge are more confident than those who have no knowledge, and they are more confident after they have learned than before.

b

And haven't you seen persons utterly ignorant, I said, of these things, and yet confident about them?

Yes, he said, I have seen such persons far too confident.

So are these confident people also courageous?

That would be a shame for courage, he replied, seeing that these people are insane.

Then who are the courageous? Aren't they the confident?

Yes, he said; I stick to that.

---

[53]The *pelta* was a light shield.

And those, I said, who, like these, are confident without
c knowledge are exposed as being not courageous in truth,
but insane? And in our former example, the wisest are also
the most confident, and being the most confident are also
the most courageous? And again in accordance with that
argument, wisdom would turn out to be courage?

No, Socrates, he replied, your recollection of what I
said in my reply is defective. When you asked me if the
courageous are confident, I agreed that they were, but I
was never asked if the confident are courageous; if you had
asked me, I would have answered "Not all of them." As for
d my claim that the courageous are confident, you have
nowhere disproved it or shown that it was mistaken. And
yet then you proceed to show that those who have knowledge are more confident than they were before they had
knowledge, and more confident than others who have no
knowledge, and from this you conclude that courage is the
same as wisdom. But by this manner of arguing you might
also conclude that strength is wisdom. You might begin by
asking if the strong are able, to which I would say "Yes";
e and then if those who know how to wrestle are not more
able to wrestle than those who do not know how to wrestle,
and more able after they had learned than before, to which
I would also assent. And when I had admitted this, it would
be open to you to use my admissions in such a way as to
prove that on my view wisdom is strength; whereas in fact
I have nowhere admitted, any more than in the other case,
that the able are strong, but only that the strong are able.
351 For ability and strength are not the same thing; the former
is given by knowledge, and also by insanity or rage,[54] but

[54]Protagoras means that sometimes madmen and people in extreme states of
anger find the ability to perform feats beyond their normal strength.

strength comes from nature and a healthy state of the body. Similarly, in the former case, confidence and courage are not the same thing; so it happens that the courageous are confident, but certainly not all the confident are courageous. For men can acquire confidence by means of art, and also, like ability, by insanity and rage; but courage b comes to them from nature and a healthy condition of the soul.

I said: Would you admit, Protagoras, that some men live well and others badly?

He assented.

And do you think that a man who lives in pain and grief lives well?

He does not.

But if a man lives pleasantly to the end of his life, won't he in that case have lived well?

It seems so to me.

Then to live pleasantly is a good, and to live unpleas- c antly an evil?

Yes, he said, if the pleasure is good and honorable.

And do you, Protagoras, like the rest of the world, call some pleasant things evil and some painful things good? What I mean is, aren't things good insofar as they are pleasant, regardless of whether or not consequences of a different nature result from them? And likewise in turn for painful things—aren't they bad insofar as they are painful?

I don't know, Socrates, he said, if I can assert in so unqualified a manner that the pleasant is the good and the d painful the evil. Looking at it from the perspective of not only my present answer, but also my whole life, it would be safer, unless I am mistaken, to say that there are some pleasant things which are not good, and that there are some painful things which are not evil and some which are, and, thirdly, that there are some things which are neither good nor evil.

And don't you call pleasant, I said, the things which
e have pleasure in them or create pleasure?

Certainly, he said.

My point in saying that insofar as things are pleasant they are good was to inquire into the nature of pleasure: Isn't it in and of itself good?

To adopt your own favorite formula, Socrates, "let us examine this," he said; and if the thesis proves reasonable, and "pleasant" and "good" are shown to be really the same, then we will agree; but if not, then we will argue it out.

And would you like to lead the inquiry? I asked. Or shall I?

You ought to take the lead, he said, for you are the originator of the thesis.

352 Then, I said, perhaps it will become clear to us from the following illustration. Suppose someone is trying to ascertain from a man's appearance the state of his health or some bodily function—he looks at his face and hands, and then he says, "Uncover your chest and back for me; I want to make a more searching examination"—that is the sort of thing which I desire in this investigation. So, having learned what your opinion is about the good and the pleasant, I have to say to you something like this: "Uncover this
b part of your mind for me, Protagoras: What is your position on knowledge? Do you agree with the majority of mankind, or not? Most people are of the opinion that knowledge is not a thing of strength, or such as to dominate or command: they do not think of it in that way, but hold that a man may often have knowledge, and yet be governed not by knowledge but by something else—by anger, or pleasure, or pain, sometimes by love, often by fear—just

as if knowledge were a slave, being dragged around by all the rest. Now is that your view? Or do you think that knowledge is noble, and such as to command a person, and that if someone knows the difference between good and evil, then it would not be possible for him to be forced by anything to do other than what knowledge ordains, but rather his intelligence would be well up to the job of rescuing him?"

I agree with you, Socrates, said Protagoras; and not only that, but I, above all other men,[55] am bound to say that wisdom and knowledge are the most powerful of human things.

Good, I said, and true. So then you are aware that the majority of mankind does not concur with us, but says that even when men know the things which are best and are free to do them, they often refuse, and prefer some other course of action? And when I have asked what is the reason for this, I am told that these people act as they do because they are "overcome by pleasure," or by pain, or by some of those forces which I was just now mentioning.

Yes, Socrates, he replied; and that is not the only point about which mankind is in error.

Suppose, then, that you and I try to instruct and inform them what is the nature of this experience which they call "being overcome by pleasure," and which they claim to be the reason why they do not always do what is best, even when they know what the best is. When we say to them: "Friends, you are mistaken, and are saying what is not true," they would probably reply: "Socrates and Protagoras, if this experience of the soul is not to be called 'being overcome by pleasure,' please tell us what it is, and what you would call it?"

---

[55] I.e., as the leading sophist, he has a special relationship with wisdom (*sophia*).

But why, Socrates, do we have to bother with examining the opinion of the many? They just say anything that happens to occur to them.

b   I believe, I said, that they may be of use in helping us to discover how courage is related to the other parts of virtue. If you are disposed to stick to our recent agreement, that I should lead us along the path by which I think our question is most likely to be cleared up, then follow; otherwise, if you prefer, I will dismiss the whole thing.

You are quite right, he said; continue as you have begun.

c   Well then, I said, let's suppose that they repeat their question, "What account do you give of what we were calling 'being overcome by pleasure'?" I would answer as follows: "Listen, Protagoras and I will try to show you. When people are overpowered by the pleasures of eating and drinking and sex, and they, knowing them to be evil, nevertheless indulge in them, isn't this what you say is to be 'overcome by pleasure'?" They would say yes. And suppose that you and I were to go on and ask them again: "In what
d   way do you say that they are evil—in that they are pleasant and give pleasure at the moment, or because they cause disease and poverty and other such evils in the future? Suppose they simply give pleasure, and bring no evil consequences, would they still be evil, merely because they cause pleasure in any way whatsoever?" Wouldn't they answer, Protagoras, that they are not evil on account of the pleasure which is immediately given by them, but on account of the after-consequences—diseases and the like?

I believe, said Protagoras, that the world in general would answer as you indicate.

"Then by causing disease pleasures cause pains? And by causing poverty they cause pains?"—they would say yes to these also, if I am not mistaken.

Protagoras assented.

"Doesn't this prove to you, people, that, as Protagoras and I maintain, what makes these evil is nothing but that they end in pain and rob us of other pleasures?" There again they would agree?

354

We both of us thought that they would.

And then we might take the question from the opposite point of view, and say: "People, when you speak of good things as being painful, don't you mean such things as gymnastic exercises, and military service, and medical treatments such as cauterization, cutting, drugging, and starving? Are these the things which are good but painful?"—they would assent?

He agreed.

"And do you call them good because they occasion the greatest immediate suffering and pain, or because, afterward, they bring health and improvement of the body's condition and the salvation of states and power over others and wealth?" They would agree to the latter alternative, if I am not mistaken?

b

He concurred.

"Are these things good for any other reason except that they end in pleasure, and get rid of and avert pain? Are you looking to any other end but pleasure and pain when you call them good?" They would acknowledge that they were not?

c

I think so, said Protagoras.

"And don't you pursue pleasure as something that is good, and avoid pain as something evil?"

He assented.

"Then this is what you think is evil—pain—and you think good is pleasure, since even enjoyment itself, you say, is in that case evil, when it robs you of greater pleasures than it gives, or causes pains greater than the pleasure. For d if your calling enjoyment itself evil is done with reference to some other outcome or standard, you would be able to show us that standard. But you will not be able to."

I do not think that they will, said Protagoras.

"And doesn't the same argument apply in turn to pain itself? You call pain good when it takes away greater pains than those that it causes itself, or gives pleasures greater than the pains. For if, when you call pain itself good, you are referring to some outcome other than the one I mention, then

e you can show what it is. But it will turn out that you can't."

True, said Protagoras.

"Then again," I said, "if you should ask me, people, 'Why are you speaking at such length and so exhaustively about this matter?' I would reply, 'Excuse me, friends, but in the first place, explaining the precise meaning of your expression "overcome by pleasure" is not an easy task; and the whole argument turns on it. And even now, if you see any-

355 thing else that you are able to call the good other than pleasure, or can call the evil other than pain, please go ahead and change your position. Is a life of pleasure without pain good enough for you, then? If it is, and if you are unable to say that any other thing is good or evil, the end result of which is not these things—pleasure or pain—then hear the consequences: if what you say is true, then I assure you that your concept becomes absurd at the point at which you affirm that often a man, even though recognizing evil for what it is, nevertheless still does it, though it is open to him not to,

b because he is led on and confused by pleasure. And, similarly, when you say that a man knows what is good but refuses to do it because he is overcome by the pleasures of the moment. And that this is ridiculous will become evident if we stop indiscriminately using a multiplicity of names, such as pleasant and painful and good and evil. Rather, since it is clear that there are two phenomena at issue, let us call them by two names—first, good and evil, and then, pleasant and painful.[56] Having adopted this principle, let us go on to c say that a man does evil knowing that he does evil. That way, if someone asks 'Why?' we will say 'Because he is overcome.' 'And by what is he overcome?' the inquirer will proceed to ask. But now it is no longer open to us to say 'By pleasure,' since pleasure has changed its name from 'pleasure' to 'the good.'[57] So let us answer him and say 'Because he is overcome'. 'By what?' he will reiterate. 'By the good,' we will have to reply, by god. Now, if our questioner happens to be an aggressive sort, he will laugh and say, 'It's a ridiculous thing to say that a man does what he knows is evil d when he ought not to because he is "overcome by good." 'Does this happen,' he will ask, 'because the good present in you does or does not outweigh the evil?' And in answer to that we shall clearly reply, 'Because it does not; otherwise he who, as we say, is overcome by pleasure, would not do wrong.' 'But in what respect,' he will reply, 'does the good not match up to the evil, or the evil to the good? Doesn't that have to mean that the one is greater than the other in size or e quantity?' This we will not be able to deny. 'So it is clear that when you speak of being overcome what you mean,' he will say, 'is that you choose a greater quantity of evil in exchange for a lesser quantity of good?' Admitted. So now let's switch the pairs of terms and substitute the names of 'plea-

[56]That is, the argument should use one pair (good and evil) or the other (pleasant and painful) consistently, and not switch between them (good and painful, or pleasant and evil).

[57]That is, by starting the argument using the term "evil," i.e., a member of the pair good and evil, we are committed to sticking to that pair of terms in formulating the rest of the argument, and therefore may not switch over to one or the other or both of the other pair, pleasant and painful (unless explicitly making such a conversion, as at 355e below).

sure' and 'pain' for 'good' and 'evil,' and say, not as we did before, that a man does what is evil, but that he does what is painful, knowing that it is painful, because he is overcome

356 by pleasure, clearly because it does not outweigh the pain. For what other measure is there of pleasure's inability to counterbalance pain than that of more and less, which means the degree to which they differ in size, number, or intensity? And now if anyone should say: 'Yes, Socrates, but pleasure in the present is a very different thing from what comes in the future, whether pleasure or pain'—to that I would reply: 'Do they differ in respect of anything but pleasure and pain? No, there can be no other measure of them. So you must proceed as if you were an expert at weight

b measurement: first, assemble all the pleasures on one side and all the pains on the other. After that, adjust the scale so that it assigns different weightings to different items according to their nearness and distance in time. And then tell us which side outweighs the other. Now, if ever you weigh pleasures against pleasures, you must of course always take the more and greater; and if ever you weigh pains against pains, you must take the fewer and the less; but if you are weighing pleasures against pains, then if the pains are outweighed by the pleasures—whether the near in time by the far, or the far in time by the near—you must choose the course of action in which the pleasures are to be found; similarly, if the pleasures are ever surpassed by the pains,

c then it is that course of action which must be avoided.[58]

[58]In other words, the hedonist—the person who equates "pleasant" with "good"—must always choose the course that will yield the maximum sum of pleasure over the course of his entire life—in effect, "whoever dies with the most, wins." Thus: the greater of two goods, the lesser of two evils, and, where good and bad are mixed (e.g., over time), the choice in which good preponderates should be taken, whereas that in which bad preponderates is to be avoided.

Would you not admit, people, that this is true?' I am confident that they cannot deny this."

He agreed with me.

"Well then," I shall go on to say to them, "if you agree so far, please answer this for me: 'Don't the same magnitudes appear larger to your sight when near, and smaller when at a distance?' " They will acknowledge that. "And the same holds for thickness and number; also sounds that are, in themselves, equal are louder when near, and softer when at a distance." They will grant that also. "Now suppose happiness consisted in doing or choosing the greater, d and in not doing or in avoiding the less, what would turn out to be the saving principle of human life? Wouldn't it be the art of measuring? Or would it be the power of appearance? Isn't it the latter that leads us astray and often makes us opt for things at one time that we repent of at another, both in our actions and in our decisions about matters great and small? But if we had then possessed the art of measurement, wouldn't it have done away with the power of appearances, and, by revealing to us the truth, wouldn't it have taught the soul at last to find rest e in the truth, and thus have saved our life?" Wouldn't people generally acknowledge that the art that would accomplish this result is the art of measurement, and not any other?

Yes, he said, the art of measurement.

"Suppose, again, that the salvation of human life depended on the correct choice of odd or even, and on that between the greater and lesser as the occasion arose, either between two odd numbers or two evens, or between an even against an odd, whether a low number or a high; what would be the saving principle of our lives? Wouldn't it be 357 knowledge? That is, a knowledge of measurement, since that is the art concerned with what is too much and too little? And when it is concerned with odd and even, can it be any art other than arithmetic?" Would people agree to this, or not?

Protagoras thought that they would.

"Well then, people," I say to them, "seeing that the salvation of human life has been found to consist in the right choice of pleasures and pains—in the choice of the more

b and the fewer, and the greater and the less, and the nearer and farther—doesn't it follow, first, that this salvation consists in measurement, since it involves a consideration of which is more and which less and which equal in relation to each other?"

But of course—necessarily.

"And since it involves measurement, it must obviously also be an art and a science?"

They will agree, he said.

"The nature of that art and science we will look into at a later date; but that it *is* such a science is sufficient to

c serve as a proof that Protagoras and I needed to make to answer the question you asked of us. At the time when you asked the question, if you remember, both of us were agreeing that there was nothing more powerful than knowledge, and that knowledge, wherever it inheres, always prevails over pleasure and all other things; and then you said that pleasure often got the advantage even over a man who has knowledge; and when we refused to agree with you, you then asked us: 'Protagoras and Socrates, what is the meaning of being overcome by pleasure if not this? Tell us what you call such a state.' If we had immedi-

d ately at the time answered 'Ignorance,' you would have laughed at us. But now, if you laugh at *us*, you will be laughing at *yourselves*: for you yourselves admitted that

people go wrong in their choice of pleasures and pains—
that is, in their choice of good and evil—from a deficiency
of knowledge; and not only from a deficiency of knowledge in general, but of that particular knowledge which
you have already agreed to be the science of measurement. And you yourselves certainly know that the wrong
action which is done *without* knowledge is done *with* igno- e
rance. So this, therefore, is the meaning of being overcome
by pleasure: supreme ignorance. And our friends Protagoras and Prodicus and Hippias declare that they are healers
of ignorance; but you, who are under the mistaken impression that something other than ignorance is the cause,
neither go yourselves nor send your children to the
sophists, who are the teachers of these things, on the
grounds that they can't be taught—you are stingy with
your money and give them none; and the result is that you
are the worse off both in public and in private life."

That, then, is what would be our answer to the world in 358
general; and now I would like to ask you, Hippias, and you,
Prodicus, as well as Protagoras (for let our discussion be
yours as well as ours), whether you think that I am speaking the truth or not?

They all were exceedingly certain that what I had said
was true.

Then you agree, I said, that the pleasant is good, and the
painful evil. And here I ask my friend Prodicus not to introduce his distinctions among words; whether you use the
word "pleasurable," or "delightful," or "joyful," or any
other conceivable name it is your pleasure to call them, I
will ask you, most excellent Prodicus, to answer according b
to my sense of the words.

Prodicus laughed and agreed, as did the others.

Then, my friends, what do you say to this? Aren't any

and all actions that conduce to making life painless and pleasant to be called honorable? And isn't the honorable also useful and good?

This was admitted.

Accordingly, I said, if the pleasant is *good*, then nobody who knows, or even thinks, that there are available things that lie within his capacity to do that are better, that is, *more* good, than what he is currently doing, continues with what c he is doing, when it is open to him to be doing better. And not to have control of oneself is merely ignorance, and to be master of oneself is wisdom.

They all assented.

Now isn't ignorance to have a false opinion and to be deceived about important matters?

To this they also unanimously assented.

Then, I said, no man voluntarily pursues evil, or what he thinks to be evil. To prefer what he believes evil to d good, it appears, is not in human nature; and when compelled to choose one of two evils, no one will choose the greater when it is possible to have the lesser.

All of us agreed to every word of this.

Well, I said, there is a certain thing called fear or terror; and here, Prodicus, I would particularly like to know whether you agree with me in defining this fear or terror as an expectation of evil.

Protagoras and Hippias agreed, but Prodicus said that e this was fear and not terror.

Never mind, Prodicus, I said; it doesn't matter; but let me ask whether, if our former assertions are true, anyone will consent to pursue what he fears when it is open to him to pursue what he doesn't? Wouldn't this be in flat contradiction to the admissions that have been already made, that a person thinks the things that he fears to be evil, and that no one will pursue or voluntarily accept what he thinks to be evil?

That also was universally admitted.   359

Then, I said, these are our premises. But now I ask Hippias and Prodicus to stand back and permit Protagoras to explain to us how he can be right in what he said at first. I don't mean the very first thing he said, for that was, as you may remember, his statement that there are five parts of virtue and none of them is like any other of them—each of them has a separate function. That statement is not the one I'm referring to now, but to the assertion he made afterward, that of the five virtues, four are nearly identical, but that the fifth, courage, differs greatly from the others. And   b he said that I would recognize he was right about this from the following evidence: "You will find, Socrates," he said, "that some of the most utterly criminal, and impious, and licentious, and ignorant of men are nonetheless remarkable for their courage; which proves that courage is very different from the other parts of virtue."[59] At the time I was very much surprised at his saying this, and I am still more surprised now that I have discussed the matter with all of you. So I asked him whether by the courageous he meant the confident. "Yes," he replied, "and the impetuous or headlong goers."[60] (You may remember, Protagoras, that   c this was your answer.)

He assented.

Well then, I said, tell us against what are the courageous ready to go against—the same dangers as the cowards?

No, he answered.

[59]At 350d.

[60]At 350e, where for "headlong goers" Protagoras said "ready to go headlong into what others are afraid to approach."

Then against something different?

Yes, he said.

Then do cowards go where there is cause for confidence, and the courageous where there is danger?

Yes, Socrates, so men say.

d Yes, that's true—they do say it, I said. But what I want to know is what *you* say that the courageous are ready to go face-to-face against—dangers, believing them to be dangers, or against what are not dangers?

But, he said, the former case was just proved by you in your previous argument to be impossible.

That again, I replied, is quite true. And if this proof was correct, then no one goes to meet what he thinks to be dangers, since lack of self-control, which makes men rush into dangers, has been shown to be ignorance.

He assented.

And yet all men, the courageous man and the coward alike, go to meet that about which they are confident; so that, from this point of view, the cowardly and the courageous go to meet the same things.

e But really, Socrates, said Protagoras, what cowards go to is the opposite of what the courageous go to; the one, for example, is ready to go to battle, and the other refuses.

And is going to battle honorable or disgraceful? I said.

Honorable, he replied.

And if it's honorable, then it has already been admitted by us to be good; for all honorable actions, we agreed, are good.

That is true; and to that opinion I shall always adhere.

Quite properly, too, I said. But which of the two types
360 are those who, as you say, are unwilling to go to war, which is a good and honorable thing?

The cowards, he replied.

And what is good and honorable, I said, is also pleasant?

It has certainly been acknowledged to be so, he replied.

And do the cowards knowingly refuse to go to what is nobler, and pleasanter, and better?

The admission of that, he replied, would belie our former admissions.

But what about the courageous man? Does he also go to meet the better, and pleasanter, and nobler?

That must be admitted.

And, in general terms, the courageous man feels no discreditable fears when he is afraid, or discreditable confidence when he feels confident? **b**

True, he replied.

And if it is not discreditable, then it's honorable?

He admitted this.

And if honorable, then good?

Yes.

But the fear and confidence of the cowardly or the rash or the insane, on the contrary, are discreditable?

He assented.

And these discreditable fears and confidences originate in obtuseness and ignorance?

It is so, he said.

Then as to the motive from which the cowards act, do **c** you call it cowardice or courage?

I would certainly say cowardice, he replied.

And haven't they been shown to be cowards through their ignorance of dangers?

Definitely, he said.

And it is because of that ignorance that they are cowards?

He assented.

And the reason why they are cowards is admitted by you to be cowardice?

He again assented.

Then the ignorance of what is and is not dangerous is cowardice?

He nodded.

But surely courage, I said, is the opposite of cowardice?

Yes.

d   Then the wisdom that knows what are and are not dangers is the opposite of the ignorance of them?

Here too he nodded.

And the ignorance of them is cowardice?

To this he very reluctantly nodded assent.[61]

And the knowledge of that which is and is not dangerous is courage, and it is the opposite of the ignorance of these things?

At this point he would no longer nod assent, but was silent.

And why, I said, do you neither assent nor dissent, Protagoras?

Finish the argument by yourself, he said.

e   I want to ask only one more question, I said. I want to know whether you still think that there are men who are extremely ignorant and yet extremely courageous?

You seem obstinately determined to make me answer, Socrates, and therefore I will gratify you, and say that it seems to me to follow from our earlier findings that this is impossible.

My only object, I said, in asking all these questions has been the desire to find out about virtue and, in particular, to define it; for if this were clear, I am very sure that the

361 other controversy which has been carried on at great length

[61]"Protagoras dies hard," remark J. and A. Adam, *Plato, Protagoras* (Cambridge University Press: 1893), p. 209.

by both of us—you asserting and I denying that virtue can be taught—would also be clarified. The present conclusion of our discussion appears to me to be scoffing and laughing at us, and if it should assume a human voice, it would say: "Protagoras and Socrates, you are inexplicable creatures; there you are, Socrates, who were saying that virtue cannot be taught, contradicting yourself now with your attempt to b prove that all things are knowledge, including justice, and prudence, and courage—all of which tends to show that virtue can certainly be taught; for if virtue were something other than knowledge, as Protagoras attempted to prove, then clearly it could not be taught; but if virtue turns out to be *nothing* but knowledge, as you are now trying to show, then it would be a miracle if it weren't capable of being taught. Protagoras, on the other hand, who started out by saying that it might be taught, seems now on the contrary eager to prove it to be almost anything other than knowledge; and if this is true, it must be completely incapable of c being taught." Now I, perceiving this outrageous confusion of our ideas, Protagoras, have a great desire that they should be cleared up. And now that we have discussed these subjects, I would like to proceed to inquire what virtue is, and to examine the question whether it is capable of being taught or not, so that that Epimetheus of yours should not trip us up and deceive us in the argument, as he forgot us in the distribution, according to your story. I pre- d ferred Prometheus to Epimetheus in the fable; and I make use of him, whenever I busy myself with these questions in Promethean care for my life in its entirety.[62] And if you have no objection, as I said at first, I would like more than anything to have your help in the inquiry.

[62]"Prometh-" means "forethought," "Epimeth-" means "hindsight."

Protagoras replied: Socrates, I applaud your energy, and your conduct of an argument. I do not think I am a base
e person in general, and in particular, I am the last man in the world to be envious. In fact, many people have heard me say that I admire you above all others whom I encounter, and far above all men of your age; and I may add that I would not be surprised if you came to be ranked among famous philosophers. Let us discuss the subject at some future time, whenever you want; at present it is high time to turn to something else.

362 By all means, I said, if that is your wish; for I ought long since to have kept the appointment I spoke of earlier—but I stayed here to oblige the fair Callias.[63]

So the conversation ended, and we went our way.

---

[63]It would appear that in claiming this appointment, Socrates is telling a lie, as we might have guessed. At any rate, at the very beginning of the work, during what gives every appearance of being a chance encounter with his unnamed friend, and which cannot therefore be the "appointment" here and earlier mentioned, Socrates says, "I have just now come from" Alcibiades (309b).

PHAEDRUS

PHAEDRUS

DRAMATIS PERSONAE

Socrates
Phaedrus

*(In the countryside outside the city walls of Athens,
Socrates encounters Phaedrus.)*

SOCRATES: Phaedrus, my friend, where are you headed, 227
and where coming from?

PHAEDRUS: I've been with Lysias,[1] Cephalus' son, and
now I'm going for a walk outside the city wall: I spent all
morning with him, sitting the entire time. *(Pause.)* I like
to take my walks out on the roads—in this I follow the
advice of your and my friend Acumenus: he says this is
more refreshing than pacing back and forth under the
colonnades.[2]   b

SOCRATES: And of course he is right. Lysias, I take it, was
in the city?

[1] It is the house of Lysias' father, Cephalus, that forms the setting for the *Republic*. Readers of that dialogue will recall that it includes, very early on, a charming conversation between Socrates and the aged Cephalus. The family was enormously rich, their wealth deriving from arms manufacture. They were not Athenian citizens, but resident aliens invited by Pericles to live in Athens. Another of Cephalus' sons, Polemarchus (also a character in the *Republic*), was murdered by the brutal oligarchical regime that briefly ruled Athens after the Peloponnesian War, called The Thirty, which had designs on the family fortune. Lysias managed, barely, to escape. He was one of the most talented writers of his generation. A body of about thirty speeches attributed to him survives.

[2] Phaedrus is shown in the *Symposium* in close association with the rather fussy doctor Eryximachus, the son of this same Acumenus, both of whom are mentioned again later on. Phaedrus appears to be something of a hypochondriac.

PHAEDRUS: Yes, at Epicrates', in the house that used to belong to Morychus—the one near the temple of Olympian Zeus.[3]

SOCRATES: And how were you occupying yourselves? Or—the obvious thing—did Lysias give you a taste of one of his works in progress?

PHAEDRUS: You'll find out, if you can spare the time to come with me and listen.

SOCRATES: What—do you imagine that I wouldn't, as Pindar puts it, "make it a matter of greater import than any mere business"[4] to hear what you and Lysias have been up to?

PHAEDRUS: Come on then.

(They walk a way together in silence.)

c SOCRATES: Please proceed with your account . . .

PHAEDRUS: In fact, Socrates, it was just your kind of thing: Lysias read us a speech, and we spent the morning going over it; it was, shall we say, *erotic*—at least in a way. You see, he represents an attempt being made on some pretty boy's virtue, not by a lover but by—well, it's in just this that his brilliant originality shows itself: for he says that you should go to bed with someone who *doesn't* love you in preference to someone who *does*.

SOCRATES: What noble generosity! I wish that he would say, Go to bed with the poor man rather than the rich, and with the old man rather than the young one, and

d whatever other conditions afflict me and the majority of us—then his little pleasantries would be truly urbane and populist. Naturally I am so inflamed with desire to

---

[3]Epicrates was a politician singled out by comic writers for his exceptionally luxuriant beard; Morychus was a notoriously high-living gourmand.

[4]From the opening of Pindar's first *Isthmian Ode*, written in honor of one Herodotus of Thebes, and still extant.

hear this speech of his that even if you walk all the way to the walls of Megara and back, as Herodicus[5] recommends, I will not fall a step behind you.

PHAEDRUS: Oh come on, Socrates. How can you imagine that an amateur could accurately reproduce an elaborate work like that, which the greatest writer of the age spent a long time composing? Not likely—though I would prefer such a talent to a large sum of money. 228

SOCRATES: Oh, Phaedrus. If I don't know Phaedrus, then I've lost my grip on myself, too. But in fact neither is the case. I am very sure that the speech of Lysias was repeated to him, not once only, but again and again—he insisted on hearing it many times over and Lysias was very willing to gratify him; at last, when nothing else b would do, he got hold of the book, and studied carefully what he most wanted to—this occupied him for the whole morning;—and then when he was tired with sitting, he went out to take a walk, but not until, by the dog,[6] as I believe, he had learned the entire speech by heart, unless it was unusually long, and he set out for a walk outside the wall in order to practice it. There he saw a certain person besotted with hearing discourses—he saw and he rejoiced: "Now," thought he, "I will have a partner in my revels." And he invited him to lead on. c But when the lover of discourse begged him to repeat the speech, he became all coy and said, "No, I cannot," as if he were not longing to do so, and were not in the end going to deliver it to some audience, whether one willing to listen or brought to do so by force. Therefore,

[5]Another well-known doctor, himself from Megara. A walk to the wall of that city, due east of Athens on the map, and back again, would be over fifty miles.

[6]One of Socrates' characteristic oaths. No one knows exactly what it means.

Phaedrus, bid him do at once what he will soon do whether bidden or not.

PHAEDRUS: It's clearly in my interest to deliver the speech however I can, since I see that you will absolutely not release me until I do deliver it, one way or another.

SOCRATES: You judge my intention correctly.

d PHAEDRUS: Then I will comply; but believe me, Socrates, I most certainly did not learn it verbatim—oh no. Still, I have a general notion of what he said, and will give you a summary of the points in which he said the lover differed from the non-lover. Let me begin at the beginning.

SOCRATES: Yes, my dear; but you must first show what you have there in your left hand under your cloak, for that roll, as I grasp it, is the actual speech itself.[7] If that is the case, then understand this about me, that I love

e you very much, but if Lysias, too, is here, then I am determined not to furnish myself to you to take your exercise upon.

PHAEDRUS: Stop. You have shattered the hope I had placed in you, Socrates, of a good workout. But where would you like us to sit and read?

229 SOCRATES: Let's turn off the road here and go by the Ilissus;[8] we will sit down at some quiet spot.

PHAEDRUS: It is opportune, as it seems, that I happen not to be wearing sandals; you of course never do. So the easiest thing is for us to get our feet wet and walk right

---

[7]Written out on sheets of papyrus, formed into a cylindrical roll.

[8]A river rising from the northern reaches of Mount Hymettus (east of Athens), descending south to the east of the city, then skirting close to the southeastern section of the city walls, and continuing past them to the west-southwest until it joins the Cephisus. Socrates and Phaedrus are most likely to the east of the city, and will follow the river downstream (i.e., west-southwest) for a ways.

along in the stream itself—*(steps in)*—and it's not unpleasant either, especially at this time of year and day.

SOCRATES: Lead on, and look out for a place where we
can sit down.

PHAEDRUS: Do you see that tallest plane-tree in the distance?

SOCRATES: Certainly.

PHAEDRUS: There are shade and gentle breezes there, and
grass on which to sit, or, if we wish, to lie down.

SOCRATES: Please lead on then.

(A few moments pass as they proceed.)

PHAEDRUS: Tell me, Socrates, wasn't it somewhere along
here where Boreas is said to have carried off Orithyia
from the banks of the Ilissus?[9]

SOCRATES: Such is the tradition.

PHAEDRUS: And is this the exact spot? Certainly the little
stream is delightful and pure and clear right through,
and very suitable for young girls to play by.

SOCRATES: I believe that the spot is not exactly here, but
about a quarter of a mile lower down, where you cross
to the shrine of Agra, and there is, I think, some sort of
an altar of Boreas at the place.

PHAEDRUS: I have never noticed it; but I beg you to tell
me, Socrates, do you believe this story?

SOCRATES: The sophisticated are doubtful, and I would
not be eccentric if, like them, I too were skeptical. I
could then come up with a rationalistic explanation that
Orithyia was playing with Pharmacia, when a northern
gust carried her over the neighboring rocks; and, having

---

[9]Orithyia was a daughter of Erechtheus, legendary founder of Athens;
Boreas is the North Wind, who was said to have carried the young princess off to
be his wife. About Pharmacia little is known except that a fountain nearby was
dedicated to her.

died in this way, she was said to have been "carried away
by Boreas." (There is a discrepancy, by the way, about
the locale: according to another version of the story, she
was taken from the Areopagus, and not from here.) But
no—though I readily acknowledge that these rational-
izations are very nice, still, the person whose task it is to
invent them is not to be envied; a great deal of labor and
ingenuity will be required of him, and when he has once
begun, he must go on and rehabilitate the hippo-
centaurs and chimeras, and then a flood of Pegasuses
inundates him, and countless other inconceivable and
portentous creatures. A person who is skeptical about
these things, and tries to reduce them one after another
to the rules of probability, using this heavy-handed sort
of knowingness, will need an enormous amount of
time.[10] Now, I myself have no leisure for such inquiries.
Shall I tell you why? I am still unable to fulfill the command of the Delphian inscription and "Know myself."
To be curious about what is not my concern, while I am
still ignorant of my own self, would be ridiculous. And
so I say good-bye to all this; the received opinion is good
enough for me. For, as I was saying, I want to know not
about this, but about myself: Am I a monster more complicated and swollen with passion than Typho, or a
creature of a gentler and simpler sort, naturally a part of
some divine, and not monstrous, dispensation? But
meanwhile, let me ask you, my friend—wasn't this the
plane-tree you were leading us to?

PHAEDRUS: Yes, this is it.

---

[10]Plenty of people were willing to expend this time; one, whose work survives in excerpted form, Palaephatus (late fourth century B.C.), certainly does exhibit the "heavy-handed sort of knowingness" Socrates suggests will be required.
Palaephatus' book is amazingly tiresome.

SOCRATES: By Hera, a fine resting place it is. Here is this lofty and spreading plane-tree, and the height and shade of the *agnus castus* are altogether lovely; since it is at its peak of blossom, it should make the spot as fragrant as possible; and the spring flowing beneath the plane-tree is deliciously cold to the feet. Judging from the ornaments and images, this must be a spot sacred to Achelous[11] and the Nymphs. If you like, in turn, how delightful and so very sweet is the breeze, and it gives a c clear and summery accompaniment to the chorus of the cicadas. But the greatest charm of all is the matter of the grass, like a pillow gently sloping to the head. My dear Phaedrus, you have been an admirable guide.

PHAEDRUS: What an incomprehensible being you are, Socrates. You really are like some stranger who is being led around by a tour guide. Do you ever go out of town d and cross the border? I tend to think that you don't exit the wall at all.

SOCRATES: I must ask your forgiveness, my good friend. I am a lover of knowledge, and the countryside and the trees decline to teach me anything, whereas the people in the city do. Though I do believe that you have found the charm with which to lure me out of the city into the country, like a hungry animal before whom a bough or a bunch of fruit is waved. For only hold up a book before me in the same way, and you can lead me all around Attica, and wherever else you want. But now, having ar- e rived, I intend to lie down, and you—you choose whatever posture you can read best in, and read.

PHAEDRUS: Listen then:

You know what my position is, and you have heard that

[11] A river god.

I believe it is to the advantage of both of us if this comes to

231 pass. I maintain that what I seek I deserve to obtain because I am *not* your lover:

First: when their passion ceases, lovers repent of the kindnesses they have shown. But to non-lovers no time of regret ever comes; for they confer their benefits not under compulsion, but freely, in accordance with the best arrangements they can make for their own interests.

Then again, lovers consider how by reason of their love they have neglected their own concerns and rendered service to others; and, adding into the account the troubles

b they have endured, they think that they have long ago made to the beloved a very ample return. But the nonlover has no such tormenting recollections: he has never neglected his affairs or quarreled with his relations; he has no troubles to add up or excuses to invent; and being well rid of all these evils, why should he not freely do what, as he supposes, will gratify the beloved?

c If you say that lovers are all the more to be esteemed because people say that they feel the greatest love for those whom they desire, and are willing to say and do what makes them hateful to other men, in order to please their beloved—if that is true, it is only proof that the lover will prefer any future love to his present one, and will injure his old love at the whim of the new. And yet how, in a matter of such infinite importance, can a man be right in trusting himself to someone who is afflicted with a malady

d that no experienced person would attempt to cure, since the patient himself admits that he is lovesick and not in his right mind, and himself acknowledges that his thought processes are gone awry, and agrees that he is unable to control himself? And if he came into his *right* mind, would he ever imagine that the desires which he conceived when in his *wrong* mind were good?

What is more, there are many more non-lovers than lovers. If you choose the best of the lovers, you will not have many to choose from; but if you choose the most congenial of the non-lovers, the choice will be larger, and you will be far more likely to find among them a person who is e worthy of your friendship.

Now, if you are anxious about public opinion, and you want to avoid discovery and reproach, in all probability the lover, who is always thinking that other men are as ready to 232 envy him as he is them, will exult in talking about it, and in his pride will make it perfectly clear to everyone that his efforts have not been in vain. But the non-lover is more his own master, and is desirous of solid good, and not of the esteem of mankind.

Again, the lover may be generally noted or seen following the beloved (this is his main occupation), and whenever they are observed to exchange a word or two, people assume that they are meeting because the impulses of lust b have either already been fulfilled or are about to be. But when non-lovers meet, no one seeks to find fault with it, because people know that talking to another is natural, whether friendship or some other pleasant matter is the occasion.

Once more, if you fear the fickleness of friendship, consider that in any other case a quarrel might be a mutual calamity; but now, when you have given up what is most c precious to you, you will be the greater loser, and therefore, you will have more reason to be afraid of the lover, since many things upset him, and he always thinks that everything is working against him. For that reason he debars his beloved from the society of others; he will not let you associate with the rich, in case they should surpass him in wealth, or with the educated, in case their wit should give them an edge; and he is equally afraid of anybody's influ-

d ence who has any other advantage over himself. So, by inducing you to make yourself hateful to them, he effectively deprives you of friends; but if, out of consideration for your own interests, you resist his strictures, then you will end up in a fight with him. But those who are non-lovers, and who achieve the satisfaction of their desire through their own merit, will not be jealous of their beloved's friends, and will rather hate those who refuse to be his associates, thinking that their favorite is slighted by the latter and benefited by

e the former; so that the affair is, in this case, likely to bring him much more friendship than enmity.

Many lovers have lusted for a youth's body before getting to know his character or obtaining experience of his circumstances, with the result that they can not be sure whether, when their passion has faded away, they will want to continue to be his friend. In the case of non-lovers, on

233 the other hand, they perform the act as established friends, and so it is unlikely that behavior from which they derive pleasure will cause their friendly affection to diminish, but rather the engagements will linger pleasantly in the memory, holding out the promise of pleasures yet to come.

Furthermore, I say that you are likely to be more improved by me than by a lover. For they praise your words and actions in the wrong way; partly, because they are afraid of offending you, but also because their judgment is

b weakened by passion. That's what love does to those who don't get their way—it makes painful things that give no pain to the rest. On the other hand, it drives the successful lover to praise behavior in the beloved that ought not to give him any pleasure, and therefore the beloved is to be pitied rather than envied. But if you listen to me, in the first place, I, in my relationship with you, will not have thought of present enjoyment alone, but also future advantage, since I will not be overwhelmed by love, but am my c own master; nor will I take up a fierce grudge against you over little matters, but even when the cause is great, will only slowly build up a small amount of wrath—unintentional offenses I shall forgive, and intentional ones I shall try to prevent; for these are the marks of a friendship which will last. Do you think that only a lover can be a firm friend? Reflect: if this were true, we would set small values d on sons, or fathers, or mothers; nor would we ever have loyal friends, for our love for them arises not from passion, but from other things that we have in common.

Furthermore, if the rule is that we ought to gratify the people who most press for it, then, on that principle, we ought in general to benefit not the most virtuous, but the most needy; for they are the ones who will be most relieved, and will therefore be the most grateful; and when you have a dinner party you should invite not your friends, e but the beggars and the hungry; for they will love you, and attend you, and come to your door, and will experience the greatest pleasure, and will be the most grateful, and will invoke many blessings upon your head. But surely you ought not to grant favors to people just because they have a very great need, but rather to those who are best able to return them; and again not to those who do no more than ask for it, but to those who deserve it; and not to those who 234 will enjoy the bloom of your youth, but to those who will share their prosperity with you as you grow older; nor to those who, having brought it off, will boast of their success to others, but to those who will be modest and tell no tales;

nor to those who are solicitous of you for a moment only, but to those who will continue to be your friends through life; nor to those who, when their passion is over, will pick a quarrel with you, but rather to those who, when the

b charm of youth has left you, will show their own virtue.

Remember what I have said; and consider yet this further point: friends admonish the lover under the idea that his way of life is bad; but no one of his intimates ever yet censured the non-lover, or thought that he was ill advised about his own interests.

Perhaps you will ask me whether I propose that you should indulge every non-lover. To which I reply that not even the lover would advise you to be so disposed toward

c all lovers, for the indiscriminate favor is less esteemed by the rational recipient, and less easily concealed by him who wants to escape the censure of the world. The matter ought to be to the advantage of both parties, and to the injury of neither.

I believe that I have said enough; but if there is anything more which you desire or which in your opinion needs to be supplied, ask.

Now, Socrates, what do you think? Isn't the speech great? Especially its style?

d SOCRATES: Yes, indescribably brilliant; the effect on me was ravishing. And this I owe to you, Phaedrus, for I observed that, while you were reading, you were in some kind of ecstasy, and, in the belief that you are more experienced in these matters than I am, I took my cue from you, and became inspired with frenzy together with you, the divine leader.[12]

---

[12]Socrates here uses language which suggests that Lysias is at the head of a group of worshipers of Dionysus, the frenzied bacchants.

PHAEDRUS: Oh. I see. You want to make a joke out of it.

SOCRATES: Me? Are you saying you don't think I'm being serious?

PHAEDRUS: Please stop it, Socrates, and let me have your e real opinion. I ask you, in the name of Zeus, the god of friendship, to tell me whether you think that any Hellene could have said more or spoken better on the same subject.

SOCRATES: Well, what do you want? Are you and I expected to praise the author for saying what the subject requires, or only the clearness, and roundness, and finish, and *tournure* of the language? As to the first, I willingly submit to your better judgment, for I am not worthy to form an opinion, having only attended to the 235 rhetorical manner; but I was doubting whether this could have been defended by even Lysias himself; I thought, though I speak under correction, that he repeated himself two or three times, either from lack of fluency in speaking at length on a single topic, or from lack of interest in such a subject; and also, he appeared to me to exult ostentatiously in showing how well he could say the same thing in two different ways.

PHAEDRUS: You are talking utter rubbish, Socrates. What b you call repetition was the special merit of the speech; for he omitted no topic of which the subject rightly allowed, and I do not think that anyone could have spoken better or more exhaustively.

SOCRATES: There I cannot go along with you. Ancient sages, men and women, who have spoken and written of these things, would rise up in judgment against me, if out of eagerness to please, I yielded to you on this point.

PHAEDRUS: Who might these be? And where did you hear c anything better than this?

SOCRATES: I am sure that I must have; but at the moment I cannot remember from whom; perhaps it was from the lovely Sappho, or the wise Anacreon;[13] or, possibly, from a prose writer. What ground have I for saying so? Why, because I perceive that my bosom is full, and that I could make another speech as good as that of Lysias, and different. Now I am certain that this is not an invention of my own, since I am well aware that I know nothing, and therefore I can only infer that I have been filled through the ears, like a pitcher, from the waters of another, though I have actually forgotten in my stupidity how this occurred, and who my informant was.

d

PHAEDRUS: Oh, this is spectacular. But never mind how you heard it or from whom; let that be a mystery not to be divulged even at my earnest request. You have committed to making another and better speech, equal in length and entirely new, on the same subject; and I, like the nine archons, promise that I will set up a golden statue at Delphi, not only of myself, but of you, too, and as large as life.[14]

e

SOCRATES: You are a dear friend, and truly priceless, if you suppose me to mean that Lysias has altogether missed the mark, and that I can make a speech from which all his arguments are to be excluded. The worst of

[13]Sappho: of the late seventh century B.C., poet of Mytilene on the island of Lesbos; since the late nineteenth century greatly honored as a poet of female love. Anacreon: Ionian poet of the later sixth century B.C., born in Teos, active in Samos and afterwards in Athens. The epithets Socrates applies here to the two seem ironical: Sappho was said to be startlingly ugly, and Anacreon's surviving work suggests just about anything besides wisdom, but most of all frivolous aestheticism and sensuality.

[14]The chief magistrates of the Athenian state, elected for a year's term. Upon entering office each swore an oath that he would dedicate a gold statue if found breaking any law.

authors will say something which hits the mark. Who, for example, could argue that one ought to gratify a non-lover rather than a lover without praising the discretion of the former and blaming the indiscretion of 236 the latter? These points are necessary to the argument, and no one will be able to find others to replace them; they must be allowed and overlooked. In making arguments like these, then, the only merit lies in their arrangement, for there is little to be done in the invention; but when you get beyond these built-in arguments and come up with harder-to-find new points, then you will win praise for originality, and not just for your arrangement.

PHAEDRUS: I admit that there is some justice to what you say, and so I too will be reasonable, and will allow you to start with the premise that the lover is more disordered b in his wits than the non-lover; if, in what remains, you make a longer and better speech than Lysias', and use some different arguments, then I say again that you shall have a statue of beaten gold, and take your place by the colossal offerings of the Cypselids at Olympia.[15]

SOCRATES: You really are annoyed, aren't you, Phaedrus? All because in teasing you I laid a finger on your little friend Lysias. Do you really imagine that I am going to try to improve upon his over-ingenuity?

PHAEDRUS: There I have you as you had me, and you must just speak "however you can." Don't force us to go c back and forth saying "You too!" as in a bad comic routine, or make me say to you as you said to me, "If I don't

[15]A dynasty of tyrants of Corinth, dating from the mid-seventh century B.C. Perhaps most famous of their treasures is a no longer extant wooden chest, elaborately decorated, described at length by Pausanias (*Description of Greece* 5. 17. 5).

know Socrates then I've lost my grip on myself," and "he was longing to speak, but became all coy." Rather, I suggest that you consider that we will not stir from this place until you have, if you will, unbosomed yourself of the speech; for here we are, all alone, and I am stronger

d   than you, remember, and younger; wherefore, "understand what I tell you,"[16] and do not prefer to speak under compulsion rather than willingly.

SOCRATES: But, my sainted Phaedrus, how ridiculous it would be of me to compete with Lysias with an extemporaneous speech! He is a master of his art and I am a mere layman.

PHAEDRUS: You see how matters stand; and therefore let there be no more pretenses; for, in fact, I know the word that is irresistible.

SOCRATES: Then don't say it.

PHAEDRUS: Yes, but I will; and my word shall be an oath. "I say, or rather swear"—but what god will be the witness of my oath?—"by this plane-tree I swear, that un-

e   less you make your speech here in the face of this very plane-tree, I will never again either recite or report to you any speech by any author."

SOCRATES: Oh, foul play, you monster! How cleverly you found the goad to drive the discourse-loving man to obey your wishes.

PHAEDRUS: Then why are you still playing your tricks?

SOCRATES: I am not going to any longer now that you have taken your oath, for I cannot allow myself to be starved.

237 PHAEDRUS: Then proceed.

SOCRATES: Shall I tell you what I will do?

---

[16]A quotation from Pindar.

PHAEDRUS: About what?

SOCRATES: I will cover up my face and race through the speech as fast as I can, for if I see you I will feel ashamed and not know what to say.

PHAEDRUS: Just give the speech; as for the rest, do whatever you want.

(Socrates stands in front of the plane-tree and arranges his cloak to cover his face.)

SOCRATES: Come, O ye Muses, be it that you have received your name Ligeiae[17] from the character of your strains, or because the Ligurians are a musical race, help, O help me in the tale which my good friend here desires me to unfold, in order that his friend whom he always deemed clever may seem to him more clever now than ever.

b

Once upon a time there was a boy, or, more properly speaking, a young man, and very beautiful he was. He had a great many lovers. One of them was especially crafty; he had persuaded the young man that he did not love him, though in fact he loved him more than did any of the rest. Now one day when this crafty lover was pursuing the young man, he used the following argument: that he ought to give his favors to the non-lover rather than the lover. His words were as follows:

No matter what the subject, there is for those who wish to deliberate well upon it always one and the same starting point: you must know what it is you are deliberating about, c or you will inevitably fail altogether. Most people, however, are not aware of their ignorance of a thing's essential

[17]"Clear-toned."

nature, and because they think they know all about it, they fail to secure agreement about the premises of their inquiry at its beginning, and as they proceed, they reap the predictable harvest of this oversight: they disagree with one another and even contradict themselves. Now, you and I must not be guilty of this fundamental error which we condemn in others; but as the question that lies before us is whether you should enter into intimacy with the lover or non-lover, let us first of all agree in defining the nature and

d power of love itself, and then, keeping our eyes upon the definition and constantly referring to it, let us further inquire whether love brings advantage or disadvantage.

Everyone sees that love is a desire, and we know that even non-lovers desire the beautiful. Now in what way is the lover to be distinguished from the non-lover? Let us note that in every one of us there are two guiding and ruling principles which lead us wherever they wish; one is the natural impulse to pleasure, the other is a consciously acquired faculty of judgment which aspires after what is best; and these two are sometimes in harmony and sometimes at

e war, and sometimes the one, sometimes the other prevails. When judgment, with the help of reason, leads us to the best, and proves superior, it is called prudence; but when desire, which is devoid of reason, rules in us and drags us

238 to pleasure, the name given to that regime is wantonness *(hubris)*. Now wantonness comes under many names, being composed of many members, and many forms, and any of these forms when very marked gives its own name to the possessor, a name neither honorable nor creditable to acquire. The desire for eating, for example, which gets the better of the higher reason and the other desires, is called

b gluttony, and he who has it is called a glutton; the tyrannical desire for drink, which inclines the possessor of the desire to drink, has a name that is only too obvious, and there can be as little doubt by what name any other appetite of the same family would be called—it will be the name of whatever happens to be dominant. And now I think that you will perceive the drift of my argument; but a matter stated explicitly is altogether clearer than if not so stated, so here I state it: the irrational desire that overcomes the tendency of judgment toward right, and is led away to the enjoyment of beauty, and, under the influence in turn of its related desires—that supreme desire, I say, which by leading conquers and by the force of passion is reinforced from this very force, receiving a name, is called the force of love.[18]

c

And now, dear Phaedrus, I shall pause for a moment to ask if you do not think me, as I appear to myself, divinely inspired?

PHAEDRUS: Yes, Socrates, a very unusual fluency has taken possession of you.

SOCRATES: Listen to me, then, in silence; for surely the place is holy; so that you must not wonder, if, as I proceed, I enter into a divine fury, for already I am not far off from uttering dithyrambics.[19]

d

PHAEDRUS: Nothing could be truer.

SOCRATES: The responsibility rests with you. But hear what follows, and perhaps the fit may be averted; all is in their hands above. I will go on talking to my young man.

We have now declared and defined the nature of the subject. Keeping the definition in view, let us now inquire

---

[18]The Greek exploits an untranslatable pun on *eros,* "love," and *erromenos rostheisa,* "strongly strengthened" (translated here as "reinforced from this very force.")

[19]The dithyramb is a song in honor of the god Dionysus; a byword for utterances of violent emotion and extravagant imagery.

e what advantage or disadvantage is likely to accrue from the lover or the non-lover to him who accepts their advances.

He who is the victim of his passions and the slave of pleasure will of course desire to make his beloved as agreeable to himself as possible. Now to him who has a diseased mind, anything is agreeable that is not opposed to him; but that which is equal or superior is hateful; and

239 therefore the lover will not brook any superiority or equality on the part of his beloved; he is always working to reduce him to inferiority. And the ignorant is the inferior of the wise, the coward of the brave, the slow of speech of the orator, the dull-witted of the clever. Such, or even graver than these, are the mental defects in which a lover will necessarily delight when they are implanted by nature; and which otherwise he must contrive to implant, or else be deprived of his immediate pleasure. But then he cannot help

b being jealous, and will debar his beloved from advantageous connections that would most tend to make a man of him, thus doing him great harm; and especially harmful is it to withdraw him from that society which would have given him wisdom. That is to say, in his excessive fear lest he should come to be despised in his beloved's eyes, he will be compelled to banish from him divine philosophy; and there is no greater injury that he can inflict upon him than this. He will contrive that his beloved shall be wholly ignorant, and shall refer all questions to him; the beloved is to be to his lover the greatest source of pleasure, to himself the greatest source of harm. Truly then, the man afflicted

c with passion is no profitable guardian and associate for him in all that relates to his mind.

Let us next see how the man whose law of life is pleasure, and not good, will condition and train the body of the youth over whom he has gained ascendancy. He will be ob-

served to choose a beloved who is delicate rather than
sturdy and strong, one brought up in half-light and not
outside in the sun, a stranger to manly exercises and the
sweat of toil, accustomed to only a soft and luxurious and
unmanly diet, instead of the hues of health, made up in the d
colors of paint and ornament, and the rest following in accordance with these—such a life as anyone can imagine
and which I need not detail at length. But I may sum up all
that I have to say in a word, and pass on. Such a physique
in war, or in any of the great crises of life, will be the anx-
iety of his friends and also of his lover, and a great source
of encouragement for his enemies.

Leaving this obvious point, let us tell what advantage or
disadvantage the beloved will receive from the guardian- e
ship and society of his lover in the matter of his property;
this is the next point to be considered. The lover will be
the first to see what, indeed, will be sufficiently evident to
all men, that he desires above all things for his beloved
to be deprived of those dearest and most kindly disposed
to him, and of his dearest and holiest possessions: father,
mother, kindred, friends—he would be glad to see him deprived of all who he thinks may be hinderers or critics of 240
that cooperative enterprise from which the lover extracts
his highest pleasure; he will even cast a jealous eye upon
his gold and silver or other property, because these make
him a less easy prey, and, when caught, less manageable;
hence a lover is of necessity displeased at his possession of
them and rejoices at their loss; and he would like him to be
wifeless, childless, homeless, as well; and the longer the
better, for what he desires is to prolong his selfish fruition
for as long as possible.

There are other ills in the world, to be sure, but some
god has mixed into the majority of them a transitory plea- b

sure, as in a flatterer, a fearsome beast and great cause of harm, but nonetheless, nature has imbued him with a capacity to cause a not unalluring pleasure; and you may say that a prostitute is a harmful thing, and disapprove of many creatures and practices of such a character, and yet for the time they are very pleasant. But the lover is not only hurtful to his love; he is also an extremely disagreeable

c companion. The old proverb says "Youth for youth, age for age"; I suppose that equality of years inclines people to the same pleasures, and similarity begets friendship; yet you may have more than enough even of this. Constraint, also, is said to be grievous to all men at all times. But the relation between the lover and his beloved, apart from their unlikeness, is as constrained as possible. For he is old and his beloved is young, and neither day nor night will he leave him if he can help it; necessity and the sting of desire

d drive him on, and tantalize him with the pleasure that he receives from seeing, hearing, touching, experiencing him through every sense organ. And for that reason he is delighted to cling to him and to be servant to him. But what pleasure or consolation can the beloved be receiving all this time? Must he not feel the extremity of disgust when he looks at an aged face from which youthful charm has faded, as indeed it has from the whole person of the lover?

e If it is disagreeable merely to hear about such things, it is much worse to be forced into daily contact with them; for he is jealously watched and guarded against everything and everybody, and has to hear misplaced and exaggerated praises of himself, and censures equally inappropriate, which are intolerable when the man is sober, and, when he is drunk, become disgusting, as well as intolerable, in their wearisome and unrestrained frankness.

And not only while the lover's love continues is he destructive and unpleasant, but when his love ceases, he becomes a perfidious enemy of him on whom he showered his oaths and prayers and promises, and yet could hardly prevail upon him to tolerate the tedium of his company 241 even from motives of interest. The hour of payment arrives, and now he is the servant of another master; instead of love and infatuation, wisdom and temperance are his lords; but the beloved has not noticed the change which has taken place in him, and when he asks for a return favor and reminds him of what was said and done before, he believes himself to be speaking to the same person, and the other, not having the courage to confess the truth, that he has changed, and not knowing how to fulfill the oaths and promises he made when under the sway of folly, and having now grown wise and temperate, does not want to do as b he did or to be as he was before. And so he runs away and is made to become a defaulter; the oyster shell has fallen with the other side uppermost[20]—he changes from pursuit to flight, while the other is compelled to pursue him with anger and imprecation, not knowing that he ought never from the first to have yielded to a demented lover instead of a sensible non-lover; and that in making such a choice c he was giving himself up to a faithless, morose, envious, disagreeable being, hurtful to his property, hurtful to his bodily health and still more hurtful to the cultivation of his mind, which there neither is, nor ever will be, anything more honored than in the eyes both of gods and men. Consider this, fair youth, and know that in the friendship of the lover there is no real kindness; he has an appetite and wants to feed upon you: as wolves love lambs, so lovers love their loves. d

---

[20]Referring to a sort of "heads or tails" game played with oyster shells.

(Socrates uncovers his face.)

That's it, Phaedrus. There's not any more for you to get out of me; let's let the speech end here.

PHAEDRUS: But I thought that you were only halfway through and were going to make a similar argument about all the advantages of accepting the non-lover. Why are you stopping now?

e SOCRATES: Didn't you notice, dear friend, that I have passed beyond dithyrambic rhythms into the heroic measure, and that too when merely uttering criticism of the lover? If I go on to praise the non-lover, what rhythms will I attain to then? Do you not perceive that my wits are plainly being overwhelmed by the Nymphs to whom you have mischievously exposed me here? So I will complete the speech with a word: all the ills that we have censured in the lover—invert them and assign the corresponding virtues to the non-lover; take it as read. And now I will say no more; there has been enough of both of them. Thus this fairy tale will suffer the fate it deserves, while I

242 will cross the river and make my way home, before you compel me to commit some greater outrage.

(Socrates moves to the stream in order to head back to Athens.)

PHAEDRUS: Not yet, Socrates; not until the heat of the day has passed; don't you see that it is almost noon? There is the midday sun standing still, as people say, in the meridian. No, let us rather stay and talk over what has been said, and then return in due time when it's cool.

(Socrates returns.)

SOCRATES: Your love of discourse, Phaedrus, is superhuman, simply miraculous, and I don't believe there is any one of your contemporaries who has either himself made or in one way or another has compelled others to b make a comparable number of speeches. I would except Simmias the Theban,[21] but all the rest are far behind you. And now I do in fact believe that you have been the cause of another, which I will now have to deliver.

PHAEDRUS: This is no declaration of war. But what do you mean?

SOCRATES: I mean to say that as I was about to cross the stream, the divine sign that characteristically comes to me intervened; when it comes, it always restrains me from doing whatever I am about to do, and so now, I c thought that I heard on the spot a voice forbidding me from departing until I had purified myself, as a sinner against the godhead. Now I am a diviner, though not a very good one, but good enough for my own use, as you might say of someone who is just barely literate, that he can read and write well enough for his own purposes; and I now perceive my error clearly. For the soul, of course, has a certain power of prophecy, my friend. That is why some time ago, while I was still speaking, I had a sort of misgiving, and, like Ibycus,[22] I was troubled "lest I might be buying honor from men at the price d of sinning against the gods." And now I recognize my error.

PHAEDRUS: What error?

SOCRATES: That was a horrible speech that you brought

[21]An associate of Socrates'; he is given a leading role in Socrates' last conversation, represented in the *Phaedo*.

[22]Poet of the mid-sixth century B.C., born in southern Italy, active in Samos, in the court of the tyrant Polycrates.

with you, simply horrible, and you made me utter one as bad.

PHAEDRUS: How so?

SOCRATES: It was fatuous, I say, and, to a certain extent, impious; could anything be more horrible?

PHAEDRUS: No, not if the speech really was such as you describe.

SOCRATES: Well, isn't Eros the son of Aphrodite, and a god?

PHAEDRUS: So men say.

SOCRATES: But that was not acknowledged by Lysias in
e   his speech, nor by you in that other speech which you by a charm drew from my lips. For if Eros is, as he surely is, a divinity, or something divine, then he cannot be evil. Yet both the speeches spoke about him as if he were such. And therefore we two both sinned against Eros. What is more, there was also a hypersophisticated silliness about the speeches: having no truth or honesty in
243   them, nevertheless they pretended to be something, hoping to succeed in deceiving a few feeble wretches and to gain celebrity among them. Therefore, my friend, I must be cleansed.

Now there is available to those who commit mythological error an ancient purgation which Homer did not know, but Stesichorus did. For when the latter was deprived of his sight for reviling Helen, he was not dumbfounded, as Homer was, but, being a man of the Muses, recognized the cause and immediately sang as follows:

> *It is not true this story,*
> *And you did not embark on well-benched ships,*
b > *And you did not come to the tower of Troy.*

When he had completed his poem, which is called "The Recantation," immediately his sight returned to him. Now I will be wiser than either Stesichorus or Homer, in that I am going to make my recantation for reviling love before I suffer any punishment; and this I will attempt, not as before, covered up out of shame, but with head bared.[23]

PHAEDRUS: Nothing could be more agreeable to me than to hear you say this.

SOCRATES: Only think, my good Phaedrus, what an utter c lack of delicacy was shown in the two speeches; I mean, in my own and in the one you recited out of the book. Wouldn't anyone who was himself of a noble and gentle nature, and who loved or ever had loved a nature like his own, when he heard us saying that lovers take up serious grudges over trivialities, and imputing to them excessive jealousy, and speaking of the harm they do their beloved, wouldn't he assume that he was hearing the words of persons who, reared among sailors, had never witnessed a liberal and gentlemanly love? And wouldn't he adamantly deny our criticisms of Eros? d

PHAEDRUS: No doubt, Socrates, by god.

SOCRATES: I blush at the thought of this person, and I am also afraid of Eros himself, and so I desire to wash the brine out of my ears with water from the spring; and I counsel Lysias not to delay, but to write another speech, which will prove that the lover's love ought to be reciprocated and the non-lover's non-love likewise.

PHAEDRUS: Be assured that he will. For if you speak the

---

[23]Stesichorus lived in the first half of the sixth century B.C. and is associated with southern Italy and Sicily. He composed long poems that seem to have fused lyric poetry with epic. Homer, of course, was legendarily blind—unlike Stesichorus, who, owing to his special insight, was only temporarily blind.

praises of the lover, then it is ordained that Lysias will be compelled by me to write another speech on the same theme.

SOCRATES: This I can believe, as long as you are who you are.

PHAEDRUS: Then take heart and speak.

SOCRATES: But where is the fair youth whom I was addressing before, and who ought to listen now; lest, if he hear me not, he should accept a non-lover before he knows what he is doing?

PHAEDRUS: Here he is, right by you, and always at your service.

SOCRATES: Know then, fair youth, that my previous speech was the work of Phaedrus, son of Pythocles, of the deme Myrrhina. The one which I am about to utter is the recantation of Stesichorus, son of Euphemus, of Himera. It is as follows:

"It is not true, this story" that urges the beloved to accept the non-lover, when he might have the lover, on the grounds that the former is sane, and the latter mad. It might be so if madness were straightforwardly an evil; but in fact the greatest of goods come to us through madness, at least through madness that is given by divine dispensation. For prophecy is a madness, and the prophetess at Delphi and the priestesses at Dodona when out of their senses have conferred great benefits on Greece, on both states and private individuals, but when in their senses few or, rather, none at all. And I might also tell you how the Sibyl and other inspired persons have foretold the future to many people and thereby saved them from disaster. But it would be tedious to tell what everyone knows.

The following evidence, however, deserves to be adduced: the ancient inventors of names did not consider

madness *(mania)* a disgrace or reproach; otherwise they
would not have woven into the noblest of arts, that by   c
which the future is foretold, this very name, and called it
the "manic" art. But believing it to be a noble thing, whenever it occurs by divine dispensation, they named it thus—
though men of the present ignorantly insert a T and call it
the "mantic" art. And this is confirmed by the name that
was given by them to the rational investigation of the future, whether made by the help of birds or other signs—
this, for inasmuch as it is an art which supplies in a rational
manner insight *(nous)* and information *(historia)* to human
understanding *(oiesis),* they originally called it "oio-no-(h)
ist-ikē," but the word has lately been altered and made
more impressive by the modern introduction of the long O   d
(oionistike).[24] Now, to the same degree as prophecy *(man-
tikē)* is more perfect and august than augury *(oionistikē),*
both in name and fact, to the same degree, as the ancients
testify, is madness superior to a sane mind, for the one is
only of human, but the other of divine, origin. Again,
where plagues and the direst woes have bred in certain
families, owing to some ancient blood-guiltiness, there
madness, inspiring and taking possession of those whom
destiny has appointed, has found deliverance, having recourse to prayers and religious rites. And learning from   e
there the use of purifications and mysteries, it has sheltered
from evil, future as well as present, the man who has some
part in this gift, and has afforded a release from his present
calamity to one who is truly possessed, and duly out of his

[24]That is, the actual Greek word, *oionistike,* does not admit the fantastic ety-
mological analysis from *nous, historia,* and *oiesis,* so Socrates pretends, as with the
equally preposterous derivation of "mantic" from "manic," that it represents a
deformation of the supposedly original oio-no-(h)ist-ikē, with a short O (or omi-
cron) instead of a long (omega).

245 mind. The third kind is the madness of those who are possessed by the Muses; which, taking hold of a delicate and virgin soul, and there inspiring frenzy, awakens lyrical and all other poetical rhythms, and with these, it adorns the myriad actions of ancient heroes for the instruction of posterity. But whoever has no touch of the Muses' madness in his soul approaches the gates of poetry and thinks that he will get into the temple by the help of art—he, I say, is not admitted, and the poetry of the sane man is utterly eclipsed by that of the inspired madman.

b I might tell of many other noble deeds which have sprung from divine madness. And therefore, let not the mere thought of this frighten us, and let us not be scared and confused by an argument which says that the temperate friend is to be chosen rather than the driven one; no, that argument must show that love is not sent by the gods for the good of the lover and the beloved; only when he has demonstrated that will we allow him to carry off the palm. And we, for our part, must prove in answer to him that the divine dispensation of madness is the gift of the gods most
c conducive to our benefit. The proof of this shall be one that the wise will receive, and the cynical reject. But first of all, let us observe the nature of the divine and human soul, its experiences and actions, and try to ascertain the truth. The beginning of our proof is as follows:

All soul is immortal. For that which is always in motion is immortal. But that which moves another and is moved by another, in having cessation of motion, has cessation of life. Only the Self-Moving, since it cannot forsake its own nature, never ceases to move, and is the fountain and be-
d ginning of motion to all else that moves. Now, Beginning is unbegotten. For that which is begotten must have a beginning, but Beginning itself cannot be begotten of anything.

For if Beginning came out of and thus after something, then it would not exist from the beginning.[25] But since it is unbegotten, it must also be indestructible. For surely if Beginning were destroyed, then it could neither come into being itself from any source, nor serve as the beginning of other things, if it is true that all things must come into being from a beginning. Thus it is proved that the Self-Moving is the beginning of motion; and this can be neither destroyed nor begotten, or else all of the universe and all of creation would collapse and stand still, and never again be able to be put into motion. And since the Self-Moving has been proved to be immortal, a person will not blush to affirm that this, self-motion, is the very essence and meaning of the soul. For every body that is moved from outside is soulless, but that which is self-moved from within is soulfull or animate.[26] But if this is true, that the soul is identical with the self-moving, it must necessarily follow that the soul is unbegotten and immortal.

e

246

Enough, then, about the soul's immortality: let us pass to the description of her form. Now, to tell what sort of thing the soul *is* would require an absolutely superhuman and lengthy narrative; but an account of what it is *like* will be briefer and within the range of human capability. Let us, then, take the latter course. We posit that the soul is like the combined functioning of a yoke-team of horses and their driver, all winged. Now the horses and the drivers of the gods are all of them noble and of noble descent, but those of other races are mixed. First, you must know that the human driver drives a pair; and next, that one of his horses is good and noble and descended from such, while

b

[25]That is, since that from which it was begotten must have existed prior to it.
[26]Greek *psyche*, soul, is conceived to be, among other things, the life force, for which the Latin is *anima*, from which comes the English "animate."

the other descends from, and is himself, the opposite nature. Necessarily, the management of the human chariot is a difficult and frustrating task. Now, it must be attempted to explain how a living creature is said to be both mortal and immortal. Soul in her totality has the care of inanimate being everywhere, and traverses the whole heaven assuming different forms on different occasions—when perfect and fully winged, she soars upward, and brings order to the whole world; whereas the imperfect soul, losing her wings and drooping in her flight, at last settles on the solid ground, and there, finding a home, she acquires an earthly body, which appears to move itself but is really moved by her power; and this compounding of soul and body is called a living creature and is given the name "mortal." For no such union can be reasonably believed to be immortal; but we, although we have not seen a god nor adequately perceived divine nature, invent in our imaginings an immortal creature with a body and a soul which are united throughout all time. Let that, however, be as the god wills, and be spoken of likewise. Let us for our part inquire into the reason why the soul loses her wings. The explanation is something like this:

The natural faculty of the wing is to lead that which gravitates downward up into the higher region, which is the habitation of the gods; the wing is the corporeal element that has the greatest share of the divine. The divine is beautiful, wise, good, and all the like; and by these qualities, the wingedness of the soul is most of all nourished, and brought to grow; but when fed upon evil and foulness and the opposite of good, it wastes away and perishes. The mighty lord of heaven, Zeus, driving a winged chariot, leads the procession in heaven, ordering all and taking care of all; and there follows him the host of gods and demigods,

marshaled in eleven bands; for Hestia stays by herself in the 247
house of heaven; of the others, those who are counted
among the princely twelve lead the lesser divinities in their
appointed order. They see many blessed sights in the inner
heaven, and there are many ways to and fro, along which the
blessed gods pass, each one doing his own work. Whoever
wishes to and can may follow, for jealousy has no place in
the celestial chorus. But when they go to banquet and feast,
then they move steeply up to the top of the vault of heaven. b
The chariots of the gods, obeying the rein, advance with
ease and in equilibrium; but the others labor, because the
wicked one of the two horses goes heavily, inclining to the
earth and weighing down any of the charioteers who have
not trained their horses well: it is here that the ultimate task
and contest is set for the soul. For these souls, being called
immortal, as soon as they arrive at the top, go forth and
stand on the upper surface of heaven; its revolution carries
them around, and they behold the things beyond. c

But of the place that is above the heavens, no earthly
poet ever has or ever will compose a song that does it justice. It is as I will describe; for I must venture to speak the
truth, especially since truth is my theme. There occupies
this place the true essence of Being: without color or
shape, and intangible, visible only to reason, the helmsman
of the soul, it is the object of the class of knowledge that is
true. Now, the intelligence of a god, because it is nourished d
upon reason and pure knowledge, and the intelligence of
every soul insofar as it is capable of receiving the nourishment proper to it, rejoices at beholding reality once more,
after so long a time, and, gazing upon truth, is replenished
and made glad, until the revolution brings her around
again in a circle to the same place. In the circuit she beholds justice itself, and she beholds prudence, and knowl-

edge—not that knowledge that has coming-into-being as a property, that shifting and variable knowledge of the

e things that we now call real—but truly real knowledge that is really present where true being is. And beholding the other true existences in like manner, and feasting upon them, she passes back down into the interior of the heavens and returns home; and when she arrives there, the driver puts up his horses at the stall and gives them ambrosia to eat and nectar to drink.

248   Such is the life of the gods; but of other souls, that which follows god best, and is most like him, lifts the head of the charioteer into the outer world, and is carried around in the circuit, being distracted all the while by the unruly steeds, and thus with difficulty beholds true being. Meanwhile, another rises and falls, and sees, and again fails to see by reason of the violent misbehavior of the horses. The rest of the souls are also yearning for the upper world, and they all follow, but not being strong enough, they are carried around below the surface, treading on one another and colliding, each trying to get ahead of the other; and

b there is confusion and competition and extreme sweat; and during this time many of them are lamed or have their wings broken as a result of the incompetent driving of the charioteers; and all of them, after suffering much toil, depart without having attained to the mysteries of true being, and, departed, they feed upon mere appearance. The reason why the souls exhibit this extraordinary eagerness to behold the Plain of Truth is that there is found there the pasturage that is suited to the highest part of the

c soul; the wings on which the soul soars are nourished with this. And there is this law of destiny—that the soul that attains any vision of truth in company with a god is preserved from harm until the next circuit, and if always able to attain this is always unharmed. But when she is unable to follow, and fails to behold the truth, and through some mishap is weighed down by a double load of forgetfulness and vice, and her wings fall from her and she drops to the earth, then the law ordains that this soul shall at her first birth pass not into any other animal, but only into man; and the soul that has seen most of truth shall be placed in the seed from which will be born a philosopher, or a seeker of beauty, or someone who is both artist and lover; and the soul that has seen truth in the second degree will be some righteous king or warrior chief; the soul that is of the third class will be a politician, or economist, or businessman; the fourth will be a lover of athletic exercise, or a doctor; the fifth will lead the life of a prophet or hierophant; to the sixth, the character of a poet or some other practitioner of the representationalist arts will be assigned; to the seventh, the life of an artisan or farmer; to the eighth, that of a sophist or demagogue; to the ninth, that of a tyrant. All these are states of probation, in which he who lives righteously improves, and he who lives unrighteously deteriorates, his lot.

Ten thousand years must elapse before the soul of each one can return to the place from which she started, for she cannot grow her wings in less time, unless it is the soul of a man who has honorably pursued philosophy, which is to say, of a man who has pursued the love of boys in a philosophical manner:[27] these, when the third thousand-year circuit comes around, if they have chosen this life three times in succession, have wings given back to them, and go away at the end of only three thousand years instead of

[27]Much of the rest of the speech is given over to explaining this startling change of subject to "the love of boys" (the Greek word used is in fact a verb formed from the noun "pederasty").

ten. But the others receive judgment when they have completed their first life, and after the judgment they go, some of them to the houses of correction which are under the earth, and are punished; others to some place in heaven to which they are lightly borne by justice, and there they live in a manner worthy of the life that they led here when in b the form of men. And in the thousandth year, both kinds go to a place where they must draw lots and choose their second life, and they may take any which they please. And now the soul of a man may pass into the life of a beast, or that which has once been a man may return again from the beast into human form. But the soul that has never seen the truth will not pass into the human form. For a man must understand something spoken at the level of generality, proceeding from the many particulars of sense, and ren- c dered by reasoning into a coherent unity. This process is the recollection of those things that our soul once saw while following god—when, ignoring the things that we now say possess being, she raised her head up toward the true being. And therefore, the mind of the philosopher alone has wings; and this is just, for he is always, according to the measure of his abilities, clinging in recollection to those things by virtue of being close to which a god is divine. And whoever employs the reminders of these things properly is constantly being initiated into perfect mysteries and alone becomes truly perfect. But, as he stands apart d from earthly interests and is fastened upon the divine, he is admonished by the multitude as if he were a lunatic; they do not see that he is inspired.

Thus far I have been speaking of the fourth and last kind of madness, which is imputed to him who, when he sees the beauty of earth, recollects the true beauty, and becomes winged and, raising his wings, is eager to fly upward, but cannot; he is like a bird fluttering and looking upward, and is careless of the world below; and he is therefore castigated for being mad. And I have shown this of all inspirations to be the noblest and highest and the offspring of the e highest to him who has or shares in it, and that he who loves the beautiful is called a lover because he partakes of it. For, as has been already said, every soul of man has by nature beheld true being; this was the condition of her passing into the form of man. But all souls are not easily 250 reminded by the things on earth of the things of the other world; they may have seen them for a short time only, or they may have been unfortunate in their earthly lot, and, having had their hearts turned to unrighteousness through some corrupting influence, they may have lost the memory of the holy things which they once saw. Only a few retain an adequate remembrance of them, and they, when they behold here any semblance of that other world, are stunned with amazement and beside themselves; but they do not recognize what this rapture means, because they do not clearly perceive. For there is no radiance in our earthly copies of justice or prudence or those other things which b are precious to souls: they are perceived by means of dull sense-organs; and there are few who, when they approach the images, behold in them the realities, and these only with difficulty. But beauty could be seen, brightly shining, by all who were with that happy band—we[28] following in the train of Zeus, others of another god; and they beheld the beatific vision and were initiated into a mystery that may be truly called most blessed, which we celebrated in c our state of innocence, before we had any experience of

[28]Presumably philosophers, though elsewhere Socrates regularly identifies himself as a follower of Apollo.

evils to come, when we were admitted to the sight of ap-
paritions innocent and simple and calm and happy, which
we beheld shining in pure light, pure ourselves and not yet
enshrined in that living tomb that we carry about and call
the body, imprisoned like an oyster in his shell.

Let the preceding digression be a gift to memory; it was
through her that our yearning for the things seen then has
caused our account to be spoken at such length. But of
beauty, I repeat that we saw her there shining in company
d with the celestial forms; and coming to earth we find her
here too, shining most clearly through the clearest aperture of sense. For sight is the most piercing of our bodily
senses, though wisdom is not seen by it—for wisdom
would cause furious passions of love if, coming into view,
she offered any such clear image of herself; and so would
the rest that are lovable. But as it is, beauty alone has this
prerogative, so that it is most visible and that which most
e excites love. Now whoever is not newly initiated or has become corrupted does not easily rise out of this world to the
sight of true beauty in the other, when he contemplates
her earthly namesake, and instead of being awed at the
sight of her, he is given over to pleasure, and like a brutish
beast he tries to mount, and to beget children; he consorts
with wantonness, and is not afraid or ashamed of pursuing
251 pleasure in violation of nature. But he whose initiation is
recent, and who has been the spectator of many of the
things in the other world, is amazed when he sees anyone
having a godlike face or bodily form, which reflects the
true beauty; and at first a shudder runs through him, and
again the old awe steals over him; then looking upon the
face of the beautiful one, as if of a god, he reveres him, and
if he were not afraid of being thought a downright madman, he would sacrifice to his beloved as to the image of a

god. Then while he gazes on him there is a sort of reaction, and the shudder passes into an unusual heat and perspiration; for, as he receives the effluence of beauty through the eyes, the wings moisten and he warms. And as he warms, the parts out of which the wing grew, and which had been hitherto closed and rigid, and had prevented the wing from shooting forth, are melted, and as nourishment streams upon him, the lower end of the wing swells and starts to grow from the root upward; and the growth extends under the whole soul—for once the whole was winged. During this process the whole soul is boiling up and overflowing— the effect is similar to the irritation and uneasiness in the gums at the time of cutting teeth. The soul bubbles up then, and has a feeling of uneasiness and tickling as it begins to sprout wings. Now, when the soul gazes upon the beauty of the boy and she receives this surpassing overflow—therefore called Sir Passion—and is refreshed and warmed by them, she then ceases from her pain with joy. But when she is parted from her beloved and her moisture fails, then the orifices of the passage out of which the wings shoot dry up and close, and block the growth of the wings; each of which, being choked up with the surpassing passion, throbbing as with the pulsations of an artery, pricks the aperture which is nearest, until at length the entire soul is pierced all around and maddened and pained, but then in turn at the recollection of the beautiful one she is again delighted. And from having both of these experiences mixed together, the soul is deeply distressed at the strangeness of her condition, and, at a loss, becomes frenzied. In her madness she can neither sleep by night nor stay in her place by day, but wherever she thinks that she will behold the beautiful one, there in her desire she runs. And when she has seen him, and bathed herself in the waters of

beauty, her previous constraint is loosened, and she is refreshed, and has no more pangs and pains; and this that she
252 then enjoys is the sweetest pleasure of all, and she will
never willingly forsake it, and she esteems the beautiful
one above all: she has forgotten her mother and brothers
and friends, and thinks nothing of the neglect and loss of
property; all the rules and proprieties of life, on which she
formerly prided herself, she now despises, and is ready to
be a servant and to sleep wherever she is allowed, as near as
possible to the desired one. For in addition to worshiping
the possessor of beauty, in him has been found the sole
b healer of her greatest pains. And this state, my dear imagi-
nary youth to whom I am talking, is by men called Eros,
and among the gods has a name at which you, in your
youth, may be inclined to laugh; but I recall that some of
the Homeridae[29] recite from the apocryphal poems two
couplets that are actually addressed to Eros. The second
couplet involves a rather grating pun, and the first is not altogether faultless metrically. At any rate, they praise the
god thus:

> It is of "Winged Eros"
>   The mortal lover sings;
> But gods prefer to call him "Pteros"
>   Who makes us all sprout wings.[30]

[29]The Homeridae were a famous and influential guild of rhapsodes, centered
on the island of Chios; they claimed to possess authoritative texts or versions of
the poems of Homer, from whom they in early days asserted descent, and were
thought to have allowed more recent compositions into the catalog of Homer's
works.

[30]*Pteros* is the Greek word for wing, as in lepido-ptera (having delicate
wings), etc. "Pteronymic," below in the text, means "wing-named," i.e., the one
called "winged" or "wing" (*pteros*).

You may believe this or not, however you prefer. At any c
rate the plight of lovers and its cause are in fact as I have
described them.

Now of those who attend upon Zeus, he who has been
taken captive by love is able to bear the burden of the
pteronymic god with greater steadiness, and can endure a
heavier burden; but all those who are squires of Ares, and
made the circuit in his company, when they are seized by
love, if they fancy that they are being at all wronged by
their beloved, are ready to become murderers and immo-
late themselves and their boy-loves. And whoever followed
in the train of any other god, for as long as he is uncor- d
rupted and the impression lasts, honors and imitates him,
as far as he is able; and he behaves after the manner of his
god in his intercourse with his beloved and with the rest of
the world, during the first period of his earthly existence.
Everyone chooses his love from the ranks of beauty according to his character, and this he makes his god, and
fashions and adorns as a sort of image that he is to fall
down and worship with rites. The followers of Zeus desire e
that their beloved should have a soul like him; and therefore they seek out someone of a philosophical and imper-
ial nature, and when they have found him and loved him,
they do all they can to confirm such a nature in him, and if
they have no prior experience of such an undertaking, they
try to learn from anyone who can teach them, and themselves pursue it. And they are well equipped for tracking
down the nature of their specific god from their own re- 253
sources, because they are constrained to gaze intensely on
him; their recollection clings to him, and they become possessed by him, and receive from him their character and
disposition, so far as man can participate in god. Giving
the credit for all this to the beloved, they love him all the

more, and if, like the Bacchic Nymphs, they draw inspiration from Zeus, they pour out their own fountain upon him, wanting to make him as like as possible to their own god.

b   Those who were the followers of Hera seek a royal love, and when they have found him they do just the same with him; and likewise the followers of Apollo and of every other god proceed to seek a boy who accords with the nature of their god, and when they win him, they themselves imitate their god, and persuade their boyfriends to do the same, bringing them into step and harmony with the disposition and style of the god as far as they each can; for no feelings of envy or jealousy are entertained by them toward their beloved, but they do their utmost to create in

c him the greatest likeness of themselves and of the god whom they honor. The desire of those who love truly, and its fulfillment, provided that they accomplish their desires in the way I prescribe, in this way is made noble, and beneficial to the beloved, by the lover who is maddened through eros, provided he is taken captive. And whoever is taken captive is captured as follows:

    At the beginning of this tale, I divided each soul into three parts—two having the form of horses and the third

d being like a driver; let this division now remain before us. Of the horses, the one, we said, was good, the other bad, but I have not explained yet in what the goodness or badness of either consists, and to that I will now proceed. The horse on the right hand—the nobler position—is upright and cleanly made; he has a lofty neck and an aquiline nose; his color is white and his eyes dark; he is one who loves honor with modesty and prudence, and is a companion of justly deserved reputation; he needs no touch of the whip, but is guided by word and admonition only. The other is a

crooked, lumbering hulk of an animal, put together any- e
how; he has a short, thick neck, and he is flat-faced and of
a dark color, with bloodshot gray eyes, and is a companion
of wantonness and arrogant pride, shag-eared and deaf,
hardly yielding to the whip and spur. Now when the driver
sees the eyes of the beloved, and his whole soul is filled
with a sensation of warmth, and is full of the prickings and
ticklings of desire, the obedient steed, then as always gov- 254
erned by a sense of shame, restrains himself from leaping
on the beloved; but the other, heedless of both the charioteer's goadings and the whip, plunges and starts violently,
giving all manner of trouble to his companion and the
charioteer, whom he forces to approach the beloved and to
remember the pleasures of sex. They at first indignantly
oppose him and will not be urged on to do terrible and un- b
lawful deeds; but at last, when he persists in plaguing them,
they yield and agree to do as he bids them. And now they
are at the spot and behold the flashing glance of the
beloved; which, when the charioteer sees, his memory is
carried to the true beauty, and again he has sight of it, in
company with prudence, standing on a holy pedestal. He
sees her, and takes fright and falls backward in adoration,
and by his fall is compelled to pull back the reins with such c
violence as to bring both the steeds on their haunches, the
one willing and unresisting, the unruly one very unwilling.
And when they have drawn back a little ways, the one is
overcome with shame and horror, and drenches the whole
soul with sweat; but the other, when the pain which the bri-
dle and the fall had given him is over, having with difficulty
caught back his breath, is full of wrath and reproaches,
which he heaps upon the charioteer and his fellow steed,
for cowardice and unmanliness, declaring that they have
been false to their agreement and guilty of desertion.

d Again they refuse, and again he urges them on, and will only reluctantly yield to their prayer to put it off until another time. When the appointed hour comes, they make as if they had forgotten, and he reminds them, fighting and neighing and dragging them on, until at length he, intent on the same purposes, forces them to approach the boy again. And when they are near, this horse stoops his head and puts up his tail, and takes the bit in his teeth and pulls

e shamelessly. Then the charioteer is worse off than ever; he falls back, and with a still more violent wrench drags the bit out of the teeth of the wild steed and covers his abusive tongue and jaws with blood, and forces his legs and haunches to the ground and delivers him into agonies. And when this has happened several times and the villain has ceased from his wanton way, he is at length tamed and humbled, and follows the will of the charioteer, and when he sees the beautiful one he is ready to die of fear. And so then at last the soul of the lover follows the beloved in modesty and holy fear.

255 Accordingly, the beloved who, like a god, has received every true and loyal service from his lover, not in pretense but in reality, being also himself naturally well disposed toward the person performing these services, even if previously he drove his lover away, because his youthful companions or others slandered him, saying that it was disgraceful to have converse with a lover, now as years advance, at the appointed age and time, is led to receive him

b into his companionship. For as fate has forbidden that evil be friend to evil, so also it forbids good not to be friend with good. And when the beloved accepts him and receives him into his friendship and intimacy, he is quite amazed at the goodwill of the lover, now that it comes into close range; he recognizes that all other friends or kinsmen offer not a fraction of the friendship provided by the inspired friend. And as they continue doing this and their association begins to include touching, both in the course of gymnastic exercises and at other times of meeting, then the fountain of that stream, which Zeus, when he was in love c with Ganymede, dubbed Sir Passion, overflows upon the lover, and some enters into his soul, and some when he is filled flows out again; and as a breeze or an echo rebounds from the smooth rocks and returns from where it came, so the stream of beauty comes back to the beautiful one, passing through the eyes, and thus arriving by way of the natural entrance to the soul, and arousing her, the stream waters and stimulates the wings to grow, and fills with love d the soul of the beloved also. And thus he loves, but he knows not what; he does not understand and cannot explain his own state; but as if he had caught an eye infection of blindness from another,[31] he is not able to tell the cause; the lover is his mirror in whom he is beholding himself, but he is not aware of this. When his lover is near, the beloved ceases from his pain, just as the other does; but when he is away, then he longs for his lover and is longed for, suffering love's image, requited love, which he calls and believes to e be not love but friendship only, and he desires in the same way in which that one desires, but more weakly; he wants to see him, touch him, kiss, embrace him, to lie down with him, and probably not long afterward his desire is accomplished. Now while they are lying together, the wanton steed of the lover has a word to say to the charioteer; he would like to have a little pleasure in return for his many pains, but the wanton steed of the beloved says not a word, 256

---

[31]It appears to have been believed that eye infections could be transmitted by visual contact alone.

for he is bursting with passion which he does not understand—he throws his arms around the lover and embraces him as his dearest friend; and, when they are side by side, he is in a state in which he would not refuse the lover anything, if he should ask him; on the other side his fellow steed together with the charioteer opposes him with the arguments of shame and reason.

b
If now the better elements of the mind which lead to order and philosophy prevail, then the life they pass here is a blessed and harmonious one: masters of themselves and orderly, enslaving the vicious and emancipating the virtuous instruments of the soul; and when the end comes, they are light and winged for flight, having conquered in one of the three heavenly or truly Olympian victories;[32] nor can human discipline or divine inspiration confer any greater blessing on man than this. If, on the other hand, they leave

c
philosophy and lead the lower life of ambition, then probably, after wine or in some other careless hour, the two wanton horses catch the two souls off their guard and bring them together, and take that choice deemed most blessed by the multitude; and having once enjoyed this, they continue to do it, yet rarely, because they have not the approval of the whole soul. These two are also worthy to be called friends, but not so much as the other pair; it is for

d
each other that they live, throughout the time of their love and afterward. They consider that they have given and taken from each other the most sacred pledges, and they may not break them and fall into enmity. At the end of their lives they pass out of the body, unwinged but eager to soar, and thus obtain no mean reward for their erotic mad-

---

[32]I.e., victories pertaining to Mount Olympus, the seat of the gods, rather than to Olympia, site of the mere mortal Olympics.

ness. For those who have once begun the heavenward pilgrimage may not go down again to darkness and the journey beneath the earth, but they live in light always, happy companions in their pilgrimage; and when the time comes at which they receive their wings, they have the same e plumage because of their love.

These then are the blessings, so great and heavenly to such a degree, which the friendship of a lover will confer upon you, my youth. Whereas the attachment of the non-lover, which is alloyed with a worldly prudence and has worldly and stingy ways of doling out benefits, will breed in your soul those vulgar qualities that the populace applaud as virtue, will send you hurtling around the earth for nine 257 thousand years, and leave you a fool in the world below.

And thus, dear Eros, I have made and paid my recantation, as well and as finely as I could; more especially in the matter of the poetical figures I was compelled to use, because Phaedrus wanted them. And now forgive my previous speech and take pleasure in the present one, and be gracious and merciful to me, and do not in thine anger deprive me of sight, or take from me the art of love which thou hast given me, but grant that I may be yet more esteemed in the eyes of the beautiful. And if Phaedrus or I myself said anything rude in our first b speeches, blame Lysias, who is the father of the brat, and let us have no more of his progeny; bid him take up philosophy, like his brother Polemarchus; and then his lover Phaedrus will no longer halt between two opinions, but will dedicate himself wholly to Eros in union with philosophical discourses.

PHAEDRUS: I join you in your prayer, Socrates, that these things, if they should be for our good, come to pass. But I c have long been amazed at how much more beautiful you have made this second oration than the first. And I begin to fear that Lysias will appear worthless in my eyes, if in the event he consents to field another speech against yours. For quite recently one of the politicians was abusing him on this very account—calling him a "speechwriter" again and again. So that a concern for his position may make him give up writing and leave us bereft.

SOCRATES: What an absurd idea, my boy. You are much
d mistaken in your friend if you imagine that he jumps at shadows so. But perhaps you think also that his assailant meant his remark as a reproach?

PHAEDRUS: I thought, Socrates, that he did. And you are undoubtedly aware that the greatest and most influential statesmen disdain to write speeches and leave behind other written compositions of their own, fearing lest they should be called sophists by posterity.

SOCRATES: You seem to be unaware, Phaedrus, that the "pleasant bend" of the proverb is really the long bend of
e the Nile.[33] And you appear to be equally unaware that the most ambitious of our great politicians love nothing more than writing speeches and bequeathing books to posterity: whenever they write something, so much love do they feel for those who praise it that they write in the names of their local admirers at the very beginning.

PHAEDRUS: What do you mean? I don't understand.

258 SOCRATES: Why, don't you know that when a politician writes, he begins with the names of his approvers?

---

[33]This proverb has so far defied persuasive explanation. The best proposal is that "pleasant bend" is an example of the figure *antiphrasis*, whereby an ill-omened or terrifying or disagreeable thing is referred to under a name denoting qualities opposed to the negative ones; thus, the Furies are called the "Kindly Ones"; the terrifyingly dangerous Black Sea is called the "Hospitable Sea." So here Socrates is going to claim that politicians do pride themselves on their writing, but they conceal it under the name lawmaking.

PHAEDRUS: How so?

SOCRATES: Why, he begins in this manner: "Be it enacted by the Council, the people, or both, on the motion of a certain person," which is our author's solemn and laudatory way of describing himself.[34] Only after this preamble does he proceed, displaying his own wisdom to his approvers in what is often a long and tedious composition. Now what is that sort of thing but a speech written out?

PHAEDRUS: No, you're right.

b

SOCRATES: And if the piece is finally approved, then the author leaves the theater in great delight; but if it is rejected and he is done out of his speechwriting, and declared unworthy to write, then he and his party are in mourning.

PHAEDRUS: Very true.

SOCRATES: So far are they from despising, or rather so highly do they value, the practice of writing.

PHAEDRUS: No doubt.

SOCRATES: And when a king or orator has the capacity to assume the power of Lycurgus or Solon or Darius[35] and c become an immortal speechwriter in his state, isn't he thought by posterity when they see his compositions, and doesn't he think himself while he is still alive, to be the equal of the gods?

PHAEDRUS: Definitely.

SOCRATES: Then do you think that anyone of this class, whoever he is and however ill disposed, would reproach Lysias simply with being a speechwriter?

PHAEDRUS: Not on your view; for according to you, he

[34]Socrates is quoting a typical opening formula for decrees of the Athenian Council or Assembly.

[35]Famous lawgivers of Sparta, Athens, and Persia, respectively.

would be casting a slur upon his own favorite pursuit.

d SOCRATES: Now, anyone can see that there is no disgrace in the mere fact of writing.

PHAEDRUS: Certainly not.

SOCRATES: The disgrace, I assume, begins when a man speaks or writes not well, but badly.

PHAEDRUS: Clearly.

SOCRATES: Well then, what is the nature of "writing well" and "writing badly"? Do we think we ought to examine Lysias on this question—him, and anyone else who has ever written or intends to write, on either a public or private subject, whether in meter, like a poet, or in prose, like an ordinary layman?

e PHAEDRUS: You're asking me? What's the point of living, if I may be so blunt, if not the joy of looking into such questions? Surely not those pleasures that have some previous pain as the condition of them, as almost all bodily pleasures have, and therefore are rightly called slavish.[36]

SOCRATES: We have enough time for the undertaking, as it seems. And I believe that the cicadas chirruping in their customary manner in the heat of the sun over our

259 heads are talking to one another and looking down at us. What would they say if they saw that we, like the many, are not conversing, but slumbering at midday, lulled by their voices, too indolent to think? Wouldn't they have a right to laugh at us? They might imagine that we were slaves, who, coming to their own retreat, like sheep lie asleep at noon around the well. But if they see us conversing, and like Odysseus sailing past them, deaf to

---

[36]Phaedrus appears to be someone who unself-consciously adopts the outlook of whomever he is with. Having spent an hour or two with Socrates, he seems suddenly to have adopted more spiritual and more Socratic aims than he began the day with.

their Siren voices, they may perhaps, out of respect, give us some of the gifts that they receive from the gods b to confer upon men.

PHAEDRUS: What gifts do you mean? I've never heard of this.

SOCRATES: A lover of the arts like yourself ought surely to have heard the story of the cicadas. It is said that they were once human beings in an age before the Muses. And when the Muses came and song appeared, it seems the cicadas were so ravished with delight that, singing always, they never took thought of eating and drinking, c until at last, without themselves noticing it, they died. It is from these men that the cicada species derives; as a special gift from the Muses, they require no nourishment, but from the hour of their birth are always singing, and never eating or drinking, until they die; and when they die they go and inform the Muses in heaven which of us honors which of them. Those who have honored Terpsichore in the dance choruses, they make even more dear to her by their report of them; those who have honored Erato in erotic matters are more endeared d to that goddess, and so on for the rest of the Muses, according to the different ways of honoring them. To Calliope, the eldest Muse, and Urania, who comes after her, they make a report of those who honor music of their kind, and spend their time in philosophy; since these are of all the Muses those who are most concerned with the heavens and with reasoning, divine as well as human, they have the sweetest utterance. For many reasons, then, we ought always to talk and not to sleep at midday.

PHAEDRUS: Then talk we must.

SOCRATES: Shall we discuss the rules of writing and e speech as we were proposing?

PHAEDRUS: Clearly.

SOCRATES: Isn't it a necessary prerequisite of excellence in speech that the mind of the speaker must be furnished with knowledge of the truth of the matter about which he is going to speak?

PHAEDRUS: And yet, Socrates, I have heard that a person who intends to become an orator has no need to learn what is really just, but only what is likely to be approved by the mob who will be rendering the verdict; nor what is truly good or honorable, but only what will appear to be, since it is from this, and not from the truth, that persuasion comes.

SOCRATES: "Not to be discounted," Phaedrus, "is any word" spoken by the wise;[37] for there is probably something in it; and therefore the meaning of this claim is not to be hastily dismissed.

PHAEDRUS: A very sound ruling.

SOCRATES: Let us put the matter thus.

PHAEDRUS: How?

b SOCRATES: Suppose that I wished to persuade you to buy a horse and go to the wars; and suppose further that neither of us knew what a horse was like, but I happened to know this much, that Phaedrus believed a horse to be that one of domesticated animals which has the longest ears.

PHAEDRUS: That would be ridiculous.

SOCRATES: No, not yet. Suppose, further, that in sober earnest I, having persuaded you of this, went and composed a speech in honor of the donkey, calling it the horse, and saying that this animal is quite invaluable to possess for domestic use and military service, and that

[37] *Iliad* 2. 361.

you may sit on his back and fight, and that he will in addition carry baggage, and be useful in other ways.

PHAEDRUS: Utterly ridiculous!

SOCRATES: Ridiculous—yes; but isn't even a ridiculous friend better than a formidable enemy?

PHAEDRUS: Certainly.

SOCRATES: And when the orator, instead of putting a donkey in the place of a horse, puts good for evil, being himself as ignorant of their true nature as the city on which he imposes is ignorant and, having studied the opinions of the multitude, falsely persuades them not about "the shadow of a donkey,"[38] which he confuses with a horse, but about good, which he confuses with evil, and induces them to do it—what will be the harvest which rhetoric will be likely to gather after the sowing of that seed?

PHAEDRUS: Not a terribly nice one.

SOCRATES: But perhaps rhetoric has been too roughly abused by us, and she might answer: "What amazing nonsense you are talking! As if I insisted that ignorance of the truth is indispensable to one who is learning to speak! If you want my advice, it would be to arrive at the truth first, and then take me on. At the same time I strongly affirm that mere knowledge of the truth, without my help, will not give you the art of persuasion."

PHAEDRUS: Won't she have made some fair points if she says that?

SOCRATES: Certainly—but will the arguments attacking her concede that she is an art at all? For I seem to hear them arraying themselves on the opposite side, declaring that she speaks falsely, and that rhetoric is a mere

[38]Proverb: "a worthless donkey."

routine and trick, not an art. Lo! A Spartan appears, and says a real art of speaking is an impossibility, now and forever, if unaccompanied by a firm knowledge of the truth.[39]

261 PHAEDRUS: These arguments must be summoned as witnesses, Socrates. Bring them out and question them: What do they say and what do they mean?

SOCRATES: Come out, fair children, and convince Phaedrus, who is the father of similar beauties, that unless he becomes a good philosopher, he will not ever be a good speaker, either—on any subject. And let Phaedrus answer your cross-examination.

PHAEDRUS: Put the question.

SOCRATES: Is not the art of rhetoric, taken generally, a technique for influencing people's minds, based on verbal argumentation, and practiced not only in courts and public assemblies, but in private houses also, the same technique applying to all matters, great as well as small,

b which, to be honest, is no more honorable when exercised on serious matters than when on trivialities? Is that what you have heard?

PHAEDRUS: No, absolutely not, by god. I would say rather that the art is said to be primarily displayed in speaking and writing in lawsuits, and in speaking in public assemblies—I have not heard it more widely extended.

SOCRATES: Then I suppose that you have heard only of the manuals of rhetoric written by Nestor and by Odysseus, which they composed in their leisure hours when at Troy, and never of the one by Palamedes?[40]

c PHAEDRUS: No more than I've heard of Nestor's, unless

---

[39]Reference unknown.
[40]On Palamedes, see note 40 on the *Apology*.

Gorgias is your Nestor,[41] and Thrasymachus or Theodorus your Odysseus.[42]

SOCRATES: Perhaps that is my meaning. Well, anyhow, let's forget them. But you tell me instead, what are the plaintiff and defendant doing in a law court—aren't they engaged in a verbal argument?

PHAEDRUS: Exactly so.

SOCRATES: About the just and unjust—that is, the matter in dispute?

PHAEDRUS: Yes.

SOCRATES: And a person who uses a technique to do this will make the same thing appear to the same people to be at one time just, at another time, if he is so inclined, to be unjust?

PHAEDRUS: Exactly.

SOCRATES: Likewise when he speaks in the assembly, he will make the same things seem good to the city at one time, and at another time the reverse of good?

PHAEDRUS: That is true.

SOCRATES: But then don't we also know that the Eleatic Palamedes uses a technique such that he can make the same things appear to his hearers like and unlike, one and many, at rest and in motion?[43]

[41]Gorgias, of Leontini in Sicily. One of the great sophists, he was born around 450 B.C. and apparently lived to a very old age, thus justifying the equation with Nestor, who, along with Odysseus, was regarded as the most eloquent of the Greeks at Troy.

[42]Thrasymachus of Chalcedon achieved great fame in Athens as a teacher of rhetoric; he is a character in the *Republic.* There is not much to be said about Theodorus of Byzantium, except that he too is said to have been a master of rhetoric.

[43]Zeno, the disciple of Parmenides, the founder of Eleatic philosophy. Zeno's paradoxes, referred to here by Socrates, are still well known: "Achilles and the tortoise," etc.

PHAEDRUS: Very true.

SOCRATES: Argumentation, then, is not confined to the
e courts and the assembly, but is one single technique involved in every use of language: this is the art, if it really is an art, by which a person will be able to find a
likeness of everything to which a likeness can be found,
and to expose to the light of day the likenesses and disguises that are used by others?

PHAEDRUS: How do you mean?

SOCRATES: I think the truth will appear if we ask this
question: When will there be more chance of decep-
tion—when the difference is large or small?

262 PHAEDRUS: When the difference is small.

SOCRATES: And you will be less likely to be found out in
passing by small degrees into the other extreme than
when you go all at once?

PHAEDRUS: Of course.

SOCRATES: Then a person who intends to deceive others,
but not be deceived himself, must know the real likenesses and differences of things exactly?

PHAEDRUS: He must.

SOCRATES: But if he is ignorant of the true nature of any
subject, how can he detect the greater or less degree of
likeness in other things to that of which by the hypoth-
esis he is ignorant?

b PHAEDRUS: He cannot.

SOCRATES: Now when men are deceived and their notions are at variance with the facts, it is clear that the
error has slipped in through some sort of misleading resemblance?

PHAEDRUS: Yes, that is the way.

SOCRATES: Then unless our orator has understood the
real nature of everything, he will not be a skilled artist

in making the gradual departure from fact into the opposite, which is effected by the help of resemblances, or in avoiding this when he is on the defensive.

PHAEDRUS: He will not.

SOCRATES: And so the "art of rhetoric" displayed by a man c who, being ignorant of the truth, has hunted after appearances, will be of a ridiculous sort, and not an art at all?

PHAEDRUS: That seems likely.

SOCRATES: Shall I propose that we look for examples of art and deficiency of art, according to our notion of them, in the speech of Lysias which you have in your hand, and in my own speeches?

PHAEDRUS: Nothing could be better; and indeed I think that our discussion so far has been too abstract and not had enough illustrations.

SOCRATES: Yes; and the two speeches happen to afford a very good example of the way in which the speaker who d knows the truth may, without any serious purpose, steal away the hearts of his hearers. This piece of good fortune I attribute to the local deities, and perhaps the prophets of the Muses who are singing over our heads may have imparted their inspiration to us. For I do not imagine that I have any rhetorical art of my own.

PHAEDRUS: Granted; if you will only please get on with it.

SOCRATES: Suppose that you read me the first words of Lysias' speech.

PHAEDRUS: "You know what my position is, and you have e heard that I believe it is to the advantage of both of us if this comes to pass. I maintain that what I seek I deserve to obtain because I am *not* your lover; for when their passion ceases, lovers . . ."

SOCRATES: Enough. Now, shall I point out the error and deficiency of art in those words?

263 PHAEDRUS: Yes.

SOCRATES: Isn't it plain to everyone that about certain types of things we are agreed, whereas about other things we differ?

PHAEDRUS: I think that I understand you; but will you explain yourself more explicitly?

SOCRATES: When anyone says the word "iron" or "silver," doesn't the same thing come into the minds of all?

PHAEDRUS: Certainly.

SOCRATES: But when anyone speaks of justice and goodness, we part company and are at odds with one another and with ourselves?

PHAEDRUS: Precisely.

b SOCRATES: Then in some things we agree, but not in others?

PHAEDRUS: That is true.

SOCRATES: In which are we more likely to be deceived, and in which has rhetoric the greater power?

PHAEDRUS: Clearly, in the uncertain class.

SOCRATES: Then the would-be exponent of the art of rhetoric ought, before all else, to make a systematic division of things, and discover a characteristic mark of each type—I mean the things that the mass of men will necessarily disagree about, and those that they will not.

c PHAEDRUS: Whoever discovers this will have gotten himself a wonderful principle.

SOCRATES: Yes; and in the next place he must have a keen eye for the observation of particulars, and not make a mistake in assigning to one of those two classes the subject on which he intends to speak.

PHAEDRUS: Certainly.

SOCRATES: Now to which class does love belong—to the debatable or to the undisputed class?

PHAEDRUS: To the debatable, clearly; for if it weren't, do you think that it would have been open to you to say as you did, that love is an evil both to the lover and the beloved, and then later that it is the greatest possible good?

SOCRATES: Excellent point. But will you tell me whether d I defined love at the beginning of my speech? For, having been in a transport of ecstasy, I can't remember well.

PHAEDRUS: Yes, indeed; that you did, very much so.

SOCRATES: Good lord! How vastly superior at the techniques of verbal argumentation, then, do you say the Nymphs of Achelous and Pan the son of Hermes,[44] who inspired me, are to Lysias, son of Cephalus. Am I completely wrong? Did Lysias in fact at the beginning of his lover's speech insist on our supposing love to be something or other that he wanted it to be, and fashion and frame the remainder of his speech with reference to e this conception? Suppose we read his beginning over again.

PHAEDRUS: If you wish; but you will not find what you want.

SOCRATES: Read, that I may have his exact words.

PHAEDRUS: "You know what my position is, and you have heard that I believe it is to the advantage of both of us if this comes to pass. I maintain that what I seek I deserve to obtain because I am *not* your lover; for when their 264 passion ceases, lovers repent of the kindnesses they have shown."

SOCRATES: Here he appears to be far from doing what we are looking for; for he has begun not from the beginning,

---

[44]Achelous: the river god mentioned at the beginning of the work. Pan: the goat-legged and goat-eared god of the countryside, and player of pipes.

172 · *Selected Dialogues of Plato*

but is swimming against the tide of the argument, from its end toward its beginning, and he starts out with just what the lover would say to his boyfriend at the end. Or did I get that wrong, Phaedrus my dear?

b PHAEDRUS: Certainly it is an end that is the subject of his speech.

SOCRATES: Then as to the rest—doesn't the structure of the speech seem to have been laid down haphazardly? Does whatever is said next seem to have demanded by any necessity to be placed next, instead of another of the arguments? I can't help supposing in my ignorance that, with an admittedly admirable boldness, he wrote down simply whatever came into his head; but can you discern any compositional necessity in the way in which he has put the parts of the speech together?

PHAEDRUS: You have too good an opinion of me if you c think that I have any such insight into his principles of composition.

SOCRATES: At any rate, you will grant that every composition ought to be like a living creature, having a body of its own and not lacking head and feet; there should be a middle, beginning, and end, adapted to one another and to the whole?

PHAEDRUS: Certainly.

SOCRATES: Can this be said of the speech of your friend? See whether you can find any more connection in his words than in the epitaph which is said by some to have been inscribed on the grave of Midas the Phrygian.[45]

d PHAEDRUS: What epitaph is that? What's the problem with it?

SOCRATES: It is as follows:

[45]The legendary king cursed with the touch of gold.

I am a maiden of bronze and lie on the tomb of Midas;
So long as water flows and tall trees grow,
So long here on this spot by his sad tomb abiding,
I shall declare to passersby that Midas sleeps below.

Now here it makes no difference what order the lines e
are spoken in, as you no doubt have noticed.

PHAEDRUS: You are making fun of that oration of ours,
Socrates.

SOCRATES: Well, I will say no more about your friend's
speech; I don't want to upset you—although I think that
it might furnish many other examples that a man might
study with profit (though it certainly wouldn't be profitable to try to emulate them). . . . But I will proceed to
the other speeches, which, as I think, are also suggestive
to students of rhetoric.

PHAEDRUS: In what way?   265

SOCRATES: The two speeches, as you may remember,
were not alike; the one argued that the lover and the
other that the non-lover ought to be gratified.

PHAEDRUS: And very manly the argument was.

SOCRATES: I thought you were going to speak the truth,
that it was spoken very "madly," which is the point I was
coming to, for, as we said, "love is a madness," didn't we?

PHAEDRUS: Yes.

SOCRATES: And of madness there were two kinds: one
produced by human weakness, the other through a divine release from the yoke of custom and convention.

PHAEDRUS: True.   b

SOCRATES: The divine madness was subdivided into four
kinds, prophetic, ritual, poetic, and erotic, having four
gods presiding over them; the first was the inspiration of
Apollo, the second that of Dionysus, the third that of

the Muses, the fourth that of Aphrodite and Eros. In the description of the last kind of madness, which was also said to be the best, we spoke of erotic passion figuratively, introducing an acceptably credible and possibly

c true though partly erroneous myth, which was also a hymn in honor of Eros, who is your lord and also mine, Phaedrus, and the guardian of beautiful children, and to him we sang the hymn in measured and solemn strain.

PHAEDRUS: Well, I know that I greatly enjoyed listening to you.

SOCRATES: Let us then seize upon this part of it—the way in which the transition was made from blame to praise.

PHAEDRUS: What do you mean?

SOCRATES: I mean to say that while the composition was mostly playful, still in these random utterances there were involved two principles, the power of which we

d would be grateful to get a description of in technical terms, if that were possible.

PHAEDRUS: What are they?

SOCRATES: First, the survey of scattered particulars, leading to their comprehension in one idea; as in our definition of love, which whether true or false certainly gave clearness and consistency to the discussion, the speaker should define each term and so make his meaning clear.

PHAEDRUS: What is the other principle, Socrates?

e SOCRATES: The second principle is that of division into species according to the natural formation, where the joint is, not breaking any part as a bad carver might. Just as our two speeches alike assumed, first of all, a single form of unreason, and then, as synonymous pairs are

266 part of the one single body, distinguished as the parts on the left and those on the right, in the same way my two speeches assumed that madness is a single class of phe-

nomena innate in us; the first speech proceeded to divide the parts of the left side of the class and did not stop dividing until it found in them an evil or left-handed love, which it justly reviled; whereas the other speech led us to the madness that lay on the right side, and found another love, also having the same name, but divine, which the speaker held up before us and applauded and affirmed to be the cause of the greatest benefits.

b

PHAEDRUS: Most true.

SOCRATES: I am myself a great lover of these processes of division and generalization, Phaedrus; they help me to speak and to think. And if I find any man who is able to see both a one and a many that are in nature, him I follow, and "walk in his footsteps as if he were a god."[46] And those who have this talent, I have up to now been in the habit of calling dialecticians; but god knows whether the name is right or not. But now I would like to know what name you and Lysias would want me to give them, and whether this may not be that famous art of speaking which Thrasymachus and others use, and by means of which they have become skilled speakers, and make others so, on the condition that their pupils are willing to bring tribute to them, as to kings.

c

PHAEDRUS: Yes, they are royal men; but they have no skill in those operations that you call, and rightly, in my opinion, dialectical. But we are still in the dark about rhetoric.

SOCRATES: What do you mean? Can anything of value be brought under rules of art, save by these processes? At any rate, if it can be, then it is not to be despised by you

d

[46]Modeled on several similar phrases in Homer.

and me, and we ought to try to say what this remaining part of rhetoric is.

PHAEDRUS: There is a great deal surely to be found in books of rhetoric?

SOCRATES: Yes; thank you for reminding me. There is the "exordium," showing how the speech should begin, if I remember rightly; that is what you mean—the niceties of the art?

e PHAEDRUS: Yes.

SOCRATES: Then follows the "statement of facts," I believe it is, and attached to that, "witnesses and evidence"; third, "proofs"; fourth, "probabilities"; the great Byzantian word-maker also speaks, if I am not mistaken, of "confirmation" and "further confirmation."

PHAEDRUS: Do you mean the excellent Theodorus?

267 SOCRATES: Who else? He tells how "refutation" or "further refutation" is to be managed, whether in accusation or defense. Ought I not also to bring forward the illustrious Parian, Evenus, who first invented "insinuations" and "indirect praises",[47] and also "indirect censures," which, according to some, he put into verse to help the memory—for the fellow is brilliant. But shall we leave to their slumbers Tisias[48] and Gorgias, who perceived that probability is superior to truth, and who, by force of eloquence, make the little appear large and the large little,

b express new ideas in old-fashioned language, old ideas in language new, and discovered a method of

[47]Another sophist, and, as the next clause suggests, a poet also, some few fragments of whose verses survive; he was probably about the same age as Socrates. In the *Apology* Socrates speaks as if he had only just heard of him (20b).

[48]An obscure figure, usually associated with the equally dim Corax, legendarily the Sicilian founders of rhetoric, in the early to mid-fifth century B.C.

speaking on every subject either concisely or at infinite length. I remember Prodicus laughing when I told him of this;[49] he said that he had himself discovered the true rule of art, that a speech should be neither long nor short, but "just right."

PHAEDRUS: Well done, Prodicus!

SOCRATES: And I cannot pass over Hippias, for I imagine that this colleague from Elis would vote with him.

PHAEDRUS: No doubt.

SOCRATES: And there is also Polus,[50] who has treasuries of tropes, such as "diplasiology," and "gnomology," and "iconology,"[51] and of words of which Licymnius made him a present; they were to give a polish.

PHAEDRUS: But didn't Protagoras have something of the same sort?

SOCRATES: Yes, my boy, rules of correct diction and many other fine precepts. But for speeches concerned with the sorrows old age and poverty, no one is better than the Chalcedonian giant;[52] he can put a whole company of people into a fury and then, once enraged, he calms them back down with his charms, as he himself claimed. He was also first-rate at inventing or disposing of any sort of calumny on any grounds or none. All of them agree in asserting that a speech should end in a "recapitulation," though they do not all agree to use the same word.

PHAEDRUS: You mean that there should be at the end a

---

[49]Of Ceos; for him, Hippias, and Protagoras, soon mentioned in the text, see the dramatis personae for the *Protagoras.*

[50]A student of Gorgias, appearing as such in the dialogue of that name.

[51]"Diplasiology": apparently, "repetition of words"; "gnomology": use of maxims; "iconology": use of imagery, similes, and the like.

[52]Thrasymachus again.

summing-up of the arguments in order to remind the
hearers of what has been said?

PHAEDRUS: Yes. Now, unless you have something else to
say about the art of speaking ...

PHAEDRUS: Not much; nothing very important.

268 SOCRATES: Let's leave the unimportant aside and instead
bring the devices we have already mentioned up into
the light of day, and ask: To what extent, and when, do
they have the force of art?

PHAEDRUS: They have a very great power in public meet-
ings.

SOCRATES: So they have. But I would like to know if you
have the same feeling as I have about the rhetoricians? To
me there seem to be a great many holes in their fabric.

PHAEDRUS: Give an example.

SOCRATES: I will. Suppose a person should come up to
your friend Eryximachus, or to his father Acumenus,[53]
and say to him: "I know how to apply drugs which shall
have either a heating or cooling effect, as I please, and if

b I want I can make a man vomit and in turn suffer diar-
rhea, and all that sort of thing; and knowing all this, as I
do, I claim to be a doctor and to make doctors by im-
parting this knowledge to others"—what do you suppose that they would say?

PHAEDRUS: They would be sure to ask him whether he
also knew to whom he ought to give each kind of treat-
ment, and when, and how much.

SOCRATES: And suppose that he were to reply: "No, I
know nothing about all that; I expect the person who
has learned what I have to teach to be able to do these

c things for himself"?

[53]See the opening of this work.

PHAEDRUS: They would say in reply that he is a madman or a pedant who imagines that he is a doctor because he has read something in a book, or has stumbled on a prescription or two, although he has no real understanding of the art of medicine.

SOCRATES: And suppose a person were to come to Sophocles or Euripides and say that he knows how to make a very long speech about a small matter, and a short speech about a great matter, and also a sorrowful speech, or a terrible or threatening speech, or any other kind of speech, and in teaching this imagines that he is d teaching the art of tragedy?

PHAEDRUS: They too would surely laugh at him if he imagines that tragedy is anything but the arranging of these elements in a manner that will be suitable to one another and to the whole.

SOCRATES: But I do not suppose that they would be rude or abusive to him: wouldn't they treat him as a musician would treat a man who thinks that he is a harmonist because he knows how to pitch the highest and lowest note; happening to meet such a person he wouldn't say to him savagely, "Fool, you are insane!" But because he e is, as a musician, himself a Muse-like man, he would say in a gentle and harmonious tone of voice: "My good friend, a man who wishes to be a harmonist must certainly know the things you know, and yet one who has not got beyond your stage of knowledge may understand nothing of harmony, for you know only the necessary preliminaries of harmony and not harmony itself."

PHAEDRUS: Very rightly.

SOCRATES: And will not Sophocles say to the display of 269 the would-be tragedian that this is not tragedy but the

preliminaries of tragedy? And will not Acumenus say
the same of medicine to the would-be doctor?

PHAEDRUS: Quite true.

SOCRATES: And if Adrastus the mellifluous or Pericles
heard of these wonderful arts,[54] brachylogies and icon-
ologies and all the rest that we have been trying to draw
into the light of day, what would they say? Instead of
losing their tempers and applying insulting epithets, as
b you and I have been doing, to those who have written of
these things and teach them as the art of rhetoric, their
superior wisdom would rather censure us: "Have a little
patience, Phaedrus and Socrates," they would say, "you
should not be so angry with those who from some deficiency of dialectical skill are unable to define the nature
of rhetoric, and consequently suppose that they have
found the art when they have studied only the necessary
c preliminaries to it and, in teaching these to others, fancy
that the whole art of rhetoric has been taught by
them; but as to using these devices in a persuasive
manner, or making the composition a whole—this they
regard as an easy thing which their disciples ought to be
able to supply for themselves in writing their own
speeches."

PHAEDRUS: I quite admit, Socrates, that the art of rhetoric
which these men teach and of which they write is such
as you describe—there I agree with you. But I still want
to know where and how the true art of rhetoric and per-
d suasion is to be acquired.

SOCRATES: The capacity to become a top-ranked oratori-

---

[54]Adrastus was a mythological king of Argos, not especially identified with
oratory, so the meaning of the reference is unclear; Pericles is, of course, the
dominant figure of fifth century B.C. Athenian democracy, and was famously eloquent.

cal performer is probably, or rather necessarily, like anything else—if you have a natural talent for it, and add to
it knowledge and practice, you will be a distinguished
speaker; but if you fall short in either of these, you will
be in that respect defective. But to whatever extent
there actually *is* an art of rheoric, the way along which
Lysias and Thrasymachus proceed to it does not appear
to me to be the right one.

PHAEDRUS: What then is?

SOCRATES: I conceive Pericles to have been the most ac- e
complished of rhetoricians.

PHAEDRUS: What of it?

SOCRATES: All the great arts require uninhibited discussion and lofty speculation about the rules of nature; for 270
it is from these that come loftiness of thought and com-
pleteness of execution. And this, as I conceive, was the
quality which, in addition to his natural gifts, Pericles
acquired from his contact with Anaxagoras,[55] who possessed these qualities himself. Pericles was thus imbued
with the higher philosophy, and attained the knowledge
of Mind and of Mindlessness, which were favorite
themes of Anaxagoras, and from these he applied what
suited his purpose to the art of speaking.

PHAEDRUS: Explain.

SOCRATES: The character of rhetoric is like that of medi- b
cine.

PHAEDRUS: How so?

SOCRATES: Why, because in both it is necessary to define
a nature—in medicine, the nature of the body, and in
rhetoric, the nature of the soul; you must do so, that is,

[55]Philosopher from Clazomenae, resident in Athens in mid-fifth century B.C.
Socrates talks somewhat less respectfully of him in the *Apology*.

if you intend to proceed, not empirically, by trial and error, but scientifically, in the one case to impart health and strength by giving medicine and food, in the other to implant the conviction or virtue which you desire, by the right application of words and training.

PHAEDRUS: There, Socrates, I suspect that you are right.

c SOCRATES: And do you think that you can know the nature of the soul intelligently without knowing it as a whole?

PHAEDRUS: If Hippocrates the Asclepiad is to be trusted, even the nature of the body cannot be understood without that sort of inquiry.[56]

SOCRATES: Yes, friend, and he was right. Still, we ought not to be content with the name of Hippocrates, but to examine and see whether reason gives any support to his statement.

PHAEDRUS: I agree.

SOCRATES: Then consider what true reasoning, as well as Hippocrates, says about nature. In examining the nature

d of anything, ought we not to consider first whether that which we desire to have, and to impart to others, namely, expert knowledge, is a simple or multiform thing, and if simple, then to inquire what power it has of acting or being acted upon in relation to other things, and if multiform, then to number its forms, and to do just what we did in the case of the simple thing for each of the multiforms, namely, to see what way it is able to act upon what, or in what way to be acted upon by what?

PHAEDRUS: You are very likely to be right, Socrates.

[56]Hippocrates is, of course, the great doctor, to whom is attributed the famous oath. He is called an Asclepiad because Asclepius, the son of Apollo, is regarded as the founder of medicine, and therefore all doctors as his heirs.

SOCRATES: The path that proceeds without this analysis is like the groping of a blind man. Yet, surely, a person who proceeds through science ought not to resemble the blind or deaf man in any way. The rhetorician, whose teaching of eloquence is scientific, will particularly set forth the essential nature of that entity to which the student will address his speeches; and this I conceive to be the soul.

PHAEDRUS: Certainly.

SOCRATES: His whole effort is directed to the soul; for in that, he seeks to produce conviction.

PHAEDRUS: Yes.

SOCRATES: Then clearly, Thrasymachus, or anyone else who teaches rhetoric in earnest as an art, will first give an exact description of the nature of the soul, which will enable us to see whether she is simple and homogeneous, or, like the body, multiform. For that is what we should call showing the nature of the soul.

PHAEDRUS: Exactly.

SOCRATES: He will explain, secondly, the mode in which she naturally acts or is acted upon.

PHAEDRUS: True.

SOCRATES: Third, having classified both speeches and the minds of men, and their kinds and the ways in which they can be affected, he will proceed to survey all the causes, and then, fitting one type of speech to one type of soul, and another to another, soon he will show what kind of soul is persuaded, or not persuaded, by what particular form of argument, and why.

PHAEDRUS: Ideally, it seems, that is how he should proceed.

SOCRATES: Yes, that is the true and only way in which any subject can be set forth or treated by rules of art, c whether in speaking or writing. But our current authors of handbooks of speaking, at whose feet you have sat, are mischievous and conceal the nature of the soul which they know quite well. Therefore, until they adopt our method of speaking and writing, let us not accept their claim that they write by rules of art.

PHAEDRUS: What method of ours is this?

SOCRATES: I cannot give you the exact details; but I am prepared to tell you, to the degree I can, how a man ought to write if he intends to proceed scientifically.

PHAEDRUS: Let me hear.

SOCRATES: Since the power of speech is a technique for influencing the soul, anyone who proposes to become

d an orator must know what kinds of souls there are. They are only so many in number and kind, and therefore some people are of this character, others of that. When this analysis has been finished, he must in turn enumerate the kinds of speech and state the character of each. Now people of one type are going to be easily persuaded to *this* action by *this* kind of speech for *this* reason; and people of another kind will be hard to persuade for *that* reason.

Now, after he has obtained a sufficient intellectual grasp of these points, a man must, if he is to derive any practical benefit from his theoretical training, rapidly

e apprehend by perception the various types when he beholds them in the context of life and action. When, finally, he can be relied upon both to judge what sort of man can be persuaded by what means, and also to assess the character of the individual whom he meets, and declare to himself: "This is the man—this, now present in

272 the flesh, is that character whom I earlier heard discussed—and in order to persuade him to *this* course, I

have to use *these* arguments in *this* way." When he is proficient in all this and has learned to recognize in addition the occasions when he should speak and when keep silent, when he should have recourse to brevity of expression, to pathos, to indignation, and all the other modes of speech which he has studied, then, but not till then, can it be said that the art has been finished and perfected; but if a man omits any of these points, whether as speaker, teacher, or writer, and yet claims to b speak by rules of art, we will be entitled to disbelieve him. "Well," our author will say,[57] "do you, Phaedrus and Socrates, think that we can accept this as an account of the art of rhetoric, or do we need a different one?"

PHAEDRUS: I doubt whether any alternative is possible, Socrates, but the work demanded by the art thus defined looks enormous.

SOCRATES: Very true; and therefore let us go through all our arguments up and down, and see if we can't find a shorter and easier road; there is no use in taking a long, rough, roundabout way if there is a shorter and easier c one. And I wish that you would try to remember whether you have heard from Lysias, or anyone else, anything that might be of use to us.

PHAEDRUS: If trying were all it took, then I might; but at the moment I can think of nothing.

SOCRATES: Suppose I tell you something which I have heard from some students of the subject.

PHAEDRUS: Certainly.

SOCRATES: Isn't it fair that even "the wolf," as the proverbs puts it, "be given a hearing"?

---

[57]This author is "Thrasymachus, or anyone else who teaches rhetoric in earnest as an art" as referred to in 271a.

d PHAEDRUS: Go ahead and say what can be said for him.

SOCRATES: Well then, they say that there is no use in putting a solemn face on these matters, or in going round and round, until you arrive at first principles; for, as I said at first, when the question concerns justice and good, or asks which men are just and good, either by nature or habit, then whoever wishes to become a skillful rhetorician has no need of truth—for in courts of law, men literally care nothing about truth, but only about

e credibility; and credibility is probability, to which the would-be orator should therefore give his whole attention. And they say also that there are cases in which the actual facts, if they are improbable, ought to be withheld, and only what is probable should be told either in accusation or defense, and that always in speaking, the orator should keep the probable always in view, and bid the truth a hearty farewell. And doing this throughout a

273 speech, they say, is what confers the whole art.

PHAEDRUS: That is what the professors of rhetoric actually do say, Socrates. I have not forgotten that we have briefly touched upon this matter already; with them the point is all-important.

SOCRATES: I am sure that you have perused Tisias pretty thoroughly? Now, we have one more thing to ask him. Doesn't he define probability as that which the many

b think?

PHAEDRUS: What else?

SOCRATES: Well, having made that brilliant scientific discovery, he wrote up a case in which a feeble but courageous man assaults a strong and cowardly one, and robs him of his coat or of something or other; he is brought into court, and then Tisias says that both parties should tell lies: the coward should say that he was not assaulted by only the one brave man; the other should refute this and prove that they were alone, and then have recourse to that well-known argument that asks "How could a weak man like me have assaulted a strong man like him?" c The complainant certainly will not want to admit to his own cowardice, and will therefore invent some other lie which his adversary will thus gain an opportunity of refuting. And there are other devices of the same kind which have a place in this art. Aren't I right, Phaedrus?

PHAEDRUS: Certainly.

SOCRATES: Good lord, what a frighteningly mysterious art this is which Tisias or some other gentleman, in whatever name or country he rejoices, discovered. But, my friend, shall we have a word with him or not?

PHAEDRUS: What shall we say? d

SOCRATES: Let's say to him, "Tisias, before you got here, we were saying that this 'probability' of which you speak won its place in the minds of the multitude by virtue of its resemblance to the truth, and we had just advanced to the further point that the person who actually knows the truth will always be the best equipped to discover the *resemblances* of the truth. So, if you have anything else to say about the art of speaking, we would like to hear it; but if not, we will abide by the conclusion we just reached, that unless a man makes an account of the various characters of his hearers and is able to di- e vide all things into general classes and to comprehend every particular under a single form, he will never be a skillful rhetorician even within the limits of human power. And even so, he will not attain this skill without a great deal of trouble, which a prudent man ought not to undergo for the sake of speaking and acting before men, but in order that he may be able to say what is acceptable to the gods and always to act acceptably to them as far as it lies in him. For, as you know, Tisias, there is a saying of wiser men than ourselves, that a man of sense should not try to please his fellow slaves (at least this should not be his first object) but his good and nobly born masters instead; and therefore, even though the way is long and circuitous, don't be surprised; for where the end is great, there we may take the longer road, but not for lesser ends such as yours. Our argument, however, says that even these are best secured as the consequence of higher aims."

PHAEDRUS: I think, Socrates, that this is admirable, if it should be practicable.

SOCRATES: But to the person attempting honorable aims, honor accrues no matter what the outcome.

PHAEDRUS: True.

SOCRATES: Enough appears to have been said by us about the true and the false art of speaking.

PHAEDRUS: Certainly.

SOCRATES: But there is something yet to be said of decorum and impropriety in writing, how it is done so as to turn out well, and how indecorously.

PHAEDRUS: Yes.

SOCRATES: Now, with regard to language, do you know how you can speak or act in a manner which will be most pleasing to god?

PHAEDRUS: No, indeed. Do you?

SOCRATES: I have heard a tradition of the ancients, whether true or not they only know; although if we had found the truth ourselves, do you think that we would care much about the opinions of men?

PHAEDRUS: Your question needs no answer; but tell me what you say you have heard.

SOCRATES: At the Egyptian city of Naucratis there was a famous old god whose name was Theuth; the bird that is called the Ibis is sacred to him, and he was the inventor of many arts, such as arithmetic and calculation and geometry and astronomy as well as checkers and dice, d but his great discovery was writing. Now in those days Thamus was the king of the whole country of Egypt around the great city of the upper region which the Hellenes call Egyptian Thebes, and Thamus himself is called by them Ammon. To him came Theuth and showed his inventions, and asserted that they ought to be distributed among the rest of the Egyptians; he enumerated them, and Thamus inquired about the uses of each of them, and praised some of them and censured others, as he approved or disapproved of them. It would e take a long time to repeat all that Thamus said to Theuth in praise or blame of the various arts. But when they came to writing, Theuth said: "Here, King, is a discipline that will make the Egyptians wiser and give them better memories; it is a prescription for both memory and wisdom." Thamus replied: "Most ingenious Theuth, the parent or inventor of an art is not always the best judge of the benefit or harm his own inventions will confer upon the users of them. And in this instance, you, who are the father of writing, from a paternal love for your own child have been led to at- 275 tribute to it a quality that it cannot have; for in fact this discovery of yours will create forgetfulness in the souls of those who learn it, because they will not use their memories; trusting to writing, their memories will be stimulated from the outside, by external written characters, and they will not remember by themselves, within themselves. And so what you have discovered is not a prescription for memory, but for being reminded. As for wisdom, it is the reputation, not the reality, that you have to offer to those who learn from you; they will have heard many things and yet received no teaching; they will appear to be omniscient and will generally know nothing; they will be tiresome company, having acquired not wisdom, but the show of wisdom."

PHAEDRUS: Yes, Socrates, it's easy to invent tales of Egypt, or of any other country, if you are so minded.

SOCRATES: There was a tradition in the temple of Zeus at Dodona that oaks first gave prophetic utterances. The men of old, far less wise than you sophisticated young men, deemed in their simplicity that if they heard the truth even from "oak or rock," it was enough; whereas you seem to consider not whether a thing is or is not true, but who the speaker is and what country the tale comes from.

PHAEDRUS: Well, you've hit me fair and square. I think that the Theban is right in his view about writing.

SOCRATES: You would have to be a very silly person, one completely ignorant of the prediction of Ammon, to suppose you might bequeath your professional knowledge to posterity in writings, or to accept such an inheritance in the hope that the written word will give anything intelligible or certain, or to believe that writing can be anything more than a reminder to a person who already knows the subject.

PHAEDRUS: That is perfectly true.

SOCRATES: I cannot help feeling, Phaedrus, that writing has one grave fault in common with painting; for the creations of the painter stand there true as life, and yet if you ask them a question they maintain a solemn silence. And the same may be said of written words. You would imagine that they had intelligence, but if, out of a desire to learn, you ask for an explanation of something that has been said, they produce the same unvarying meaning, over and over again. And once they have been written down, they promiscuously knock about the e world anywhere at all, among those who understand them, and equally among those for whom they are completely unsuitable; they do not know to whom they should or should not speak; and if they are mistreated or unjustly slandered, they always require the author of their being to rescue them; for the book cannot protect or defend itself.

PHAEDRUS: That again is perfectly true.

SOCRATES: Isn't there another kind of word far better 276 than this, one having far greater power—a son of the same family, but lawfully begotten?

PHAEDRUS: Who do you mean, and what is his origin?

SOCRATES: I mean the word of knowledge that is inscribed in the soul of the learner, which can defend itself, and knows with whom to speak and with whom to be silent.

PHAEDRUS: You mean the word of the man who knows, a word that is living and has a soul, and of which the written word might properly be called no more than an image?

SOCRATES: Yes, of course that is what I mean. And now b tell me this: Would a farmer, if he is a man of sense, take seeds which he values and which he wants to bear fruit, and in sober seriousness plant them during the heat of summer, in some garden of Adonis,[58] in order that he might have the pleasure of seeing them come up nicely

[58]Plants were quickly forced for the festival of Adonis.

in eight days? At least he would do so, if at all, only for the sake of amusement and for show. But when he is being serious he employs his art of husbandry and sows in fitting soil, and is satisfied if in eight months the seeds which he has sown arrive at perfection?

c PHAEDRUS: Yes, Socrates, that will be his way when he is being serious; he might act otherwise for the reasons which you give.

SOCRATES: And can we suppose that the person who possesses true knowledge of the just and good and honorable has less understanding than the farmer about his own seeds?

PHAEDRUS: Certainly not.

SOCRATES: Then he will not when being serious want to write his thoughts in water (not even in the black water called ink), sowing words which can neither speak for themselves nor teach the truth adequately to others?

PHAEDRUS: No, that is not likely.

d SOCRATES: No, it is not—in the garden of letters he will sow and plant, but only for the sake of recreation and amusement; he will write them down as memorials to be treasured against the forgetfulness of old age, by himself, or by any other man who is treading the same path. He will rejoice in beholding their tender growth; and while others have recourse to other amusements, refreshing themselves with drinking parties and the like, this will be the pastime in which his days are spent.

e PHAEDRUS: A pastime, Socrates, as noble as the other is ignoble, the pastime of a man who can be amused by serious talk, spinning fantasies about justice and the like.

SOCRATES: True, Phaedrus. But nobler by far is the serious pursuit of these matters when it is done by one who employs the art of dialectic, and, finding a congenial soul, by the help of science sows and plants therein words that are able to defend themselves and him who planted them, and are not unfruitful, but have in themselves a seed from which sprout other words, brought up in different soils, and thus in each case render the seed immortal, and making the possessors of it happy to the utmost extent of human happiness. 277

PHAEDRUS: Well, that is a nobler pursuit, certainly.

SOCRATES: And now at last, Phaedrus, having agreed upon this, we may decide the original question.

PHAEDRUS: Oh? What question was that?

SOCRATES: I mean those problems with which, in trying to solve, we have made our way to this point. We wished to get to the bottom of the insult directed at Lysias for his speechwriting, and to distinguish speeches composed with art from those composed without it. And I think that we have now pretty well distinguished the artistic from its opposite. b

PHAEDRUS: Yes, I entirely agree; but remind me again how we did it?

SOCRATES: Until a man knows the truth of the several particulars about which he is writing or speaking, and is able to define each of them as it is, and, having defined them, again in turn knows how to divide them according to type until they can be no longer divided; and until he proceeds in the same manner with regard to the nature of the soul and, discovering the different modes of discourse which are suitable for different natures, he c arranges and disposes them in such a way that the simple form of speech may be addressed to the simpler nature, and the complex form, with many variations of key, to the more complex nature—until he has accomplished all this, he will be unable to handle arguments according to rules of art, as far as their nature allows them to be subjected to art, either for the purpose of teaching or persuading. Such is the view that is implied in the whole preceding argument.

PHAEDRUS: Yes, that was our conclusion, certainly.

d SOCRATES: What now about the question whether speaking or composing speeches is a fine or disgraceful thing to do, and which manner of doing either would justly incur censure, and which not—didn't what was said a little while ago make all this clear?

PHAEDRUS: What was that?

SOCRATES: That whether Lysias or any other writer that ever was or will be, whether private man or statesman, proposes laws and so becomes the author of a political treatise, imagining that there is any great certainty and clearness in his performance, the fact of his so writing is only a disgrace to him, whatever men may say. For not to know the nature of justice and injustice, and good and evil, and not to be able to distinguish a dream from reality, cannot in truth be otherwise than a disgrace, even if the great unwashed multitude sings its praises.

PHAEDRUS: Certainly.

SOCRATES: But whoever thinks that in the written word, whatever its subject, there is necessarily much that is not serious, and that no discourse worthy of study has ever yet been written in poetry or prose, and that spoken ones are no better if, like the recitations of rhapsodes, they are delivered for the sake of persuasion, and not with any view to criticism or instruction, and whoever thinks that even the best of writings are nothing

278 but a device for reminding those who know of what they know, and that only in principles of justice and goodness and nobility taught and communicated orally

for the sake of instruction and inscribed on the soul, which is the true way of writing, is there clearness and perfection and seriousness, and that such principles should be deemed a man's as it were legitimate offspring—being, first and foremost, the principle that he discovers in himself, and second, the first one's siblings and descendants and relations, which have been duly implanted by him in the souls of others where deserved, b and he cares for these and no others. This is the right sort of man; and you and I, Phaedrus, must pray that we may become like him.

PHAEDRUS: That is most assuredly my desire and prayer.

SOCRATES: And now I think we have played sufficiently with the subject of speeches and writings. Go and tell Lysias that we went, you and I, down to the fountain and school of the Nymphs, and heard from them speeches that commanded us to tell him and other c composers of speeches—Homer and other writers of poems, whether recitative or sung, and Solon and others who have composed writings in the form of political discourses which they call laws—to all of them we are to say that if their compositions are based on knowledge of the truth, and they can defend or prove them, when they are put to the test, by spoken arguments, then they are to be called not only poets, orators, legislators, but are worthy of a higher name, befitting the serious pursuit of their life. d

PHAEDRUS: What name would you assign to them?

SOCRATES: Wise, I may not call them; for that name is too great and belongs to god alone—"lovers of wisdom," or philosophers, would be a more harmonious and befitting title.

PHAEDRUS: Very suitable.

SOCRATES: And whoever cannot rise above his own com-
pilations and compositions, which he has been long
patching and piecing together, adding some and taking
away some, may be justly called poet or speechmaker or
lawmaker.

PHAEDRUS: Certainly.

SOCRATES: Now go and tell this to your companion.

PHAEDRUS: What of you? What are you going to do? For
you too have a friend who ought not to be neglected.

SOCRATES: Who is that?

PHAEDRUS: Isocrates the fair.[59] What message will you
send to him, and how shall we describe him?

SOCRATES: Isocrates is still young, Phaedrus; but I am
willing to hazard a prophecy concerning him.

PHAEDRUS: What would you prophesy?

SOCRATES: I think that he has a genius which soars above
the orations of Lysias, and that his character is cast in a
finer mold. It would not in fact surprise me if, as he
grows older, he comes to excel all former rhetoricians in
the kind of speech he now attempts, making them seem
mere children; nor would it surprise me if he finds this
insufficient, but is urged by some more divine impulse
to things higher still. For he has an element of philosophy in his nature. This is the message of the gods
dwelling in this place, and which I will myself deliver to

[59]An older contemporary of Plato's, and competitor in the education business; legitimately accounted a true heir of the sophists, his instruction was aimed
at preparing young men of the upper classes for political careers, and he defended his approach as a truer "philosophy" than that propagated at Plato's
Academy and elsewhere. His works, of which more than a sufficiency survive, are
polished and lacking in intellectual adventure and penetration. The apparent
praise of him here—written certainly at a time by which Plato and he had established a rivalry—has puzzled scholars endlessly. Is it sincere, or mordantly sar-
castic? No firm answer is likely to emerge.

my beloved, Isocrates; and you give the other to Lysias, who is yours.

PHAEDRUS: I will; and now, as the heat has abated, let us depart.

SOCRATES: Should we not offer up a prayer first to the local deities?

PHAEDRUS: By all means.

SOCRATES: Beloved Pan, and all ye other gods who haunt this place, give me beauty in the inward soul; and may the outward and inward man be at one. May I reckon the wise to be the wealthy, and may I have such a quantity c of gold as a temperate man and he only can bear and carry.

Anything more? That prayer, I think, is enough for me.

PHAEDRUS: Ask the same for me, for friends should have all things in common.

SOCRATES: Let us go.

SYMPOSIUM

DRAMATIS PERSONAE

Apollodorus: *The narrator, who repeats to his companions the report that he had heard from Aristodemus, and had already narrated to Glaucon a few days before.*[1]

Unidentified Companions of Apollodorus

Aristodemus: *A devoted disciple of Socrates.*

Agathon: *The greatest of Athenian tragic poets after Aeschylus, Sophocles, and Euripides. Little of his work survives. He was born around 450 B.C. and, some time before 405, left Athens for Macedon, where he died. The* Symposium *takes place after his first victory in the tragic festivals, which we know to have been won in 416 B.C.*

Socrates

Pausanias: *Agathon's lover.*

Aristophanes: *Lived from the mid-fifth century B.C. to the early fourth, and is regarded as the greatest comic playwright of Greece. Eleven of his plays survive whole, many others fragmentarily.*

---

[1]One of the most notable features of the form of this work is its "I heard it from X, who heard it from Y" structure; it is difficult for his readers to guess Plato's motives for taking this approach. It is extraordinarily difficult for his translators to harmonize the successive nestings of direct speech, reported speech, reported-reported speech, etc., with the limited resources of English punctuating conventions. My basic solution is as follows: Within the Prologue the exchanges reported by Apollodorus in his recent meeting with Glaucon are put into double quotation marks; once the Prologue is over (and we are in Apollodorus' report of what Aristodemus told *him*), double quotation marks are used for the utterances of the participants in the symposium itself.—For information on Apollodorus, see note 32 to the *Apology*.

Eryximachus: *A doctor.*

Phaedrus: *Socrates' interlocutor in the dialogue of the same name.*

Alcibiades: *See the Dramatis Personae of the* Protagoras.

A Crowd of Unidentified Revelers

PROLOGUE

APOLLODORUS: Actually, it turns out that I am quite well
up on the matter you are asking about, since just the
other day, when I was heading for the city from my
house in Phalerum, one of my acquaintances caught
sight of me from behind and called out playfully from a
ways off, and said, "O Phalerian one!—Hey, Apollodorus!—Won't you wait up?" So I stopped and waited,
and he said, "Why, I was looking for you, Apollodorus,
only just now, to ask you about the speeches in praise of
love given by Socrates, Alcibiades, and others, at that   b
dinner party of Agathon's. Phoenix, the son of Philip,
told someone else, who told me of them; his account
was very unclear, but he said that you knew—so please
relate them to me. After all, who better is there to report
the words of your friend than you? But first tell me," he
said, "were you at the party yourself?"

"Your informant, Glaucon," I said, "must have been
very unclear indeed, if you imagine that the occasion was   c
recent, or that I could have been a member of the party."

"Well, yes," he replied, "I did have that impression."

"Impossible," I said. "Are you unaware that it has been many years since Agathon has lived in Athens, and not three have elapsed since I became acquainted with Socrates, and have made it my daily business to know all that he says and does? There was a time before then when I used to run about the world, fancying myself to be accomplishing something, but I was really a very miserable person—no better than you are now, in fact: I thought that I ought to do anything rather than be a philosopher."

173

"Well," he said, "joking apart, tell me when the dinner party took place."

"In our boyhood," I replied, "when Agathon won the prize with his first tragedy, on the day after the one on which he and his chorus offered the victory sacrifice."

"It must have been a really long time ago," he said. "And who told you—did Socrates?"

b

"Oh no," I replied, "but the same person who told Phoenix. He was a little fellow, who never wore any shoes, Aristodemus, of the deme of Cydathanaeum.[1] He had been at Agathon's feast, and I think that in those days there was no one who was a more passionate admirer of Socrates. Furthermore, I have asked Socrates about the accuracy of some parts of his narrative, and he confirmed them."

"Then," said Glaucon, "let us have the tale over again; isn't the journey to Athens just made for conversation?"

And so we walked, and talked of the speeches about

---

[1] Attica, the territory of Athens, was divided into smaller communities called demes.

love; and that is how it happens that, as I said at first, I am well practiced on this subject, and will now have another run-through of the speeches if you like. To talk or to hear others talk of philosophy always gives me the greatest pleasure, to say nothing of the profit. On the other hand, when I hear certain other kinds of talk, especially, for example, that of you rich people and businessmen, I am profoundly depressed, and I pity you who are my companions, because you think that you are doing something when in reality you are doing nothing. I imagine that you pity me in return, and think me an unhappy creature, and very probably you think right. But, you see, I *know* of you what you only *think* of me—there is the difference.

ONE OF APOLLODORUS' PRESENT COMPANIONS: I see, Apollodorus, that you are just the same: speaking ill always of yourself—and especially of others. I do believe that you pity all mankind, with the exception of Socrates, yourself first of all. How you ever came by your nickname "Tenderheart" I will never understand; for you are always raging, as now, against yourself and everybody but Socrates.

APOLLODORUS: Yes, friend, and of course it's obvious that thinking thus about myself and about you, I must be mad or demented; no other evidence is required.

COMPANION: No more of that, Apollodorus; but let me renew my request that you repeat the conversation.

APOLLODORUS: Well, the tale of love was like this— But perhaps I had better begin at the beginning, and try to give you the exact words of Aristodemus.

AGATHON'S DINNER PARTY

Aristodemus said that he met Socrates fresh from the bath, and with sandals on; and as Socrates was only rarely shod, he asked him where he was going that he had been transformed into such a fop.

"To a dinner party at Agathon's," he replied, "whose invitation to his victory sacrifice I refused yesterday, fearing a crowd, but I promised that I would come today instead. And so I have put on my finery, because he is such a fine man. What do you say to going with me without an invitation?"

174b

"I will do as you bid me," I replied.

"Follow then," he said, "and let us demolish the proverb 'To the feasts of inferior men the good unbidden go,' instead of which our proverb will run, 'To the feasts of the good the good unbidden go.'[2] And this alteration may be

[2]Socrates is making a pun on the name Agathon ("Goodman") and the Greek word for "good," *agathos*, as if we should say, "To Goodman's feast good men unbidden go."

supported by the authority of Homer himself, who not only demolishes but literally outrages the proverb. For, after picturing Agamemnon as a man exceptionally *good* at war, he makes Menelaus, who is only a fainthearted warrior, come unbidden to the banquet of Agamemnon,[3] who is feasting and offering sacrifices, not the better to the worse, but the worse to the better."

"I am worried, Socrates," said Aristodemus, "that this may still be my case, and that, like Menelaus in Homer, I shall be a mediocrity who 'to the feasts of the brilliant unbidden goes.' But I shall say that I was bidden by you, and then you will have to make an excuse."

" 'Two going together,' " he replied, with the Homeric verse,[4] "one or other of us may invent an excuse along the way. But let's go."

This was the style of their conversation as they went along. But then as they proceeded, Socrates became lost in thought and started steadily dropping behind, finally urging Aristodemus, who was waiting, to go on before him. When Aristodemus reached the house of Agathon, he found the doors wide open, and a comical thing happened. A slave coming out met him, and led him at once into the dining room, in which the guests were reclining, for the dinner party was about to begin. "Welcome, Aristodemus," said Agathon, as soon as he appeared. "You are just in time to sup with us; if you come on any other matter, put it off and join us, as I was looking for you yesterday to invite you, but I could not find you. But what have you done with Socrates?"

I turned round, but Socrates was nowhere to be seen;

[3] *Iliad* 2. 408.
[4] *Iliad* 10. 224.

and I had to explain that he had been with me a moment before, and that I came by his invitation to the supper.

"You were quite right in coming," said Agathon, "but where is he himself?"

175 "He was coming along behind me just now," he said, "and I cannot think what has become of him."

"Go and look for him, boy," said Agathon, "and bring him in; and meanwhile, please, Aristodemus, take the place by Eryximachus."

A slave then helped him to wash, and he lay down. Soon another slave came in with an announcement: "Socrates is here, but he has gone up onto the portico of the house next door," he said. "There he stands, and when I call him he refuses to come."

"How strange," said Agathon. "Then you must call him again, and keep calling him."

b "Let him alone," said my informant. "He has a way of stopping anywhere and abstracting himself. I am certain that he will soon appear, so do not disturb him."

"Well, if you think so, I will leave him," said Agathon. And then, turning to the slaves, he added, "Let us have supper without waiting for him. Whenever there is no one to give you orders, which I have never done, you always serve up whatever you please. So now imagine that you are our hosts, and that I and the company are your guests; treat c us well, and then we shall commend you."

After this, supper was served, but still no Socrates; and during the meal Agathon several times expressed a wish to send for him, but Aristodemus objected; and at last when the feast was about half over—for the fit, as usual, was not of long duration—Socrates entered. Agathon, who was reclining alone at the end of the table, begged that he would take the place next to him, that "I may touch you," he said, "and have the benefit of that wise thought which came into d your mind in the portico, and is now in your possession; for I am certain that you would not have come away until you had found what you sought."

"How I wish," said Socrates, sitting down on the couch, "that wisdom could be infused by touch, out of the fuller into the emptier man, as water runs siphoned on a string of wool out of a fuller cup into an emptier one; if that were so, how greatly I would value the privilege of reclining at e your side. For you would fill me full with a stream of wisdom plenteous and fair; whereas my own is without a doubt of a very slight and even illusory sort, like a dream. But yours is bright and full of promise, and shone forth in all the splendor of youth the day before yesterday, in the presence of more than thirty thousand Hellenes."

"Don't be cruel, Socrates," said Agathon. "Before long you and I will have to settle the question who bears off the palm of wisdom—of this Dionysus shall be the judge. But at present you are better occupied with supper."

Socrates reclined, and supped with the rest; and then li- 176 bations were offered, and after a hymn had been sung to the god, and there had been the usual ceremonies, they were about to commence drinking, when Pausanias said, "And now, my friends, how can we drink with least injury to ourselves? I can assure you that I feel severely the effect of yesterday's drinks, and need a respite; and I suspect that most of you are in the same predicament, since you were at the party yesterday. Consider then: What would be the least injurious approach to drinking?" b

"I entirely agree," said Aristophanes, "that we should, by all means, avoid hard drinking, for I was myself one of those who were yesterday drowned in drink."

"I think that you are right," said Eryximachus, the son of

Acumenus, "but I should still like to hear one other person speak: Is Agathon able to drink hard?"

"I am not up to it," said Agathon.

c   "Then," said Eryximachus, "the weak heads, like myself, Aristodemus, Phaedrus, and others who never can drink, are fortunate in finding that the stronger ones are not in a drinking mood. (I do not include Socrates, who is able either to drink heavily or to abstain, and will not mind, whichever we do.) Well, as none of the company seems disposed to drink much, perhaps I will be forgiven for say-

d ing, as a physician, that heavy drinking is a bad practice, which I never follow, if I can help it, and certainly do not recommend to others, least of all to anyone who still feels the effects of yesterday's carouse."

"I always do what you advise, and especially what you prescribe as a physician," responded Phaedrus of the deme Myrrhinus, "and the rest of the company, if they are wise, will do the same."

e   It was agreed that drinking was not to dominate the evening's activities, but that they were all to drink only so much as they pleased.

"Then," said Eryximachus, "as you are all agreed that drinking is to be voluntary, and that there is to be no coercive toasting or the like, I move, in the next place, that the flute-girl, who has just made her appearance, be told to go away and play to herself, or, if she likes, to the women within. Today let us have conversation instead; and, if you will allow me, I will tell you what sort of conversation."

177   This proposal having been accepted, Eryximachus proceeded as follows:

"I will begin," he said, "after the manner of Melanippe in Euripides, 'Not mine the word' which I am about to speak, but that of Phaedrus.[5] For often he says to me in an indignant tone: 'What a strange thing it is, Eryximachus, that, whereas other gods have poems and hymns made in their honor, so venerable and great a god as Love has not even one encomiast among all the poets, who are so many.[6] There are the worthy sophists too—the excellent Prodicus, for example—who have descanted in prose on the virtues of Heracles and other heroes. That is not all that amazing, but I have come across a philosophical work of which salt was the subject, and was given extraordinary encomiums for its usefulness; and you could find many other equally worthy things have had equal honor bestowed upon them. And to think that there should be eager interest in such things as these, and yet to this day no one has ever undertaken to hymn Love in a manner worthy of him! *That* is how utterly this great deity has been neglected.'

"Now in this Phaedrus seems to me to be quite right, and therefore I want to offer him a contribution; furthermore, on this occasion I cannot think of anything better suited to those present than to honor the god Love. If you agree with me, there will be no lack of conversation; for I mean to propose that each of us in turn, going from left to right, shall make as fair a speech as he can in honor of Love, and Phaedrus, because he is sitting first on the left hand, and because he is the father of the proposal, shall begin."

[5]From Euripides' play *Melanippe the Wise*, which survives only fragmentarily.

[6]Sophocles' *Antigone* (lines 781–800) and Euripides' *Hippolytus* (lines 525–564) contain "poems in honor of" Love, and both were written and performed prior to the dramatic date of the *Symposium* (416 B.C.). Phaedrus' complaint is therefore premised on what is likely to have been intended to be recognized as a falsehood.

"No one will vote against you, Eryximachus," said Socrates. "How, for example, could *I* oppose your motion, I, who profess to understand nothing but matters of love;[7] nor, I imagine, will Agathon and Pausanias;[8] and there can e be no doubt of Aristophanes, whose sole concern is with Dionysus and Aphrodite; nor will anyone else of those whom I see around me disagree. The proposal, as I am aware, seems rather hard upon us whose place is last; but we shall be contented if we hear some good speeches first. Let Phaedrus begin the praise of Love, and good luck to him."

All the company expressed their assent, and urged him to do as Socrates suggested.

178 Now, Aristodemus did not recollect all that each speaker said, and I do not recollect all that he himself related to me; but I will tell you what of the things said by the chief speakers I thought was most worthy of remembrance.

---

[7]Does Socrates profess to understand nothing but "matters of love" (i.e., the emotion) or "matters of Love" (i.e., the god)? And what is the difference? Greek thought seems to have flowed more easily than ours between an abstract and its personification (*èros* and *Eros*, love and Love), and the writing system, lacking a lower-case alphabet, did not force any decision between "love" and "Love." In the translation I have tried to use "love" where the abstract emotion seems meant, and "Love" for the personified deity, but it will be clear to readers, especially in the speeches of Pausanias and Eryximachus, that the decision for one or the other sometimes fails to do justice to the subtle modulations in the speakers' usages.

[8]Open lovers. Their relationship was unusual for ancient Athens in that it did not, as was the norm for love affairs between younger and older males (the older partner, called the lover, as opposed to the younger, the beloved), coexist with heterosexual marriage, but appears to have been the primary relationship of both participants, and continued (again anomalously) after the younger partner had left boyhood far behind. As we see on the present occasion, Agathon, still jocularly referred to by his companions as a "boy" or "lad," is a full-grown adult who has written successful dramas. It is reported that when Agathon left Athens for Macedonia, Pausanias went with him.

———

Phaedrus began with an argument to the effect that Love is a mighty god and an object of wonder and admiration among gods and men for many different reasons, but especially for his birth. "For he is the eldest of the gods, which is a source of honor to him; and a proof of his claim to this honor is b that there is no record of his parents; no poet or prose writer has ever affirmed that he had any. As Hesiod says:[9]

> First Chaos came, and then broad-bosomed Earth,
> The everlasting seat of all that is,
> And Love.

"And Acusilaus agrees with Hesiod. Also Parmenides says about Birth,

> She devised
> Love first of all the gods.[10]

Thus there are numerous witnesses who acknowledge c Love to be the eldest of the gods. And not only is he the eldest, he is also the source of the greatest benefits to us. For I know no greater blessing to a young man who is beginning life than a virtuous lover, or to a lover than a beloved youth. For the principle that ought to be the lifelong guide of men who wish to live nobly—that principle, I say, neither kinship ties, nor honor, nor wealth, nor anything else is able to implant so well as love. Of what principle am I d speaking? Of the sense of honor and dishonor, without which neither states nor individuals ever do any good or great work. And I say that a lover who is detected in doing any dishonorable act, or submitting through cowardice

[9]Hesiod, *Theogony* 116–120, with omissions.
[10]Parmenides, *Fragment* 13.

when any dishonor is done to him by another, will be more pained at being detected by his beloved than at being seen by his father, or by his companions, or by anyone else. The
e beloved, too, when he is found in any disgraceful situation, has the same feeling about his lover. And if there were only some way of contriving that a state or an army should be made up of lovers and their loves, they would be the very best governors of their own city, abstaining from all dishonor, and emulating one another in honor; and when
179 fighting at each other's side, although a mere handful, they would overcome the world. For a lover would prefer for all mankind to see him abandon his post or throw away his arms than that his beloved should see him do such things. He would be ready to die a thousand deaths rather than endure that. Then again, who would desert his beloved or fail him in the hour of danger? No one is so cowardly that Love could not inspire him to heroism, equal to that of the
b bravest, at such a time. That courage which, as Homer says, the god breathes into the souls of some heroes, Love infuses from his own nature into the lover.

"And as for dying on someone else's behalf—only lovers consent to do this, not only men, but even women. Of this, Alcestis, the daughter of Pelias, is a monument to all Hellas; for she was willing to lay down her life on behalf of her husband, when no one else would, although he had a father
c and mother; but because of her love she so far exceeded them in devotion that she made them seem to be strangers in blood to their own son, and related to him in name only. So noble did this action of hers appear to the gods, as well as to men, that among the many who have done noble deeds, she is one of the very few to whom, in admiration for her magnificent act, they have granted the privilege of
d returning alive to earth; that is how exceedingly great is

the honor paid by the gods to the devotion and virtue of love. But Orpheus, the son of Oeagrus, the harper, they sent away empty-handed, and presented to him only an apparition of her whom he sought,[11] but herself they would not give up, because he showed no spirit; he was only a harp player and did not dare, like Alcestis, to die for love, but was scheming how he might enter Hades alive. Moreover, they afterward caused him to suffer death at the hands of women, as the punishment of his cowardliness, whereas, very differently, they honored Achilles, the son of e Thetis, and sent him to the Isles of the Blest, because, though he had learned from his mother that he would die if he killed Hector, but if he did not, he would return home and live to a good old age, he dared nonetheless to go to the aid of his lover, Patroclus, and, after avenging him, not merely to die on his lover's behalf but to follow him in 180 death. And the gods, overawed by this deed, honored him exceptionally, because his zeal on behalf of his lover was so exceptional. (Aeschylus, incidentally, talks nonsense in saying that Achilles was the lover, Patroclus the beloved; for Achilles was more beautiful not only than Patroclus but than all the other heroes, and as Homer informs us,[12] he was still beardless and younger by far.) And greatly as the gods honor a lover's love, still, since the lover is more divine (seeing that he is inspired by god), the return of love b on the part of the beloved to the lover is more admired and valued and rewarded by them. Wherefore the gods honored Achilles even above the lover Alcestis, and sent him to the Islands of the Blest.

"These are my reasons for affirming that Love is the el-

---

[11]His wife, Eurydice.
[12]*Iliad*, 11. 786–7.

dest and noblest and mightiest of the gods, and the chiefest author and giver of virtue and happiness to men, both in life and after death."

c   This, or something like this, was the speech of Phaedrus. Some other speeches followed, which Aristodemus did not remember; the next that he repeated was that of Pausanias:

"Phaedrus," he said, "the argument has not been set before us, I think, quite in the right form: we should not be called upon to praise Love in such an indiscriminate fashion. If there were only one Love, then what you said would be well enough; but since there are more Loves than one, you should have begun by determining which of them was

d   to be the theme of our praises. I will amend this defect; and first of all I will tell you which Love is deserving of praise, and then I will try to formulate my praise in a manner worthy of the god.

"We all know that Love is inseparable from Aphrodite, and if there were only one Aphrodite, there would be only one Love; but as there are two Aphrodites, there must be two Loves. And am I not right in asserting that there are two Aphrodites? The elder one, having no mother, who is called the heavenly Aphrodite—she is the daughter of Uranus;[13] the younger, who is the daughter of Zeus and

e   Dione—her we call common, and the Love who is her fellow worker is rightly named common, as the other Love is called heavenly.

"It is axiomatic that all the gods must be praised, and in doing so in this case I must try to state the provinces and

---

[13]Uranus—in Greek not a planet, but the heavens conceived as a god, contrasted and partnered with Earth; hence, Aphrodite, daughter of Uranus, is "heavenly Aphrodite."

prerogatives of the two Loves. Now, the nature of any action—that is, whether it is good or bad—varies according to the manner of its performance. Take, for example, what we are now doing—drinking, singing, and talking; these 181 actions are not in themselves either good or evil, but they turn out in this or that way according to the mode of performing them, and when well done they are good, and when wrongly done they are evil. And in like manner not every kind of love, or rather, not every kind of Love, but only that which has a noble purpose, is noble and worthy of praise. The Love who is the offspring of the common Aphrodite is essentially common, and does whatever pre- b sents itself. This Love is the one that the more vulgar sort of men feel, and such men are apt to love women no less than boys, and the bodies of those whom they crave rather than their souls, so they aim for those who are as empty-headed as possible, since they look only toward bringing the deed off and do not care if they do so honorably or otherwise—for which reason it inevitably turns out that they do whatever opportunity offers, good, and, just as happily, ill. The goddess who is the mother of this Love is far younger than the other, and she was born of the union c of the male and female, and partakes of both. But the offspring of the heavenly Aphrodite is derived from a mother in whose birth the female has no part—she is from the male only; this is that Love which is of boys, and the goddess being older, there is nothing of wantonness in her. Those who are inspired by this Love turn to the male, delighting in the more valiant and intelligent nature. Anyone may recognize the pure enthusiasts of this Love in the very nature of the pederasty. For they love not little boys but in- d telligent beings whose reason is beginning to be developed, about the time at which their beards begin to grow. And in

choosing young men to be their companions, they mean to be faithful to them and pass their whole life in company with them, not to take them in their juvenile inexperience, and deceive them, and then abandon them with ridicule, to run off with another. But the love of little boys should be
e forbidden by law, because their future is uncertain; they may turn out good or bad, either in body or soul, and much serious effort may be thrown away upon them. In this matter the good are a law to themselves, and the coarser sort of lovers ought to be restrained by force, as we restrain or attempt to restrain them from fixing their affections on
182 women of free birth. These are the persons who bring a reproach on love, with the result that some people have the nerve to claim that it is disgraceful to grant sexual gratification to lovers. They say this looking at the vulgar type, observing their impropriety and lawlessness—for surely nothing that is decorously and lawfully done can justly be censured?

"Now, here and in Lacedaemon the rules about love are perplexing, but in most cities they are simple and easily in-
b telligible. In Elis and Boeotia, and in countries having no gifts of eloquence, they are very straightforward; the law is simply that gratifying lovers is a noble thing to do, and no one, whether young or old, has anything to say to the lovers' discredit, the reason being, as I suppose, that they are men of few words in those parts, and therefore the lovers do not like the trouble of pleading their suit.

"In as many parts of Ionia and other places as are subject to the barbarians, the custom is held to be dishonorable; love affairs with youths share the evil repute in which philosophy and gymnastics are held, because they are in-
c imical to tyranny; for the interests of rulers require that their subjects should be weak in spirit, and that there

should be no strong bond of friendship or society among them, which love, above all other motives, is likely to inspire, as our Athenian tyrants learned by experience; for the love of Aristogeiton and the constancy of Harmodius had a strength which undid their power.[14] And, therefore, where illegality and shame have been attached to the act of gratifying lovers, the responsibility is to be ascribed to the d evil condition of those who make the laws; that is to say, to the self-seeking of the governors and the cowardice of the governed. On the other hand, the indiscriminate honor that is given to this act in some countries is attributable to the spiritual sloth of the lawmakers.

"In our own country a far better principle prevails, but, as I was saying, the explanation of it is rather perplexing. For observe that open loves are held to be more honorable than secret ones, and that the love of the noblest and highest, even if they are physically less beautiful than others, is especially honorable. Consider, too, how great is the encouragement given by all to the lover—not only is he not thought to be doing anything dishonorable, but if he succeeds he is praised, and if he fails he is blamed! And the e custom of our city grants that in the pursuit of his love he be praised for doing many strange things, which would garner bitter censure if he should dare to do them pursuing and trying to achieve any consummation other than 183 this one. For if, from any motive of financial interest or wish for office or power, he should be willing to do what lovers do in pursuit of their darlings—pray, and entreat,

[14]According to Athenian popular belief, the regime of the Peisistratids fell at the end of the sixth century as a result of the assassination of Hipparchus, who was in fact only the brother of the ruling tyrant, Hippias. The assassins were Harmodius and his lover Aristogeiton, seeking to prevent and punish Hipparchus' erotic pursuit of Harmodius.

220 · *Selected Dialogues of Plato*

and supplicate, and swear oaths, and sleep outside the beloved's door, and voluntarily endure a slavery worse than that of any slave—in any other case his friends and enemies alike would be ready to prevent him; but in the
b case of love there is no friend who will be ashamed of him and admonish him, and no enemy will charge him with servility or flattery. There is an ennobling charm to a lover doing all these things, and it is granted by custom that he do them without censure, since he is trying to accomplish something magnificent. And what is strangest of all, the lover alone may swear and forswear himself (so men say), and the gods will forgive his transgression, for they say that
c a lover's oath is not binding. Such is the total liberty that gods and men have allowed the lover, according to the custom that prevails in our part of the world. From this point of view a man might suppose that in Athens to be a lover and to be a lover's 'friend' is held to be a very honorable thing. But when their fathers forbid the beloveds to talk with their lovers, and place them under the care of a tutor, who is appointed to see to these things, and their companions and coevals cast in their teeth anything of the sort that
d they may observe to happen, and their elders refuse to silence the reprovers and do not rebuke them for rudeness—anyone who reflects on all this will, on the contrary, think that we hold these practices to be most disgraceful. But, as I was saying at first, the truth, as I imagine, is that the matter is not a straightforward one. Such practices are in and of themselves neither honorable nor dishonorable; rather, they are honorable when done honorably, dishonorable when done dishonorably. There is dishonor in yielding to the base, or in a base manner; but there is honor in yielding to the good, or in an honorable manner. Base is
e that vulgar lover who loves the body rather than the soul,

inasmuch as he is not even stable, because he loves a thing
that is in itself unstable, and therefore when the bloom of
youth that he was desiring is over, he 'takes wing and flies
away,'[15] dishonoring all his words and promises; whereas
the lover with the noble disposition is constant for life, because he becomes one with the everlasting. The custom of
our country would have both of them proven well and 184
truly, and would have the beloved yield to the one sort of
lover and avoid the other, and therefore encourages lovers
to pursue, and beloveds to flee, testing both the lover and
beloved in contests and trials until they show to which of
the two classes they respectively belong. And this is the
reason why, in the first place, a hasty surrender is held by
custom to be dishonorable, because time is the true test of
this as of most other things; and second, there is dishonor
in being overcome by the love of money, or of wealth, or of
political power, whether a man is frightened into surrender b
by the loss of them, or, having experienced the benefits of
money and political corruption, is unable to rise above the
seductions of them. For none of these things is of a permanent or lasting nature; not to mention that no generous
friendship ever sprang from them. There remains, then, according to our custom, only one path by which a beloved
might honorably gratify his lover; for, as we saw that our
custom allows that any service that the lover does for his
beloved is not to be accounted flattery or be reviled, so the c
beloved has one way only of voluntary service that is not a
source of censure, and this is the service of virtue.

"For we have a custom, and according to our custom
anyone who does service to another under the idea that he
will be improved by him, either in wisdom or in some

[15] *Iliad* 2. 71.

other particular of virtue—such a voluntary service, I say, is not to be regarded as a dishonor, and is not open to the charge of flattery. And these two customs, the one concerned with boy-love, and the other with the practice of

d philosophy and virtue in general, ought to meet in one, and then the beloved may honorably indulge the lover. For when the lover and beloved come together, having each of them a law, and the lover thinks that he is right in doing any service that he can to his compliant beloved, and the other that he is right in submitting to any service that he can for him who is making him wise and good, the one ca-

e pable of communicating intelligence and virtue, the other seeking to acquire them with a view to education and wisdom; when the two laws of love are fulfilled and meet in one—then, and then only, may the beloved yield with honor to the lover. Nor when love is of this disinterested sort is there any disgrace in being deceived, but in every other case there is equal disgrace in being or not being de-

185 ceived. For he who is gracious to his lover under the impression that he is rich, and is disappointed of his gains because he turns out to be poor, is disgraced all the same: for he has done his best to show that he would give himself up to anyone's 'uses base' for the sake of money, and this is not honorable. And on the same principle, if someone should give himself to a lover because he seems a good man, and in the hope that he will be improved by his company, and should in the end be deceived, even though the

b object of his affection turn out to be a villain, and to have no virtue, still, the error is a noble one. For he too has shown his true nature, that for the sake of virtue and improvement he will eagerly do anything for anybody, and there can be nothing nobler than this.

"Thus it is noble in every case to gratify another for the

sake of virtue. This is that love which is the Love of the heavenly goddess, and is heavenly, and of great value to individuals and cities, making the lover and the beloved alike eager in the work of their own improvement. But all other loves are the offspring of the other, who is the common c goddess.

"To you, Phaedrus, I offer this my contribution in praise of Love, which is as good as I could make extempore."

Pausanias came to a pause—this is the balanced way in which I have been taught by the experts to speak;[16] and Aristodemus said that the turn of Aristophanes was next, but either because he had eaten too much, or from some other cause, he had the hiccoughs and was obliged to change turns with Eryximachus, the physician, who was d reclining on the couch below him. "Eryximachus," he said, "you ought either to stop my hiccoughs, or to speak in my turn until I have gotten rid of them."

"I will do both," said Eryximachus: "I will speak in your turn, and then you speak in mine; and let me recommend that while I am speaking you hold your breath, and if after you have done so for some time the hiccough is no better, then gargle with a little water; and if it still continues, e tickle your nose with something and sneeze; and if you

---

[16]The Greek, meaning literally "Pausanias having ceased," runs *Pausaniou de pausamenou,* and forms a symmetrical rhythmic pattern. Wordplay and rhythmical balance ("the balanced way in which I have been taught by the experts to speak") were the distinctive features of the style of the sophist Gorgias of Leontini, closely imitated by, among others, the historical Agathon, as shown in his surviving fragments, and by the Platonic Agathon in his speech later on in the *Symposium.* Because he was a sophist, Gorgias and all his works were, for Plato, objects of intense suspicion, as readers of the dialogue *Protagoras* above will know. As to the pleasantry in the text ("Pausanias came to a pause"), it is worth remarking that this is one of the few places in which our narrator, Apollodorus, makes something resembling an editorial intervention; its exact significance, if it has any beyond sheer playfulness, is hard to gauge.

sneeze once or twice, even the most violent hiccoughs are sure to go away." "I will do as you prescribe," said Aristophanes, "and now get on with your speech."

Eryximachus spoke as follows:

"Seeing that Pausanias made a fine beginning, but a 186 lame ending, I must try to make up his deficiency. I think that he has rightly distinguished two kinds of love. But my art further informs me that the double love is not an affection toward the beautiful found exclusively in the soul of man, but is to be found, with a multitude of different objects, elsewhere besides—in the bodies of all animals, for example, and in productions of the earth, and I may say in all that is; such is the conclusion that I am convinced I have seen supported from my own art of medicine, namely, that b the deity of love is great and wonderful and universal, and his empire extends over all things, divine as well as human. And I will begin my speech with medicine in order that I may do honor to my art.

"It is in the nature of human bodies that they comprise the two types of love. For it is agreed that in bodily terms that which is healthy and that which is diseased are different and unlike, and furthermore that unlike things desire and love unlike objects; it follows that the love in the healthy is one thing, and that in the diseased is different. Just as Pausanias has said, that to gratify good men is hon- c orable, and licentious men dishonorable, so too it stands in the case of the body that it is noble and necessary to gratify the good and healthy elements—and this is what has the name of medicine—and the bad elements and the elements of disease are not to be indulged but to be discouraged, if someone is going to prove to be a truly expert practitioner. For medicine may be regarded generally as the knowledge of the loves and desires of the body and

how to satisfy them or not; and the best physician is he who d
is able to separate fair love from foul, or to convert one into
the other; and he who knows how to eradicate and how to
implant love, whichever is required, is a skillful practitioner. For it is necessary that he be able to reconcile the
most hostile elements in the constitution and make them
loving friends. Now, the most hostile are the most opposite,
such as hot and cold, bitter and sweet, moist and dry, and
the like. It was thanks to his knowing how to implant e
love—that is, accord—in these elements that my ancestor,
Asclepius,[17] created our art, as our friends the poets here
tell us, and I believe them.

"Now, not only medicine in every branch, but the arts of
gymnastic and husbandry are governed by the god Love.
Anyone who pays the least attention to the subject will also 187
perceive that in music there is the same reconciliation of
opposites; and I suppose that this must have been the
meaning of Heraclitus, although his words are not accurate; for he says that 'The One is united by disunion, like
the harmony of the bow and the lyre.'[18] There is an absur-
dity in saying that harmony is discord or is composed of
elements that are still in a state of discord. But what he
probably meant was that harmony is composed of differing
notes of higher or lower pitch, which disagreed once but b
are now reconciled by the art of music; for if the higher
and lower notes still disagreed, there would be no harmony—clearly not. For harmony is symphony, and symphony is an agreement; but there cannot be an agreement
of disagreements so long as they disagree; for that which

---

[17]Asclepius, son of Apollo and the legendary inventor of medical art, is
claimed by Eryximachus as an "ancestor" in the sense that as a doctor, Eryximachus (like all doctors) is Asclepius' heir.

[18]Heraclitus, *Fragment* 51, modified.

disagrees cannot harmonize. Similarly, rhythm is compounded of elements short and long, once differing and
c now in accord. And as in the former instance, medicine, so in all these other cases, it is music that implants this accord, making love and unison to grow up among them; and thus music, too, is knowledge of the principles of love in their application to harmony and rhythm. Again, in the essential nature of harmony and rhythm there is no difficulty in discerning love that has not yet become double. But when you
d want to use them in actual life, either in the composition of songs or in the correct performance of tunes or meters composed already, which latter is called education, then the difficulty begins, and the good artist is needed. It is the same story all over again: one must gratify those men who are orderly, in such a way that those who are not yet orderly may become so, and to preserve the love of these or-
e derly men—this is that noble and heavenly love, the Love of Urania the muse. And again, there is the common Love, that of Polyhymnia,[19] which a person must apply, to whomever he applies it, cautiously, in order that the pleasure be enjoyed but may not generate licentiousness; just as in my own art it is a great matter so to regulate the desires of the epicure that he may gratify his tastes without the attendant evil of disease. Whence I infer that in music, in medicine, in all other things human as well as divine, both Loves ought to be noted as far as may be, for they are both present.
188 "The course of the yearly seasons is also full of both these principles; and when, as I was saying, the elements of

---

[19]Pausanias in his speech had distinguished two Aphrodites, the heavenly or Uranian one, and the vulgar one. Eryximachus here assigns to the former the name Urania, drawn from Hesiod's catalog of the Nine Muses (*Theogony* 75–9), from which source he also borrows a name, Polyhymnia ("She of many songs"), for the vulgar Aphrodite.

hot and cold, moist and dry, attain the orderly Love of one another and blend in temperance and harmony, they bring to men, animals, and plants health and plenty, and do them no harm; whereas the wanton Love, getting the upper hand and affecting the seasons of the year, is very destructive and injurious, being the source of pestilence, and bringing b many other kinds of diseases on animals and plants; for hoarfrost and hail and blight spring from the excesses and disorders of these elements of love, the knowledge of which, in relation to the revolutions of the heavenly bodies and the seasons of the year, is termed astronomy. Furthermore, all sacrifices and the whole province of divination, which is the art of communion between gods and men— c these, I say, are concerned only with the preservation of the good and the cure of the evil Love. For all manner of impiety is likely to ensue if, instead of accepting and honoring and reverencing the harmonious Love in all his actions, a man honors the other Love, whether in his feelings toward gods or parents, toward the living or the dead. Wherefore the business of divination is to see to these Loves and to heal them, and divination is the peacemaker of gods and men, working by a knowledge of the religious d or irreligious tendencies that exist in human loves.

"Such generally is the great and mighty, or rather omnipotent, force of Love. And the Love, more especially, that is concerned with the good and is realized in company with temperance and justice, whether among gods or men, has the greatest power, and is the source of all our happiness and harmony, and makes it possible for us to be friends with the gods, who are above us, and with one another.

"I daresay that I too have omitted several things that might be said in praise of Love, but this was not inten- e tional, and you, Aristophanes, may now supply the omission or take some other line of commendation; for I perceive that you are rid of the hiccoughs."

189   "Yes," said Aristophanes, who followed, "the hiccoughs did stop, not, however, until I applied the sneezing, and I wonder whether the 'orderly' part of the body has a love of such noises and ticklings as go into a sneeze, for I no sooner applied the sneezing than I was cured."

    Eryximachus said: "Watch out, Aristophanes my friend; by starting your speech with such pleasantries you compel b me to stand guard over it, looking out to see if you will say something derisive—though you *could* speak without disturbing the peace between us."

    "You are quite right," said Aristophanes, laughing. "I will unsay my words, and please do not stand guard over me, as I fear that during the speech I am about to make, instead of others laughing with me, which would be all to the good and appropriate to my particular muse, I shall only be laughed at by them."

    "Do you expect to hurl your dart and then just get off scot-free, Aristophanes? Well, perhaps if you are very c careful and bear in mind that you will be called to account, I may be induced to let you off."

    "In fact, Eryximachus, I intend to take a different line from that taken by you and Pausanias. For it seems to me that mankind has never at all understood the power of Love, since if they had understood him, they would surely have built noble temples and altars, and would offer solemn sacrifices in his honor; but this is not done, and most certainly ought to be done, since of all the gods he is d the best friend of men, the helper and the healer of the ills that are the great impediment to the happiness of the race. I will therefore try to initiate you into the mysteries of his power, and you shall be the instructors of others.

"In the first place, let me discuss man's native constitution and its sufferings—for our original constitution was not like the present, but quite different. The sexes were three in number, not, as they are now, two, male and female; there was also as a third the union of the two, having e a name corresponding to this double nature, which had once a real existence, but is now lost, and the word 'androgynous' is preserved only as a term of reproach. In the second place, the primeval humans were round, their backs and sides forming a circle; and they had four hands and four feet, one head with two faces, looking opposite ways, 190 set on a round neck and precisely alike; also four ears, two sets of genitals, and the remainder to correspond. They could walk upright as people do now, backward or forward as they pleased, and they could also roll over and over at a great pace, pushing off with their four hands and four feet, eight in all, like tumblers going over and over with their legs in the air; this was when they wanted to run fast. Now, the sexes were three, and such as I have described them, b because the sun, moon, and earth are three; and the male was originally the child of the sun, the female of the earth, and the man-woman of the moon, which is made up of sun and earth, and they were all round and moved round and round like their parents.

"Terrible was their might and strength, and the thoughts of their hearts were great, and they made an attack upon the gods; the tale told by Homer of Otys and Ephialtes actually refers to the original humans: they dared to scale heaven, and would have laid hands upon the gods.[20] Doubt reigned in the celestial councils. Should they kill them and c annihilate the race with thunderbolts, as they had done the

[20] *Iliad* 5. 385ff.

giants? But then there would be an end of the sacrifices and worship that people offered to them. On the other hand, how could the gods suffer this insolence to go unchecked? At last, after a good deal of reflection, Zeus discovered a way. He said: 'I think I've found a plan that will humble their pride and improve their manners: humans

d shall continue to exist, but I will cut them in two, and then they will be diminished in strength and increased in numbers; this will have the advantage of making them more profitable to us. They shall walk upright on two legs, and if they continue to be insolent and will not be quiet, I will split them again and they shall hop about on a single leg.' He spoke and cut all the humans in two, like a sorb apple that is

e halved for pickling, or as you might divide an egg with a hair; and as he cut them one after another, he ordered Apollo to give the face and the remaining half of the neck a turn in order that the person might contemplate the dissection of himself (they would thus learn a lesson of humility), and to heal the rest of his wounds, too. So Apollo gave the face a turn and pulled the skin from the sides all over what is now called the belly, and he made one mouth at the center, which he fastened, like a drawstring purse, with a knot

191 (the same which is called the navel); he also molded the chest and took out most of the wrinkles, using a tool like that used by a shoemaker smoothing leather upon a last; he left a few, however—those in the region of the belly around the navel—to be a memorial of this primeval suffering.

"After the division the two parts of the whole human, each yearning for his other half, came together, and, throwing their arms about each other, and intertwining in mutual embraces out of a desire to grow into one, they started

b dying off from hunger and self-neglect, because they did not like to do anything apart; and when one of the halves died and the other survived, the survivor sought another mate, man or woman, as we call them—being the sections of entire males or females—and clung to that. They were dying out, when in pity for them Zeus devised a new plan: he turned their genitals around to the front, for this had not always been their position, and they sowed their seed no longer, as hitherto, like grasshoppers in the ground, but in- c side one another; and he effected this transposition, and caused the male to generate in the female, in order that their mutual embraces might be procreative, in the case of man joining woman, and that thus the race be continued, or, if male came to male, that they might at least derive satisfaction from the coition, and rest, and go their ways to the business of life: so ancient is the desire for one another that is implanted in us, reuniting our original nature, trying to d make one of two, and healing the state of man. Each of us, sliced in two like a flat fish, is but the half of a human— from one, two. And each is always looking for his other half.

"Now men who are a section of that double nature that was once called androgynous are lovers of women; adulterers are generally of this breed, and also adulterous e women who lust after men.

"Women who are a section of the woman do not care for men, but are more inclined toward women: lesbians spring from this type.

"Finally, those who are a section of the male pursue the male, and while they are young, being slices of the original man, they love men and enjoy lying down with and intermingling with men, and they are themselves the best of 192 boys and youths, because they have the most manly nature. Some indeed assert that they are shameless, but this is not true; for they do not act thus from any want of shame, but because they are valiant and manly, and have a manly

countenance, and they embrace that which is like them. And these, when they grow up, become politicians, and these only, which is a great proof of the truth of what I am saying. When they reach manhood they are lovers of
b youth, and are not naturally inclined to marry or beget children—if at all, they do so only in obedience to the law; but they are satisfied if they may be allowed to live with one another unwedded; and such a nature is prone to love and ready to return love, always embracing that which is akin to him. And when one of them meets with his other half, the actual half of himself, whether he be a lover of boys or a lover of another sort, the pair are lost in an amazement of love and friendship and intimacy, and one
c will not be out of the other's sight, as I may say, even for a moment: these are the people who pass their whole lives together; yet they could not explain what they desire from each other. No one could plausibly think that it is just sexual relations that makes them enjoy each other's company with so much intensity; rather, the soul of each manifests a desire for something else, but what that is it is unable to
d say, and gives only obscure, oracular pronouncements of its wishes, and makes riddles.

"Now, suppose Hephaestus, with his tools, were to come to the pair as they are lying side by side and to say to them, 'What do you people want of each other?' They would be unable to explain. And suppose, further, that when he saw their perplexity he said, 'Do you desire to be wholly one, always day and night to be in each other's company? For if this is what you desire, I am ready to fuse and weld you to-
e gether, so that being two, you shall become one, and while you live, live a common life as if you were a single man, and after your death in the world below still be one departed soul instead of two—I ask whether this is what you

lovingly desire, and whether you are satisfied with this?' There is not a one of them who, when he heard this proposal, would refuse or prove to want something else, but he would simply think that in this meeting and melting into each other, this becoming one instead of two, he had heard what he now recognized to be the articulation of his long-time yearning. And the reason for this is that the human constitution was originally one and we were a whole, and the desire and pursuit of the whole is called love. There was a time, I say, when we were one, but now, because of 193 the wickedness of mankind, God has dispersed us, as the Arcadians were dispersed into villages by the Lacedaemonians. And if we are not obedient to the gods, there is a danger that we shall be split up again and go about in bas-relief, like the profile figures having only half a nose that are sculptured on monuments, and that we shall be like tallies.[21] Wherefore let us exhort all men to piety, that we may avoid evil and obtain the good, of which Love is to us the b lord and minister; and let no one oppose him: whoever opposes him is the enemy of the gods. For if we are friends of the god and at peace with him we shall find our own true loves, which rarely happens in this world at present. I am serious, and therefore I must beg Eryximachus not to make fun or to find in what I am saying any allusion to Pausanias and Agathon, who, as I suspect, are both of the all-male constitution, and belong to the class I have been describ- c ing. But my words have a wider application—they include men and women everywhere; I believe that if our loves were perfectly accomplished, and each one, restored to his

[21]A token or tally was an object, typically a knucklebone (used also for dice), that was broken into two asymmetrical pieces that were used for identification: I can securely identify as my (newborn) child the one on whose necklace hangs the tally corresponding to that on mine.

primeval nature, had his original true love, then our race would be happy. And if this would be best of all, the next best under present circumstances must be the nearest approach to such a union; and that will be the attainment of a congenial love. Wherefore, if we want to praise him who

d has given us this benefit, we must praise the god Love, who is our greatest benefactor, both leading us in this life back to our own nature, and giving us high hopes for the future, that if we are pious, he will restore us to our original state, and heal us and make us happy and blessed.

"This, Eryximachus, is my discourse of Love, which, although different from yours, I must beg you to leave unassailed by the shafts of your ridicule, in order that each may

e have his turn; each, or rather, either, for Agathon and Socrates are the only ones left."

"Indeed, I am not going to attack you," said Eryximachus, "for I thought your speech charming, and if I did not know that Agathon and Socrates are masters in the art of love, I would be really afraid that they will have nothing to say, after the great variety of things that have been said already. But, for all that, I am optimistic."

194 Socrates said: "You performed well when it was your turn, Eryximachus; but if you were in the position I am in now, or rather shall be in when Agathon has spoken, you would, indeed, be very apprehensive, even desperate, as am I."

"You are trying to jinx me, Socrates," said Agathon, "hoping that I will be thrown off by the audience's powerful expectation that I shall speak well."

"It would be strange of me to forget, Agathon," replied

b Socrates, "the courage and magnificence of spirit you showed when your own compositions were about to be exhibited, and you came upon the stage with the actors and faced the vast theater altogether undismayed, if I thought that your nerves could be fluttered at a small party of friends."[22]

"Do you think, Socrates," said Agathon, "that my head is so full of the theater as not to know how much more formidable to a man of sense a few good judges are than many fools?"

"No," replied Socrates, "it would be very wrong of me to attribute to you, Agathon, that or any other want of refinement. And I am quite aware that if you happened to meet with anyone whom you thought wise, you would care for his opinion much more than for that of the many. But there is no possibility that we here are these wise men you refer to, for we were then in the audience and were a part of the 'many fools'—but I know that if you chanced to be in the presence, not of one of ourselves, but of some really wise man, you would be ashamed of disgracing yourself before him—would you not?"

"Yes," said Agathon.

"But before the many you would not be ashamed, if you thought that you were doing something disgraceful in their presence?"

Here Phaedrus interrupted them, saying: "Do not answer him, my dear Agathon; for if he can only get a partner with whom he can talk, especially a good-looking one, he will no longer care about the completion of our plan. Now I love to hear him talk; but just at present I am obliged to remember the encomium on Love that I have to exact from each one of you. When you and he have paid your tribute to the god, then you may converse."

[22]In the *proagon*, held a few days before the dramatic performances, the poets and actors were presented to the public.

e   "Very good, Phaedrus," said Agathon. "I see no reason why I should not proceed with my speech, as I shall have many other opportunities of conversing with Socrates.

"I desire first to speak of how I ought to speak, and then to speak. For the previous speakers, instead of praising the god Love, seem more to have congratulated mankind on the benefits for which the god is responsible. The actual nature of him who has given these gifts, however, no one
195 has stated. But there is only one right way of praising anything, namely, to explain in detail both the qualities of the subject and the qualities of those things of which he is the cause. Thus the correct order for us is: praise Love first for his nature and qualities, then praise his gifts.

"I solemnly aver—if I may say it without impiety or offense—that of all the blessed gods Love is the most blessed because he is the most beautiful and the best. And he *is* the most beautiful: for, in the first place, he is the youngest, and
b   of his youth he is himself the witness, fleeing out of the way of Age, who is obviously swift, swifter truly than most of us like. Love has an innate hatred of him and will not come anywhere near him; but of the young he is, and with the young he lives—like to like, as the proverb says.

"Now of the things said by Phaedrus about Love there are many in which I agree with him, but with this I disagree: he says that Love is older than Iapetus and Kronos.
c   Not so. I maintain him to be the youngest of the gods, and young forever. The ancient doings among the gods of which Hesiod and Parmenides spoke, if they spoke true, were done of Necessity and not of Love; had Love existed in those days, there would have been no chaining or mutilation of the gods, or other violence, but peace and sweetness, as there is now in heaven, since the rule of Love began. Love is young, then, and in addition to young, ten-

der; he ought to have a poet like Homer to display his tenderness, as Homer says of Ate[23] that she is a goddess and d
tender (for if 'her feet are tender,' then she must be tender
in her entirety):

> *Her feet are tender, for she sets her steps,*
> *Not on the ground but on the heads of men.*[24]

Herein is an excellent proof of her tenderness, that she
walks not upon the hard but upon the soft. Let us adduce a
similar proof of the tenderness of Love; for he walks not e
upon the earth, nor even upon the skulls of men, which are
not so very soft, but in the softest of all that is he walks and
dwells; for it is in the hearts and souls of both gods and
men that he makes his home, though not in every soul
without exception, for where there is hardness of heart he
departs, where there is softness there he settles down; and
nestling always not only with his feet but with his whole
body in the softest of soft places, how can he be other than
the softest of all things? Of a truth he is the tenderest as 196
well as the youngest, and in addition he is of flexible form;
for if he were hard and without flexure he could not enfold
all things, or wind his way undiscovered into and out of
every soul of man. And a proof that his form is flexible and
well shaped is his gracefulness, which is universally admitted to be in a special manner the attribute of Love; grace-
lessness and love are always at war with each other. The
fairness of his complexion is indicated by his habitation
among the flowers; for he dwells not amid bloomless or b
fading beauties, whether of body or soul or anything else,

[23] Ate is delusion personified.
[24] *Iliad* 19. 92f.

but in the place of flowers and scents, there he sits and abides.

"Concerning the beauty of the god I have said enough; and yet there remains much more that I might say. Of his virtue I have now to speak: his greatest glory is that he neither does wrong nor is wrong done, to or by any god or man; for he suffers not by force if he suffers; force comes
c not near him, neither when he acts does he act by force. For all men in all things serve him of their own free will, and where there is voluntary agreement, there, as the laws that are the lords of the city say, is justice. And not only is he just but exceedingly temperate, for Temperance is the acknowledged ruler of the pleasures and desires, and no pleasure ever outdoes Love; he is thus their master and they are his servants, and if he is superior to them, then, being superior to all pleasures and desires, he must be temperate indeed. As to courage, 'even Ares, the God of War,
d is no match for him,'[25] for Ares does not have Love, Love has Ares—love of Aphrodite, that is, as the tale goes[26]— and the possessor is stronger than the possessed. And if he conquers the bravest of all others, he must be himself the bravest. Of the courage and justice and temperance of the god I have spoken, but I have yet to speak of his wisdom; and according to the measure of my ability I must try to do my best. In the first place he is a poet (and here, like Eryx-
e imachus, I magnify my art), and he is also the source of poesy in others, which he could not be if he were not himself a poet. And at the touch of him everyone becomes a poet, even if he had no music in him before; this also is a proof that Love is a good poet and accomplished in all the

[25]Sophocles, Fragment 256, from his lost play *Thyestes.* Sophocles actually says that Ares is no match for *Necessity,* not Love.

[26]As related in *Odyssey* 8. 266–366.

fine arts; for no one can give to another that which he has
not himself, or teach that of which he has no knowledge.
Who will deny that the creation of the animals is his doing? 197
Are they not all the products of his special expertise, born
and begotten of it? And as to the artists, do we not know
that only he of them whom Love inspires has the light of
fame? He whom Love touches not walks in darkness. The
arts of archery and medicine and divination were discovered by Apollo, under the guidance of love and desire; so
that he too must be a disciple of Love. And the Muses b
learned music, Hephaestus metallurgy, Athene to weave,
Zeus to govern gods and men—all at the school of Love.
And so the spheres and activities of the gods were established and determined only once Love had come to be
among them—obviously, love of beauty, for there is no
love of ugliness. In the days of old, as I began by saying,
dreadful deeds were done among the gods, for they were
ruled by Necessity; but ever since this god was born, every
good in heaven and earth has arisen from loving the beautiful.

"Therefore, Phaedrus, I say of Love that he is the most c
beautiful and best in himself, and the cause of what is most
beautiful and best in all other things. And it comes upon
me to speak in verse and say that the god who makes

> *Peace among men, the deep sea's windless calm,*
> *Pause for tempest, the troubled's hypnic balm*

—this is he who empties men of disaffection and fills them d
with affection, who makes them to meet together at ban-
quets such as these: in sacrifices, feasts, dances, he is our
lord—who sends courtesy and sends away discourtesy,
who gives kindness ever and never gives unkindness; the

friend of the good, the wonder of the wise, the amazement of the gods; desired by those who have no part in him, and precious to those who have the better part in him; parent of delicacy, luxury, desire, fondness, softness, grace; regardful of the good, regardless of the evil: in every word, work, wish, fear—savior, pilot, comrade, helper; cosmic princi-ple for all gods and men, leader best and brightest: in whose footsteps let every man follow, sweetly singing in his honor and joining in that sweet strain with which Love charms the thought of gods and men.

"Such is the speech, Phaedrus, half-playful, yet having a certain measure of seriousness, which, according to my ability, I dedicate to the god."

198   When Agathon had done speaking, Aristodemus said, there was a general cheer; the young man was thought to have spoken in a manner worthy of himself, and of the god. And Socrates, looking at Eryximachus, said: "Tell me, son of Acumenus, did I fear then a fear not to be feared?[27] Or was I not a true prophet when I said that Agathon would make a wonderful oration, and that I should be left high and dry?"

"The part of the prophecy which concerns Agathon," replied Eryximachus, "appears to me to be true; but not the other part—that you will be left high and dry."

b   "Why, my dear friend," said Socrates, "must not I or anyone be helpless who has to speak after he has heard such a rich and varied discourse? It was all marvelous, but I am especially struck with the beauty of the concluding words and expressions—who could listen to them without

[27]With the tortuous formulation "fear a fear not to be feared" Socrates is par-odying Agathon's verbal style; compare, for example, from the second-to-last paragraph of Agathon's speech above, "who sends courtesy and sends away dis-courtesy, who gives kindness ever and never gives unkindness."

amazement? As I reflected that I would be able to produce not one utterance even approaching the beauty of these, I would have run away for shame, if I had had some way out. For the speech reminded me of Gorgias,[28] so that I literally c had that experience mentioned in Homer: I feared that in his speech Agathon would send up against *my* speech a head of Gorgias, dread rhetorician, and turn me to stone with speechlessness.[29] And then I perceived how ridiculous I had been when I consented to take my turn with you in praising Love, and said that I was a past master in matters d of Love, when I really had no conception how anything ought to be praised. For in my simplicity I imagined that it was necessary to state the facts about any given topic for praise, and that this was to be the groundwork, and from these facts the speaker was to choose the best and set them forth in the most fitting manner. And I felt quite proud, thinking that I knew the nature of true praise and should speak well. Whereas I now see that all along the right way to praise something was not that, but rather to attribute to it every species of greatness and glory, whether really be- e longing to it or not, without regard to truth or falsehood— that was no matter; for the original proposal seems to have been not that each of you should really praise Love, but only that you should appear to praise him. And so you attribute to Love every imaginable form of praise that can be gathered anywhere; and you say that 'he is all this,' and 'the cause of all that,' making him appear the most beautiful 199 and best of all to those who know him not, for you cannot

[28]On Gorgias, see note 16, above.

[29]Socrates refers to *Odyssey* 11. 633–635, where Odysseus, leaving the under-world, is anxious lest Persephone send up a "head of Medusa the Gorgon, dread monster," which according to tradition turned the beholder into stone. Socrates substitutes for Homer's "Gorgon" the name of Agathon's style-master, Gorgias.

impose upon those who know him. And a noble and solemn hymn of praise you have rehearsed. But since I misunderstood the nature of the praise when I said that I would take my turn, I must ask to be absolved from the promise that I made in ignorance: 'My tongue swore, but my heart did not' (as Euripides would say).[30] Let's say good-bye, then, to that approach: for I do not praise in that way; no, in fact, I cannot. But if you wish to hear the truth about Love, I am ready to speak in my own manner, though
b I will not make myself ridiculous by entering into any rivalry with you. Say then, Phaedrus, whether you would like to have the truth about Love, spoken in any words and in any order that may happen to come into my mind at the time."

Aristodemus said that Phaedrus and the company urged him to speak in any manner he thought best. "Then," Socrates added, "let me have your permission first to ask Agathon a few more questions, in order that I may get his agreement on some points before I give my speech."

c "I grant the permission," said Phaedrus. "Put your questions." Socrates then proceeded as follows:

"I very much think that you started off your speech in the right way, my dear Agathon, in proposing to describe the nature of Love first and afterward his works—that is a way of beginning which I very much approve. And as you have spoken so eloquently of his nature, may I ask you further,
d ther, Is Love such a sort of thing as to be of something or somebody, or is it of nothing or nobody? Now, I am not asking if Love is 'of somebody' in a sense of being genealogically derived *from,* or of belonging *to,* some mother or father. And, of course, to ask if Love is erotic love *of,* that

[30] *Hippolytus* 612.

is, *for*, a mother or father would be grotesque. But actually that grotesquerie points at the usage I *am* getting at: just as if I should pose this very question about 'father' instead of about Love, I would say, Is a father a father *of* somebody or not? And obviously you would reply, if you were of a mind to reply cooperatively, by saying that a father is a father *of* a son or a daughter. Or am I wrong?"

"You are clearly right," said Agathon.

"And you would say the same of a mother?"

He assented.

"Yet let me ask you one more question in order to illus-   e trate my meaning: Is not a brother to be regarded essentially as a brother of something?"

"Certainly," he replied.

"That is, of a brother or sister?"

"Yes," he said.

"And now," said Socrates, "I will ask about Love: Is Love of something or of nothing?"

"Of something, surely," he replied.

"That something of which Love is—precisely *what* it is   200 please remember and save for later; for now only tell me whether Love desires it; that is, does Love desire that something of which Love is?"

"Yes, surely."

"And does he possess, or does he not possess, that which he loves and desires?"

"Probably not, I should say."

"Consider whether 'necessarily' is not rather the word," Socrates said, "instead of your 'probably.' The inference that he who desires something lacks it, and that he does not   b desire something if he does not lack it, is in my judgment, Agathon, absolutely and necessarily true. What do you think?"

"I agree with you," said Agathon.

"Very good. Would he who is large want to be large, or he who is strong want to be strong?"

"That would be inconsistent with our previous admissions."

"True. For he who *is* anything cannot be in lack of those things which he is?"

"Very true."

"And yet," added Socrates, "if a man who was strong wanted to be strong, or who was swift wanted to be swift, or who was healthy wanted to be healthy, in that case it might be thought, in connection with these attributes and all such things, that those who *are* such and possess these attributes c also *want* these attributes which they already possess. I give the example in order that we may avoid misconception. For the possessors of these qualities, Agathon, must be supposed to have their respective advantages at the time, whether they like it or not; and who can want that which he has? Therefore, when a person says, 'I am healthy and want simply to be healthy,' and 'I am rich and want to be rich'— to him we shall reply: 'You, my friend, having wealth and d health and strength, want to have the continuance of them; for at this moment, whether you choose to or not, you have them. And when you say, "I want that which I have," isn't your meaning that you want to have what you now have also in the future?' He must agree with us—mustn't he?"

"He must," replied Agathon.

"Then," said Socrates, "he desires that these things, preserved for him and supplied to him, be his in the future, which is equivalent to saying that he desires something which is not yet available to him, and which as yet he has not got."

e "Very true," he said.

"Then he and every one who desires, desires that which he does not have already, and with which he is not supplied, and which he does not possess, and which he is not, and of which he is in want—these are the sorts of things that love and desire seek?"

"Very true," he said.

"Now then," said Socrates, "let us recapitulate the argument. First, isn't Love *of* something, and, then, isn't that 'something' whatever thing he is supplied with lack of?"[31]

"Yes," he replied.

"This being so, recall to mind what you said in your speech was Love's object. If you wish, I will recall it for you: You said that the spheres and activities of the gods were established and determined by love of the beautiful; for there is no love for the ugly. Did you not say something of that kind?"

"Yes," said Agathon.

"Yes, my friend, and the remark was a just one. And if this is true, Love is the love of beauty and not of ugliness?"

He concurred.

"And has not the admission already been made that Love is of what is lacked and not now possessed?"

"Yes," he said.

"Then Love lacks and does not possess beauty?"

"Necessarily," he replied.

"And would you call that beautiful which wants and does not possess beauty in any way?"

"Certainly not."

"Then would you still say that Love is beautiful?"

Agathon replied, "I fear that I did not know what I was saying."

[31]The Greek is intentionally paradoxical: "lack is in ready supply."

c   "And yet you made a very good speech, Agathon," replied Socrates. "But there is still one small question that I would like to ask you: Isn't the good also beautiful?"

"Yes."

"So if Love lacks the beautiful, and the good is beautiful, then Love also lacks the good."

"Far be it from me to contradict you, Socrates," said Agathon. "Let us assume that what you say is true."

"Say instead, beloved Agathon, that you cannot refute the truth; for Socrates is easily refuted.

d   "And now, taking my leave of you, Agathon, I will rehearse a tale of love that I heard from Diotima of Mantineia, a woman wise in this and in many other kinds of knowledge, who once, before the plague came,[32] effected for the Athenians a ten-year postponement of the disease, through sacrifice. She was my instructress in the art of Love, and I shall repeat to you what she said to me, beginning with the points on which Agathon and I agreed, and I shall speak both parts myself as well as I can. As you,

e   Agathon, suggested, it is necessary first to give an account of the identity and nature of Love, and then of his works. In view of this it seems to me easiest to proceed in the way the foreign woman did long ago in examining me—for, among other things, I said to her, in nearly the same words that Agathon just used to me, that Love was a mighty god, and the beautiful his objects; and she proved to me, as I proved to him, that by my own showing, Love was neither beautiful nor good.

" 'What do you mean, Diotima?' I said. 'Is Love then ugly and evil?' 'Hush,' she cried: 'Must whatever is not

202 beautiful be ugly?' 'Certainly,' I said. 'And if something is

---

[32]In 430 B.C., at the beginning of the great war between Athens and Sparta.

not wise, must it be ignorant? Do you not see that there is a middle ground between wisdom and ignorance?' 'And what may that be?' I said. 'Right opinion,' she replied, 'which, as you know, since it is incapable of giving a reason, is not knowledge (for how can knowledge be devoid of reason?), nor again, ignorance (for neither can ignorance attain the truth), but is clearly something that is a mean between ignorance and wisdom.' 'Quite true,' I replied. 'Do not insist then,' she said, 'that what is not beautiful is of b necessity ugly, or what is not good, evil; or infer that because, as you agree, Love is not beautiful and good, he is therefore ugly and evil; for he occupies a middle ground between them.' 'Well,' I said, 'Love is surely admitted by all to be a great god.' 'When you say by "all" do you mean by those who know or by those who do not know?' 'By *everyone*.' 'And how, Socrates,' she said with a smile, 'can Love be c acknowledged to be a great god by those who say that he is not a god at all?' 'And who are they?' I said. 'You and I are two of them,' she replied. 'How can that be?' I said. 'Elementary,' she replied; 'for you yourself would acknowledge that the gods are happy and beautiful—of course you would—or would you dare to say that any god was not?' 'Certainly not,' I replied. 'And you mean by the happy, those who are the possessors of things good or beautiful?' 'Yes.' 'And you admitted that Love, because he lacks d the good and beautiful, desires them, the very things that he lacks?' 'Yes, I did.' 'But how can he be a god who has no share in what is either good or beautiful?' 'It's impossible.' 'Then you see that you also deny the divinity of Love.'

" 'What then is Love?' I asked. 'Is he mortal?' 'Of course not.' 'Well—then *what*?' 'As in the former instance, he is neither mortal nor immortal, but a mean between the two.'

'What is he, Diotima?' 'He is a great spirit [*daimon*];[33] for
e every spirit-like [*daimonion*] thing is intermediate between
the divine and the mortal.' 'And what,' I said, 'is his power?'
'He communicates,' she replied, 'between gods and men,
conveying and taking across to the gods the prayers and
sacrifices of men, and to men the commands and replies of
the gods; he is the mediator who fills the chasm that di-
vides them, and therefore in him all is bound together, and
through him the arts of the prophet and the priest, their
sacrifices and mysteries and charms, and all prophecy and
203 incantation find their way. For God mingles not with
man;[34] but through Love, all the intercourse and converse
of God with man, whether awake or asleep, is carried on.
The man wise in these matters is the spiritual [*daimonios*]
man; he who is expert in other matters, such as arts or
handicrafts, is mean and vulgar. Now these spirits or intermediate powers are many and diverse, and one of them is
Love.' 'And was he born,' I said, 'of a father and a mother?'
b 'The tale,' she said, 'will take time; nevertheless I will tell
you. On the day of Aphrodite's birth there was a feast of
the gods, at which the god Poros, or Efficacy, who is the son
of Metis, or Intelligence, was one of the guests. When the
feast was over, Penia, or Poverty, as is the manner on festive
occasions, came about the doors to beg. Now Efficacy, who
was the worse for nectar (there was no wine in those days),
went into the garden of Zeus and fell into a heavy sleep;

[33]The Greek word *daimon* has none of the connotations of its English de-
scendant "demon," so it has been translated as "spirit" here and throughout. See
also note 15 to the *Apology,* below.

[34]The Greek verb for "mingles" *(meignutai)* can refer to both sexual and non-
sexual social contact, like our word "intercourse." It was Greek tradition that
after the age of the heroes, who were the products of divine unions with mortals,
the gods ceased to "mingle" directly, in any sense, with mortals.

and Poverty, considering her own straitened circumstances, plotted to have a child by him, and accordingly she lay down at his side and conceived Love, who, partly because he is naturally a lover of the beautiful, and because Aphrodite is herself beautiful, and also because he was conceived on her birthday, is her follower and attendant. And as his parentage is, so also are his fortunes. In the first place, he is always poor, and anything but tender and fair, as the many imagine him; and he is rough and squalid, and has no shoes, nor a house to dwell in; on the bare earth exposed he always lies under the open heaven, by the roadsides or at the doors of houses, taking his rest; and, like his mother, he is always in need. Then too, in the manner of his father, he is always scheming after what is beautiful and good; he is bold, enterprising, intense, a mighty hunter, always weaving some intrigue or other, keen in the pursuit of wisdom, fertile in resources; a lifelong philosopher,[35] awesome as an enchanter, sorcerer, sophist. He is by nature neither mortal nor immortal, but alive and flourishing at one moment when he is in plenty, and dead at another moment, and again alive by reason of his father's nature. But that which is always flowing in is always flowing out, and so he is never in want and never in wealth; and, further, he is in a mean between ignorance and knowledge. The truth of the matter is this: no god is one of wisdom's lovers[36] or desires to become wise, for he is wise already; nor is any man

c

d

e

204

[35]On the word "philosopher" see the next note.

[36]The words "is one of wisdom's lovers" (or "are wisdom's lovers") here and throughout are used in an effort to represent Socrates'/Diotima's idiosyncratic interpretation and use of the Greek verb *philosopheo*, which elsewhere normally means "to be a *philosophos* (philosopher)," "to do what a *philosophos* does." *Philosophos*, the noun on which *philosopheo* is based, itself implies a verb-object proposition, "to love" (*philo-*) "wisdom" (*-sophos*). Socrates/Diotima emphasize the *philo-* part of *philosopheo* and thus proceed as if "to be a *philosophos*, i.e., wisdom

who is wise one of wisdom's lovers. Neither are the ignorant wisdom's lovers, nor do they desire to become wise. For herein is the evil of ignorance, that he who is neither good nor wise is nevertheless satisfied with himself: he has no desire for that of which he feels no want.' 'But who then, Diotima,' I said, 'are wisdom's lovers, if they are neither

b the wise nor the foolish?' 'A child may answer that question,' she replied; 'they are those who are in a mean between the two; and Love must be one of them. For wisdom is a most beautiful thing, and Love is of the beautiful; so it necessarily follows that Love is also a philosopher, that is, one of wisdom's lovers, and being one of wisdom's lovers, he is in a mean between the wise and the ignorant. And of this too his birth is the cause; for his father is a man of means and is wise, and his mother indigent and foolish. Such, my dear Socrates, is the nature of the spirit [*daimon*]

c Love. The error in your conception of him was very natural, and as I imagine him from what you say, you thought that Love was the beloved, not the lover, which made you think that love was all-beautiful. For the beloved is the truly beautiful, and delicate, and perfect, and blessed; but the principle of love is of another nature, and is such as I have described.'

"I said, 'Well then, madam—since you explain so well—assuming Love to be such as you say, what is his function

---

lover," were the same as "to be one of Wisdom's (romantic) lovers," somewhat as if we should understand "He is a Proust lover" to mean "He is one of Proust's lovers." This move permits Socrates/Diotima to assimilate "philosophy" (and all kinds of pursuits: see Diotima's comments on moneymaking and gymnastics below in the text) to love as generally defined in their account, the yearning for that which one ipso facto does not possess—in the case of philosophers, wisdom. The paradox of this argument is like that of someone's arguing that a philharmonic (i.e., symphony orchestra) is composed of "lovers of, i.e., seekers after, harmony," thus of persons lacking and not attaining musical harmony.

for mankind?' 'That, Socrates,' she replied, 'I will attempt d
to teach you next: his nature and birth I have already
stated; and you acknowledge that Love is of the beautiful.
But someone might ask us: "Why is Love of the beautiful,
Socrates and Diotima?"—or, rather, let me put the question more clearly and ask: When a man loves the beautiful,
what does he desire?' I answered her: 'That the beautiful
may be his.' 'Still,' she said, 'the answer suggests a further
question: What is given by the possession of beauty?' 'To
that question,' I replied, 'I have no answer ready.' 'Then,'
she said, 'let me put the word "good" in the place of "the e
beautiful," and repeat the question once more: If he who
loves, loves the good, what is it then that he loves?' 'The
possession of the good,' I said. 'And what does he gain who
possesses the good?' 'Happiness,' I replied; 'there is less difficulty in answering that question.' 'Yes,' she said, 'the
happy are made happy by the acquisition of good things. 205
Nor is there any need to ask why a man desires happiness;
the answer is already final.' 'You are right,' I said. 'And is
this wish and this desire common to all? And do all men always desire their own good, or only some men? What do
you say?' 'All men,' I replied; 'the desire is common to all.'
'Then why,' she rejoined, 'are not all men, Socrates, said to
love, but only some of them? Whereas you say that all men b
are always loving the same things.' 'I myself wonder,' I said,
'why this is.' 'There is nothing to wonder at,' she replied;
'the reason is that one part of love is separated off and receives the name of the whole, but the other parts have
other names.' 'Give an illustration,' I said. She answered
me as follows: 'There is poetry, which, as you know, is complex and manifold. All creation or passage of nonbeing into
being is poetry, which literally means "making," and the c
processes of all arts are poetic, or making, processes; and

the masters of arts are all poets or makers.' 'Very true.' 'Still,' she said, 'you know that they are not called poets, but have other names; only that portion of the art which is separated off from the rest and is concerned with music and meter is termed poetry, and they who possess poetry in this sense of the word are called poets.' 'Very true,' I said.

d 'And the same holds of love. For you may say generally that all desire of good and happiness is only "the great and subtle power of love";[37] but they who are drawn toward him by any other path, whether the path of moneymaking or gymnastics or philosophy, are not said to be in love and are not called lovers—the name of the whole is appropriated to those whose affection takes one form only; for them alone is reserved "love" and they alone are said to be "lovers." ' 'It seems most likely,' I replied, 'that you are right.' 'Yes,' she added, 'and you hear people say that lovers are seeking for

e their other half;[38] but I say that they are seeking neither for the half of themselves, nor for the whole, unless the half or the whole is also a good. And they will cut off their own hands and feet and cast them away if they are evil; for they do not love what is their own, unless by chance there should be someone who calls what belongs to him the good, and what belongs to another the evil. For there is

206 nothing that men love but the good. Is there anything?' 'Certainly I would say there is nothing.' 'Then,' she said, 'the simple truth is that men love the good.' 'Yes,' I said. 'To which must be added that they love the possession of the good?' 'Yes, that must be added.' 'And not only the possession, but the everlasting possession of the good?' 'That must be added too.' 'Then love,' she said, 'may be described

---

[37]This phrase appears to be a quotation, but its source is unknown.

[38]An unmistakable reference to Aristophanes' speech earlier, which, of course, no real Diotima long ago could possibly have known of.

generally as the love of the everlasting possession of the good?' 'That is most true.'

" 'Then if this is the eternal nature of love, can you tell b me further,' she said, 'by pursuing it *what* way and in *what* activity would the eagerness and exertion of its pursuers be rightly called love? What really is the object that they have in view? Answer me.' 'No, Diotima,' I replied, 'if I had known, I would not have been so amazed at your wisdom, nor would I have come so regularly for instruction at your hands.'[39] 'Well,' she said, 'I will teach you: The object they have in view is birth in beauty, whether of body or soul.' 'I do not understand you,' I said; 'the oracle requires an explanation.' 'I will make my meaning clearer,' she replied. 'I c mean to say that all humans are pregnant in their bodies and in their souls. There is a certain age at which human nature is desirous of giving birth—birth that must be in beauty and not in ugliness. The union of man and woman is this procreation, and it is a divine thing; for conception and generation are an immortal principle in the mortal creature, and in the inharmonious they can never be. But the ugly is always incompatible with the divine, and the d beautiful compatible. Beauty, then, is the Goddess of Destiny and the Birth Goddess, who preside at birth,[40] and therefore, when approaching beauty, the conceiving power is propitious and delighted, and dissolves, and begets and bears fruit: at the sight of ugliness she frowns and contracts

[39]Some scholars have suspected an underlying joke here: Socrates goes to the wise Diotima "regularly for instruction" in love inasmuch as she is actually a prostitute. Plato's model for such a "learned courtesan" would have been Aspasia, Pericles' mistress, whose intellectual gifts and attainments were such that she was popularly rumored to be Pericles' (uncredited) speechwriter (cf. Plato's *Menexenus*).

[40]The goddesses Moira (Destiny) and Eileithyia (Parturition) were thought to preside over every birth.

and has a sense of pain, and turns away, and shrivels up, and not without a pang refrains from conception. And this is the reason why, when the hour of conception arrives, and the teeming nature is already full, there is such a flutter
e and ecstasy about beauty, whose approach is the alleviation of the pain of travail. For love, Socrates, is not, as you imagine, the love of the beautiful only.' 'Of what, then?' 'The love of generation and of birth in beauty.' 'Yes,' I said. 'Yes, indeed,' she replied; 'but why of generation? Because to the mortal creature, generation is a sort of eternity and
207 immortality, and if, as has already been admitted, love is of the everlasting possession of the good, all men will necessarily desire immortality together with good: wherefore love is of immortality.'

"All this she taught me at various times when she spoke of love. And I remember her once saying to me, 'What is the cause, Socrates, of love, and the attendant desire? Do you not see how all animals, birds, as well as beasts, in their desire for procreation, are in agony when they take the in-
b fection of love, which begins with the desire for union; to which is added the care of offspring, on whose behalf the weakest are ready to battle against the strongest even to the uttermost, and to die for them, and will let themselves be tormented with hunger or suffer anything in order to maintain their young. Man may be supposed to act thus from reason; but why should animals have these passionate
c feelings? Can you tell me why?' Again I replied that I did not know. She said to me, 'And do you expect ever to become a master in the art of love if you do not know this?' 'But I have told you already, Diotima, that my ignorance is the reason why I come to you; for I am conscious that I want a teacher; tell me, then, the cause of this and of the other mysteries of love.' 'If you believe,' she said, 'that love

is of the immortal, as we have several times acknowledged, then do not be amazed; for here again, in the case of animals, and on the same principle, too, the mortal nature is seeking as far as is possible to be everlasting and immortal: and this is only to be attained by generation, because generation always leaves behind a new existence in the place of the old. For over the period in which each living thing is pronounced "alive," it is also said to be the same—for example, a man is called the same man from youth to old age, but in fact he is undergoing a perpetual process of loss and renewal—hair, flesh, bones, blood, and the whole body are always changing. Which is true not only of the body, but also of the soul, whose habits, tempers, opinions, desires, pleasures, pains, fears, never remain the same in any one of us, but are always coming and going. What is still more surprising is that this is true also of the bodies of knowledge that we possess, some of which are growing and developing, others fading away, so that in respect of them we are never the same; and within each body of knowledge individually the same thing happens—for there exists such a thing as "studying" only because knowledge departs from us. For "forgetting" is the departure of knowledge, while "study" preserves knowledge by introducing a renewed memory to replace the knowledge that has left, with the result that it appears to be the same. For this is the way in which all mortal things are preserved, not absolutely the same always, as the divine is, but through substitution—the old worn-out mortality leaving another new and similar existence behind. And by this mechanism, Socrates, the mortal body, or mortal anything, has its share of immortality (the immortal has it by a different mechanism). So do not then be amazed at the love that all men have of their offspring; for that universal love and interest is for the sake of immortality.'

"I was astonished at her words, and said: 'Is this really true, O thou wise Diotima?' And she answered with all the authority of an accomplished sophist: 'Of that, Socrates, you may be assured—think only of the ambition of men, and you will wonder at the senselessness of their ways, unless you consider how they are stirred by the love of an immortality of fame. They are ready to run risks far greater than they would have run for their children, and to spend money and undergo any sort of toil, and even to die, for the sake of "leaving behind them a name which shall be eternal."[41] Do you imagine that Alcestis would have died to save Admetus, or Achilles to avenge Patroclus, or you Athenians' own Codrus[42] in order to preserve the kingdom for his sons, if they had not imagined that the memory of their virtues, which still survives among us, would be immortal? No,' she said, 'I am persuaded that all men do all things, and the better they are the more they do them, in the hope of winning a glorious fame of immortal virtue; for they desire the immortal. Those who are pregnant in the body only betake themselves to women and beget children—this is the character of their love; their offspring, as they hope, will preserve their memory and give them the blessedness and immortality which they desire for all future time. But those who are pregnant in their souls—for there certainly exist men who generate within their souls, rather than in their bodies—conceive the kinds of things that it is proper for the soul to conceive and give birth to. And what things are these? Wisdom and virtue in general. And such creators are poets and all artists who are deserv-

[41]A verse, from an unknown work, in the epic meter.

[42]Mythical king of Athens who, when it was foretold to an enemy that Athens could not be conquered if Codrus were killed, disguised himself and allowed himself to be killed, and thus saved the Athenians from subjugation.

ing of the name inventor. But the greatest and fairest sort of wisdom by far is that which is concerned with the ordering of states and families, and which is called temperance and justice. And he who in youth has the seed of these implanted in him and is himself inspired, when he comes b to maturity desires to beget and generate. He wanders about seeking beauty in which to beget offspring—for in ugliness he will beget nothing—and because he is in pain of travail he embraces the beautiful rather than the ugly body; above all, when he finds a beautiful and noble and talented soul, he embraces the two in one person, and to such a one he is full of speech about virtue and the nature and c pursuits of a good man; and he tries to educate him; and by touching the beautiful and consorting with him he gives birth to and propagates that which he had conceived long before, both when with him and through recollecting him when apart, and together with him he tends that which was brought forth; and they are married by a far nearer tie and have a closer friendship than those who beget mortal children, for the children who are their common offspring are fairer and more immortal. Who, when he thinks of Homer d and Hesiod and other great poets, would not rather have their children than ordinary human ones? Who would not emulate them in the creation of children such as theirs, which have preserved their memory and given them everlasting glory? Or who would not have such children as Lycurgus[43] left behind him to be the saviors not only of Lacedaemon but of Hellas, as one may say? There is Solon, too, who is the revered father of Athenian laws; and many others there are in many other places, both among Hellenes e and barbarians, who have given to the world many noble

---

[43]The legendary framer of the Spartan constitution.

works, and have been the parents of virtue of every kind;
and many temples have been raised in their honor for the
sake of children such as theirs; whereas none were ever
raised in honor of anyone for the sake of his mortal children.

" 'These are the lesser mysteries of love,' she said, 'into
which you also, Socrates, may be initiated; to the greater
210 and more hidden ones which are the crown of these, and to
which, if you pursue them in a right spirit, they will lead, I
know not whether you will be able to attain. But I will do
my utmost to inform you, and do you follow if you can.[44]
For he who would proceed aright in this matter should
begin in youth to visit beautiful bodies; and first, if he is
guided by his instructor aright, to love one such body only,
and in it he should engender beautiful thoughts; and soon
he will of himself perceive that the beauty of one body is
b akin to the beauty of another; and then, if beauty of appearance is his pursuit, how foolish would he be not to recognize that the beauty present in all bodily forms is one
and the same! And when he perceives this, he will abate his
violent love of the one, which he will despise and deem a
small thing, and will become a lover of all beautiful bodily
forms; in the next stage he will consider that the beauty of
the soul is more honorable than the beauty of the body, so
that someone even of slight beauty, but virtuous in soul,
c satisfies him, and he loves and cares for him, and brings to
birth arguments of the kind to improve the young, until he
is compelled to contemplate and see the beauty of institutions and laws, and to understand that the beauty of them
all is of one family, and that personal beauty is a trifle; and
after laws and institutions he will go on to the sciences, that

[44]From this point through to the end of her speech, Diotima's language draws
heavily on that of the Eleusinian mysteries, celebrated annually in Attica.

he may see their beauty, being not servilely in love with d
the beauty of one youth or man or institution, himself a
slave, mean and small-minded, but drawing toward and
contemplating the vast sea of beauty, he will create many
fair and noble thoughts and notions in boundless love of
wisdom; until on that shore he grows and waxes strong, and
at last the vision is revealed to him of a single science,
which is the science of beauty everywhere. To this I will e
proceed; please give me your very best attention.

" 'He who has been instructed thus far in the things of
love, and who has learned to see the beautiful in due order
and succession, when he comes toward the end will suddenly have a vision of wondrous beauty (and this, Socrates,
is the ultimate aim of all our former toils)—a beauty that
in the first place is everlasting, not growing and decaying, 211
or waxing and waning; secondly, not beautiful in one point
of view and ugly in another, or at one time or in one relation or at one place beautiful, at another time or in another
relation or at another place ugly, as if beautiful to some
and ugly to others, nor will beauty appear to him in the
likeness of a face or hands or any other part of the bodily
frame, or in any form of expression or knowledge, or exist-
ing in any other being, as for example, in an animal, or in
heaven, or in earth, or in any other place; but beauty will b
be revealed to him to be absolute, separate, simple, and
everlasting, which, without diminution and without in-
crease, or any change, is imparted to the ever-growing and
perishing beauties of all other things. He who, ascending
from these by means of proper and correct pederastic love,
begins to perceive *that* beauty is not far from the end. And
the correct order of going, or being led by another, to the c
things of love is to begin from the beauties of earth and
mount ever upward for the sake of that other beauty, using

these as steps only, and from one going on to two, and from two to all beautiful bodies, and from beautiful bodies to beautiful practices, and from beautiful practices to beautiful notions, until from beautiful notions he arrives at the notion of absolute beauty, and at last knows what the

d essence of beauty is. This, my dear Socrates,' said the stranger from Mantineia, 'is that life above all others which man should live, in the contemplation of beauty absolute; a beauty that, if you once beheld it, you would see not to be like that of gold, and garments, and beautiful boys and youths, whose presence now entrances you; and you and many a one would be content to live seeing them only and conversing with them, without food or drink, if that were possible—you only want to look at them and to be with them. But what if man had eyes to see the true

e beauty—the divine beauty, I mean, pure and clear and unalloyed, not clogged with the pollutions of human flesh and complexion and all the other vanities of mortal life—do you think it an ignoble life for a person to be gazing *there*

212 and contemplating *that* with the suitable instrument, the mind's eye, and consorting with *that*? Do you not perceive that *there* alone will it happen to him, when he sees the beautiful with that instrument with which it must be seen, to give birth not to images of virtue, since he is not laying hold of an image, but to her true progeny, since he has hold of true virtue? And is it not possible for him, by giving birth to and nourishing true virtue, to become the beloved of God, and to become, if any of humankind does, immortal?'

b   "Such, Phaedrus—and I speak not only to you, but to all of you—were the words of Diotima; and I am persuaded of their truth. And being persuaded of them, I try to persuade others that in the attainment of this end, human nature will not easily find a helper better than Love. And therefore, also, I say that every man ought to honor him as I myself honor him, and I myself honor his works and cultivate them intensively, and exhort others to do the same, and praise the power and manliness of Love, according to the measure of my ability, now and forever.

"The words which I have spoken, you, Phaedrus, may c call an encomium of Love, or anything else you please."

When Socrates had done speaking, the company applauded, and Aristophanes was beginning to say something in answer to the allusion that Socrates had made to his own speech, when suddenly there was a great knocking at the door of the house, as if by revelers, and the voice of a flute-girl was heard. Agathon told the slaves to go and see who were the intruders. "If they are friends of ours," he d said, "invite them in, but if not, say that the drinking is over." A little while afterward they heard the voice of Alcibiades in the court, intensely drunk, bellowing and demanding, "Where is Agathon? Lead me to Agathon." And at length, supported by the flute-girl and some of his attendants, he found his way to them. "Gentlemen! Hello!" he said, appearing at the door crowned with an extravagant e garland of ivy and violets, his head flowing with ribbons. "Will you have a very drunken man as a companion of your revels? Or shall I crown Agathon, which was my intention in coming, and go away? For I was unable to come yesterday, and therefore I am here today, carrying on my head these ribbons, in order that, taking them from my own head, I may crown the head of this most beautiful and most accomplished of men. Will you laugh at me because I am drunk? Yet I know very well that I am speaking the truth, although you may laugh. But first tell me, if I come 213 in, shall we have the understanding of which I spoke? Will you drink with me or not?"

The company were vociferous in begging that he would take his place among them, and Agathon specially invited him. Thereupon he was led in by the people who were with him; and as he was being led, intending to crown Agathon, he took the ribbons from his own head and held them in front of his eyes; he was thus prevented from seeing Socrates, who made way for him when he saw him, and

b Alcibiades took the vacant place between Agathon and Socrates, and in taking the place he embraced Agathon and crowned him. "Take off his sandals," said Agathon, "and let him make a third on the same couch."

"By all means; but who makes the third partner in our revels?" said Alcibiades, turning round and starting up as he caught sight of Socrates. "By Heracles," he said, "what is this? Is Socrates here? You lay here, once again ambush-

c ing me, as your way is, leaping out where I least expected you would be. And now what have you to say for yourself: why are you lying *here,* where I perceive that you have contrived to find a place not by a joker or lover of jokes, like Aristophanes, but by the most beautiful of the company?"

Socrates turned to Agathon and said, "I must ask you to protect me, Agathon; for my love affair with this man has become quite a troublesome problem. Since I became his

d lover, I have never been allowed to speak to any other beauty, or so much as to look at him. If I do, he goes wild with envy and jealousy, and not only abuses me but can hardly keep his hands off me, and at this moment he may do me some harm. Please see to this, and either establish peace between him and me, or, if he attempts violence, protect me, as I am in bodily fear of his mad and passionate attempts."

"There can never be reconciliation between you and

me," said Alcibiades; "but for the present I will defer your punishment. And I must beg you, Agathon, to give me back e some of the ribbons that I may crown this extraordinary head of his—I would not have him complain of me for crowning you, and neglecting him, who in conversation is the conqueror of all mankind; and this not only once, as you were the day before yesterday, but always." Whereupon, taking some of the ribbons, he crowned Socrates, and again reclined.

Then he said, "You seem, my friends, to be sober, which is completely intolerable; you must drink—for that was the agreement under which I was admitted—and I choose as master of the feast, until you are well drunk, myself. Let us have a large goblet, Agathon, or rather," he said, addressing the slave, "bring me that wine cooler." The wine cooler that had caught his eye was a vessel holding more than two quarts—this he filled and drank off,[45] and he then bade the 214 slave fill it again for Socrates. "Observe, my friends," said Alcibiades, "that this ingenious trick of mine will have no effect on Socrates, for he can drink any quantity of wine and not be at all nearer being drunk." Socrates took a drink after the slave poured for him.

Eryximachus said, "What is this, Alcibiades? Are we to have neither conversation nor singing over our cups, but b simply to drink as if we were parched?"

Alcibiades replied, "Hail, worthy son of a most wise and worthy sire!"

"The same to you," said Eryximachus; "but what shall we do?"

"That I leave to you," said Alcibiades. " 'For a doctor's

[45]It is beyond normal human capacity to gulp down two quarts of wine when already "intensely drunk." Such superhuman over-consumption is characteristic of Heracles, as depicted on the comic stage.

life is worth many others.'"[46] Therefore prescribe and we will obey. What do you want?"

"Well," said Eryximachus, "before you appeared we had passed a resolution that each one of us in turn should make
c a speech in praise of Love, and as good a one as he could. The turn was passed round from left to right; and as all of us have spoken, and you have not spoken but have well drunken, you ought to speak, and then impose upon Socrates any task you please, and he on his right-hand neighbor, and so on."

"That is good, Eryximachus," said Alcibiades, "and yet the comparison of a drunken man's speech with those of sober men is hardly fair; and I should like to know, O holy one, whether you really believe what Socrates was just now
d saying; for I can assure you that the very reverse is the fact, and that if I praise anyone but himself in his presence, whether god or man, he will hardly keep his fists off me."

"Hush," said Socrates.

"No, by god, don't contradict me," said Alcibiades, "for with *you* here I couldn't praise *anyone* else."

"Well, then," said Eryximachus, "if you like, praise Socrates."

e "What do you think, Eryximachus?" said Alcibiades. "Shall I attack him and inflict his punishment in front of you all?"

"Hey! Just what do you have in mind?" said Socrates. "Are you going to make fun of me? Is that the meaning of your praise?"

"I am going to speak the truth, if you will permit me."

"I not only permit, but I command you to speak the truth."

[46]*Iliad* 11. 514.

"Then I will begin at once," said Alcibiades, "and if I say anything that is not true, you may interrupt me, if you will, and say, 'That is a lie,' though my intention is to speak the truth. But you must not wonder if I speak every which way 215 as things come into my mind; for the fluent and orderly enumeration of all your singularities is not an easy task for a man in my condition.

"And now, gentlemen, I shall praise Socrates in a figure that will appear to him to be a caricature, and yet I speak not to make fun of him but only for the truth's sake. I say that he is exactly like the busts of Silenus, which are set up b in the statuaries' shops, holding pipes and flutes in their mouths; and when they are made to open in two, they are revealed to have images of gods inside them. I say also that he is like Marsyas the satyr. You yourself will not deny, Socrates, that your face is like that of a satyr. Yes, and there is a resemblance in other points too. For example, you are a bully, as I can prove by witnesses, if you will not confess. And are you not a flute player? That you are, and a performer far more wonderful than Marsyas. He indeed with instruments used to charm the souls of men by the power c of his breath, and the players of his music do so still: for the melodies of Olympus are derived from Marsyas,[47] who taught them to Olympus, and these, whether they are played by a great master or by a miserable flute-girl, have a power that no others have; they alone possess the soul and reveal those who have need of gods and mysteries, because their music is divine. But you produce the same effect with your words only, and do not require the flute: that is the only difference between you and him. When we hear d any other speaker, even a very good one, he produces ab-

---

[47]On Marsyas and Olympus, see note 11 to the *Ion*, above.

solutely no effect upon us, or not much, whereas the merest fragments of your words, even at secondhand, and however imperfectly repeated, amaze and possess the souls of every man, woman, and child who comes within hearing of them. And if I were not afraid that you would think me hopelessly drunk, I would have testified under oath to the influence that they have always had and still
e have over me. For my heart leaps within me, more than that of any Corybantic reveler, and my eyes rain tears when I hear this man's talk. And I observe that many others are affected in the same manner. I have heard Pericles and other great orators, and I thought that they spoke well, but I never had any similar feeling; my soul was not thrown into a tumult by them, nor was it angry at the thought of my own slavish state. But this Marsyas has
216 often brought me to such a pass that I have felt as if I could hardly endure the life that I am leading (this, Socrates, you will admit); and I am still now conscious that if I should lend my ears to him, I would not withstand him but would suffer the same thing again. For he makes me confess that I ought not to live as I do, neglecting the wants of my own soul, and busying myself with the concerns of the Athenians; therefore I hold my ears and tear my unwilling self away from him, in order that I not grow old sitting here at his feet. And he is the only person who ever made me
b ashamed, which you might think not to be in my nature; there is no one else before whom I feel shame. For I know that I cannot answer him or say that I ought not to do as he bids, but when I leave his presence, the love of advancement gets the better of me. And therefore I run away from him like a fugitive, and when I see him, I am ashamed of what I have confessed to him. Many a time have I wished
c that he were dead, and yet I know that I should be much

more sorry than glad if he were to die: so that I am at my wit's end.

"And this is what I and many others have suffered from the flute-playing of this satyr. Yet hear me once more while I show you how exact the image is, and how marvelous his power. For let me tell you, none of you know him, but I will reveal him to you; having begun, I must go d on. You have all observed that he is sexually attracted to the beautiful. He is always with them and is always being smitten by them, and then again he knows nothing and is ignorant of all things—such is the appearance he puts on. Is he not like a Silenus in this? To be sure, he is: his outer mask is the carved head of the Silenus; but, O my companions in drink, when he is opened, what temperance there is residing within! I can assure you that it doesn't matter a whit to him if a person is beautiful—he is contemptuous of the whole thing to a degree not one of you could imagine; likewise with wealth and any other attribute worshiped by e the masses. He regards all these possessions as worthless, and, I tell you, he regards *us* as worthless: all his life is spent mocking and flouting mankind. But there is seriousness in him. I don't know if any of you have seen him opened up, and the sacred relics that lie within; but I saw once, and they seemed so golden and of such fascinating beauty that 217 I concluded that whatever Socrates commanded must be done.

"Now, I fancied that he was seriously enamored of my youthful beauty, and I thought that I should therefore have a grand opportunity of hearing him tell what he knew, for I had a wonderful opinion of the attractions of my youth. In the prosecution of this design, when I next went to him, I sent away the attendant who usually accompanied me (I b will confess the whole truth, and beg you to listen; and if I speak falsely, then you, Socrates, expose the falsehood). Well, he and I were alone together, and I thought that when there was nobody with us, I should hear him speak the language that lovers use to their loves when they are by themselves, and I was delighted. Nothing of the sort; he conversed as usual, and spent the day with me and then

c went away. Afterward I challenged him to the palaestra; and he wrestled and closed with me several times when there was no one present; I fancied that I might succeed in this manner. Not a bit; I made no headway with him. Last, as I had failed hitherto, I thought that I must make a direct assault and, as I had begun, not give him up, but see how matters stood between him and me. So I invited him to sup with me, just as if he were a comely youth and I a designing lover. He was not easily persuaded to come; he did, however, after a while accept the invitation, and when he came the first time, he wanted to go away at once as soon as

d supper was over, and I had not the nerve to detain him. The second time, still in pursuit of my design, after we had supped, I went on conversing far into the night, and when he wanted to go away, I pretended that the hour was too late and insisted that he remain. So he lay down on the couch next to mine, the same on which he had supped, and there was no one but ourselves sleeping in the apartment.

e All this may be told without shame to anyone. But what follows I could hardly tell you if I were sober. Yet as the proverb says, 'In vino veritas,' both with boys and without them;[48] and therefore I must speak. Nor, again, should I be justified in concealing the lofty actions of Socrates when I

---

[48]The exact meaning of the proverb quoted, or adapted, by Alcibiades—especially the words "both with boys and without them" (which can also mean "with slaves and without them")—is not known.

come to praise him. Moreover I have felt the serpent's sting; and he who has suffered, as they say, is willing to relate his sufferings to his fellow sufferers only, as they alone will be likely to understand him, and will not be extreme in 218 judging the sayings or doings that have been wrung from his agony. For I have been bitten by more than a viper's tooth; I have known in my soul, or in my heart, or in some other part, that worst of pangs, more violent in a not-untalented youth than any serpent's tooth, the pang of philosophy, which will make a man say or do anything. And you whom I see around me, you Phaedruses and Agathons and Eryximachuses and Pausaniases and Aris- b todemuses and Aristophaneses,[49] all of you, and I need not say Socrates himself, have had experience of the same madness and passion in your longing after wisdom. Therefore listen and excuse my doings then and my sayings now. But let the house slaves and other profane and unmannered persons close up the doors of their ears.

"When the lamp was put out and the slaves had gone away, I thought that I must be plain with him and have no c more ambiguity. So I gave him a shake, and I said, 'Socrates, are you asleep?' 'No,' he said. 'Do you know what I am meditating?' 'What are you meditating?' he said. 'I think,' I replied, 'that of all the lovers I have ever had, you are the only one who is worthy of me, and you appear to be too modest to raise the subject with me. Now, this is how matters stand with me: I feel that I would be a fool to refuse you this or any other favor, and therefore I come to lay at your feet all that I have and all that my friends have, in the hope that you will assist me in the way of virtue, which I d

[49]The plurals suggest "Phaedrus and people like him," etc., but also raise the possibility that Alcibiades is seeing double.

prize above all things, and in which I believe that you can help me better than anyone else. And I would certainly have more reason to be ashamed of what wise men would say if I were to refuse to gratify a man such as you, than of what the world, who are mostly fools, would say of me if I did.' To these words he replied in the ironical manner which is so characteristic of him: 'Alcibiades, my friend, you are, as it seems, a very shrewd bargainer, if what you

e say is true, and if there really is in me any power by which you may become better; obviously you must see in me some rare beauty of a kind infinitely higher than any that I see in you. And therefore, if you mean to share with me and to exchange beauty for beauty, you will have greatly the advantage of me; you will gain true beauty in return for

219 the appearance of beauty—like Diomedes, "gold in exchange for bronze."[50] But look again, blessed friend, and see whether you have failed to notice that I am in fact nothing at all. The mind's eye begins to grow critical when the bodily eye fails, and it will be a long time before you get old.' Hearing this, I said, 'I have told you my purpose, which is quite serious, and so please consider what you think best for you and me.' 'That is good,' he said; 'at some

b other time then we will consider and act as seems best about this and about other matters.' At which words I fancied that he was smitten, and that the words I had uttered like arrows had wounded him, and so, without waiting to hear more, I got up and, throwing my coat about him, crept under his threadbare cloak, as the time of year was

---

[50]In *Iliad* 6. 232–236 the Trojan ally Glaucus offers as a gesture of guest-friendship to exchange armor with the Greek Diomedes: Glaucus' armor was made of gold, Diomedes' of bronze, and Homer comments after the exchange is made that Zeus had removed Glaucus' wits. "Gold for bronze" (or "Bronze for gold") became and remains proverbial.

winter, and there I lay during the night, having this won- c
derful monster in my arms. This again, Socrates, will not
be denied by you. And yet, notwithstanding all, he was so
superior to my solicitations, so contemptuous and derisive
and disdainful of my beauty—which really, as I fancied,
had some attractions—hear, O judges, for judges you shall
be of the haughty virtue of Socrates: in the morning (let
all the gods and goddesses be my witnesses) I got up, together with Socrates, having passed the night no differently than if I had shared a bed with a father or an elder d
brother.

"What do you suppose must have been my feelings,
after this rejection, at the thought of my own dishonor?
And yet I could not help wondering at his natural temperance and self-restraint and manliness. I never imagined
that I could have met with a man such as he is in wisdom
and endurance. And therefore I could not be angry with
him or renounce his company, any more than I could hope
to win him. For I well know that if Ajax could not be e
wounded by steel, much less could he by money; and my
only chance of captivating him by my personal attractions
had failed. So I was at my wit's end; no one was ever more
hopelessly enslaved by another. All this happened before
he and I went on the expedition to Potidaea;[51] there we
messed together, and I had the opportunity of observing
his extraordinary power of sustaining hardship. His endurance was simply incredible when, being cut off from
our supplies, we were compelled to go without food—on
such occasions, which often happen in time of war, he was
superior not only to me but to everybody; there was no one

---

[51]A coastal city in Northern Greece, subject to Athens. The expedition was
sent in 432 B.C. to put down a rebellion.

220   to be compared with him. Yet at feasts, in times of abundance, he was the only person who had any real powers of enjoyment; in particular, though not willing to drink, he could, if compelled, beat us all at that; and what is most astounding of all, no human being has ever seen Socrates drunk—and his powers, if I am not mistaken, will be tested tonight before long. His fortitude in enduring cold was also

b   extraordinary. There was a severe frost, for the winter in that region is really tremendous, and everybody else either remained indoors or, if they went out, had on an amazing quantity of clothes, and were well shod, and had their feet swathed in felt and fleeces: in the midst of this, Socrates, with his bare feet on the ice and in his ordinary dress, marched better than the other soldiers, who had shoes, and they looked daggers at him because he seemed to despise them.

"I have told you one tale, and now I must tell you an-

c   other, which is worth hearing, 'of the doings and sufferings of this mighty man,'[52] while he was on the expedition. One morning he was thinking about something that he could not resolve; he would not give it up, but continued thinking from early dawn until noon—there he stood fixed in thought; and at noon attention was drawn to him, and the rumor ran through the wondering crowd that Socrates had been standing and thinking about something ever since the break of day. At last, in the evening after supper, some Ion-

d   ians, out of curiosity (I should explain that this was not in winter but in summer), brought out their mats and slept in the open air in order to watch him and see whether he would stand all night. There he stood until the following morning; and with the return of light he offered up a

[52]*Odyssey* 4. 242, spoken in reference to Odysseus.

prayer to the sun, and went his way. I will also tell, if you wish—and indeed I am bound to tell—of his courage in battle; for who but he saved my life? Now this was the engagement in which I received the prize of valor: for I was wounded and he would not leave me, but he rescued me and my weapons; and he ought to have received the prize of valor, which the generals wanted to confer on me partly on account of my rank, and I told them so (this, again, Socrates will not impeach or deny), but he was more eager than the generals that I and not he should have the prize. There was another occasion on which his behavior was very remarkable—in the flight of the army after the battle of Delium, where he served among the heavy-armed infantry. He and Laches[53] were retreating, for the troops were in flight, and I met them and told them not to be discouraged, and promised to remain with them. On this occasion I had a better opportunity of seeing him than at Potidaea (for I was myself on horseback, and therefore comparatively out of danger), especially of seeing how much he surpassed Laches in presence of mind. He seemed to me there, Aristophanes, just as he is in the streets of Athens, as you describe,[54] 'stalking like a pelican, and looking from side to side,' calmly contemplating enemies as well as friends, and making very intelligible to anybody, even from a distance, that whoever attacked *this* man would be guaranteed to meet with a stout resistance; and in this way he and his companion escaped—for as a rule this is the sort of man who is never touched in war; only those are pursued who are running away headlong.

[53]An Athenian with a distinguished military career.
[54]Alcibiades adapts line 362 of Aristophanes' viciously hostile comedy about Socrates, *The Clouds*.

"Many are the marvels that I might narrate in praise of Socrates; most of his ways might perhaps be paralleled in another man, but his absolute unlikeness to any human being that is or ever has been is perfectly astonishing. You may imagine Brasidas[55] and others to have been like Achilles; or you may imagine Nestor and Antenor[56] to have been like Pericles; and the same may be said of other

d famous men, but of this strange being and his talk you will never be able to find any likeness, however remote, either among men who now are or who ever have been—other than that which I have already suggested of Silenus and the satyrs; and they represent in a figure not only himself, but his words. For although I forgot to mention this to you

e before, his words are like the images of Silenus that open; they are ridiculous when you first hear them; he clothes himself in language that is like the skin of the wanton satyr—for his talk is of pack asses and smiths and cobblers and curriers, and he is always repeating the same things in the same words, so that any ignorant or inexperienced

222 person might feel disposed to laugh at him; but he who opens the bust and sees what is within will find that they are the only words that have a meaning in them, and also the most divine, abounding in beautiful images of virtue, and of the widest comprehension, or rather extending to the whole duty of him who would be a good and honorable man.

"This, friends, is my praise of Socrates. I have added my blame of him and told you of his ill-treatment of me; and

b he has ill-treated not only me, but Charmides the son of Glaucon, and Euthydemus the son of Diocles, and many

[55]Spartan general who died in 422 B.C.
[56]The legendary wise councillors of the Greeks and Trojans, respectively, during the Trojan War.

others in the same way—beginning as their lover, he has ended by reversing roles and making *them* pay their addresses to *him*. Wherefore I say to you, Agathon, 'Be not deceived by him; learn from me and take warning, and do not be "a fool and learn by experience," as the proverb says.' "[57]

When Alcibiades had finished, there was a laugh at his c outspokenness; for he seemed to be still in love with Socrates. "You are sober, Alcibiades," said Socrates, "or you would never have gone to such lengths to hide the purpose of your praises, for all this long story is only an ingenious circumlocution, of which the point comes in almost as an afterthought at the end, as if you hadn't spoken the whole speech with this aim in mind: to cause a quarrel between me and Agathon. Your notion is that I ought to love you d and nobody else, and that you and only you ought to love Agathon. But the plot of this Satyric or Silenic drama has been detected, and you must not allow him, Agathon, to set us at variance."

"I believe you are right," said Agathon, "and I am dis- e posed to think that his intention in placing himself between you and me was only to divide us; but he shall gain nothing by that move; for I will go and lie on the couch next to you."

"Yes, yes," replied Socrates, "by all means come here and lie on the couch below me."

"Oh no!" said Alcibiades. "Once again I am abused by this man; he is determined to get the better of me at every turn. I beseech you, at least allow Agathon to lie between us."

[57]The proverb alluded to occurs at *Iliad* 17. 32 (among other places): "When something is over and done even a fool recognizes it."

"Certainly not," said Socrates; "as you praised me, and I in turn ought to praise my neighbor on the right, he will be out of order and praise me again, won't he, when he ought rather to be praised by me. So I must entreat you to con-
223 sent to this, and not be jealous, for I have a great desire to praise the youth."

"Hurrah!" cried Agathon. "There is no possibility that I will stay here, Alcibiades, but I will change places immediately, in order to be praised by Socrates."

"This is *just* what I was talking about—the usual way," said Alcibiades; "where Socrates is, no one else has any chance with the pretty; and now how readily has he invented a specious reason for attracting Agathon to himself."

b   Agathon arose in order to take his place on the couch by Socrates, when suddenly a band of revelers entered and spoiled the order of the banquet. Someone who was going out having left the door open, they had found their way in and made themselves at home; great confusion ensued, and everyone was compelled to drink large quantities of wine. Aristodemus said that Eryximachus, Phaedrus, and others went away—he himself fell asleep and, as the nights were

c long, took a good rest: he was awakened toward daybreak by a crowing of cocks, and when he awoke, the others were either asleep or had gone away; there remained only Socrates, Aristophanes, and Agathon, who were drinking out of a large goblet, which they passed round, and Socrates was discoursing to them. Aristodemus was only

d half awake, and he did not hear the beginning of the discourse; the chief thing that he remembered was Socrates compelling the other two to acknowledge that the genius of comedy was the same as that of tragedy, and that the true artist in tragedy was an artist in comedy also. To this they were constrained to assent, being drowsy, and not quite following the argument. And first of all Aristophanes dropped off, then, when the day was already dawning, Agathon. Socrates, having seen them to sleep, rose to depart, Aristodemus, as his manner was, following him. At the Lyceum he took a bath, and passed the day as usual. In the evening he retired to rest at his own home.

APOLOGY

*In 399 Socrates was prosecuted on a charge of impiety. The word
"apology" in this context has nothing to do with saying you are
sorry, but is simply Greek for "defense speech," which is what the
present work purports to be: the speech spoken by Socrates in his
trial. The only other speaker in the work is Meletus, one of Socrates'
prosecutors, briefly interrogated by Socrates. Two briefer speeches
are appended, one spoken after the rendering of the verdict (guilty),
the other after sentencing (death). Socrates was executed a month
later.*

How you, men of Athens,[1] have been affected by my ac-   17
cusers, I cannot tell; but I know that they almost made me
forget who I was—so persuasively did they speak; and yet
they have hardly uttered a word of truth. But of the many
lies told by them, there was one that quite amazed me—I
mean when they said that you should be on your guard and
not allow yourselves to be deceived by the force of my eloquence. To say this, when they were certain to be detected   b
as soon as I opened my mouth and proved myself to be
anything but a great speaker, certainly did seem to me to
be extremely shameless—unless by "the force of eloquence" they mean "the force of truth"; for if that is their

[1]The jury before whom Socrates was tried was composed of five hundred
Athenian citizens. There was no presiding magistrate, so the jury served also as
judge. The procedure was straightforward: the prosecution made its speeches and
presented its witnesses, then the defense likewise; the jury then voted its verdict;
in the event of a guilty finding, the prosecution proposed a penalty, and the defense made a counterproposal; the jury then chose between them. All was over
within a day.

meaning, I must admit that I am eloquent at a very superior level to theirs. Well, as I was saying, they have scarcely spoken the truth at all; from me, you shall hear the whole truth, but not delivered the way they did theirs, in a virtuoso oration tricked out with fine words and phrases. No, you will hear improvised arguments spoken in whatever words occur to me at the moment, for I am confident in the justice of my case—and don't any of you expect otherwise: at my time of life I ought not to come before you, men of Athens, contriving ingenious arguments like an adolescent boy. But I must urgently beg of you to grant me this favor—if you hear me defending myself in the same language that I customarily use in the agora,[2] at the bankers' stands, and elsewhere, I ask you not to be surprised, and to restrain yourselves from any outcry on this account. For it's like this: I am more than seventy years of age, and this is the first time I have appeared before a court of law; the language of this place is quite literally foreign to me. Therefore, just as you would indulge me if I really were a foreigner, and spoke in the dialect and manner I had been brought up in, so I ask you, especially in view of the present circumstances, the favor—a fair one, I think—of letting pass the style of my speech, which may or may not be good, and instead to consider and attend only to whether what I say is just or not. For that is the proper measure of a judge, as it is of a speaker to speak the truth.

It is fair that I should first respond to the first charges falsely laid against me, and to my first accusers; then I will go on to the later ones. For I have had many accusers, starting from long ago in the past, who have accused me falsely

[2]The marketplace of Athens, in effect, the center of town. Socrates spent much of his time there, conversing, as described later in the speech.

to you over many years; and I am more afraid of them than of Anytus and his associates, who are dangerous too, in their own way.[3] But far more dangerous are the others, who, taking most of you into their tutelage when you were still children, tried to turn you to their way of thinking, and made utterly false accusations against me, saying, "There is a certain man Socrates, a 'wise man,' a theorizer about celestial phenomena, and an expert in everything subterranean, too; he makes the worse argument appear c the better." The men who have disseminated this slander are the accusers whom I fear; for their hearers are apt to think that people who investigate these kinds of things also do not believe in the existence of the gods. Furthermore, these accusers are numerous, and their charges against me are of long standing now, and they were made by them in the days when you would be most impressionable—in childhood, or it may have been in youth—and the case went by default, since there was no one there to speak for the defense. And what is hardest of all is that I cannot ascertain and tell the names of my accusers, except in the d chance case of a comic poet.[4] Those who have persuaded you out of envy and malice—and others who were themselves persuaded and then persuaded yet others—all this class of men are most difficult to deal with; for I cannot have any of them up on the stand here, and cross-examine them, and so I must literally fight with shadows in my own defense, and cross-examine when there is no one answering. Accordingly, I will ask you to take it from me that my

[3]Three men brought the case against Socrates: Anytus, a very prominent politician of late fifth and early fourth century B.C. Athens; Meletus (identity uncertain); and Lycon (again little is known for sure). Meletus appears to have taken the lead, and is singled out as the chief prosecutor by Socrates.

[4]That is, Aristophanes, discussed by Socrates just below.

opponents are of two kinds: one recent, the other from the
e past; and I hope that you will see the propriety of my answering the latter first, for these accusations you heard
long before others, and much more often.

Well, then, I must make my defense, and try to remove
19 from your minds in a short time a slander which you have
had a long time to take in. I would like for that to happen,
if it would be at all for my good and yours, and for my defense to be successful. But the task is not an easy one; I understand that entirely. Nevertheless, though the outcome
must be as the god pleases, still the law must be obeyed,
and a defense must be undertaken.

I will begin at the beginning, and ask what is the accusation that has given rise to the slander of me, which in turn
b has encouraged Meletus to bring this charge against me.
Well, what do the slanderers say? They shall be my prosecutors, and this is the affadavit they swear against me:
"Socrates is guilty of—and gives no rest to himself or others in—investigating matters subterranean and celestial, in
c making the worse argument appear stronger, and in teaching these same things to others."[5] It is something like that.
You have yourselves seen such things in the comedy of
Aristophanes, who brought onto stage a man whom he calls
Socrates, swinging about in a basket and claiming that he is
walking on the air, and talking a great deal of nonsense on
subjects about which I make no pretense of knowing anything, great or small[6]—not that I mean to speak disparag-

---

[5]The "crimes" Socrates is pretending to be charged with here in the "affadavit" of these early informal "prosecutors" are, of course, not legal crimes at all;
so Socrates dilutes the legal language he ascribes to the "affadavit" ("Socrates is
guilty of ...") with language expressive simply of anti-intellectual prejudice and
intolerance ("gives no rest to himself or others ...").

[6]On Aristophanes, see the Dramatis Personae of the *Symposium*, above. He

ingly of anyone who possesses such knowledge; god forbid that Meletus ever bring so great a charge against me. But the simple truth is, Athenians, that I have nothing to do with physical speculations. As witnesses to the truth of this, I offer most of you present; and I think it right that you instruct one another very clearly about this, all of you who have ever heard me talking—many of you have—so make it clear to one another if any of you have ever heard me talk, either a little or a lot, on such subjects.... You have heard their answer. And from what they say of this part of the charge, you will be able to judge the truth of the rest.

In fact, none of these charges is true, nor if you have heard anyone say that I am a teacher of men, and take money, does this accusation have any more truth in it than the other. Though this too seems to me a fine thing, if a person should really be able to instruct mankind. There is Gorgias of Leontium, and Prodicus of Ceos, and Hippias of Elis,[7] who go around to each of the cities, and are able to persuade the young men to leave their own citizens, whose protégés they might be for free, and come to them whom they not only pay, but are thankful to be allowed to pay. Why, there is at this very moment a Parian philosopher residing in Athens, of whom I have recently heard. The way I came to hear of him was this: I ran into a man who has

staged a play, devoted to ridiculing Socrates, called *The Clouds*, in the late 420s. It was not a popular success: a revised second version survives; the Socrates therein depicted bears little resemblance to the man we meet in the works of Plato. In the *Symposium* Plato makes Socrates and Aristophanes guests at the same dinner party; at the end of that work they are shown engaging in perfectly companionable conversation. It is hard to know how to reconcile that account with this one.

[7]These three and Protagoras are the four greatest of the so-called sophists, active in the mid- to late fifth century B.C.; on Gorgias see note 41 to the *Phaedrus* and note 16 to the *Symposium;* on the others see the Dramatis Personae of the *Protagorus.*

spent more money on the sophists than the rest of the world put together, Callias,[8] the son of Hipponicus, and knowing that he had sons, I asked him: "Callias," I said, "if your two sons had been born colts or calves, there would be no difficulty in finding someone to put in charge of them; we would hire a horse trainer, or a farmer probably, who would make them gentlemanly stallions or bulls, cultivated

b in the appropriate virtue and excellence; but seeing that they are human beings, whom are you thinking of putting in charge of them? Is there anyone who understands human and civic virtue? You must have thought about the matter, since you have sons; is there anyone, or not?" "There is," he said. "Who is he?" said I. "And of what country? And what does he charge?" "Evenus," he replied; "from Paros. Five minas." Blesséd is Evenus, I said to myself, if he really possesses this skill, and teaches at such a moderate charge. If I

c had his expertise, I would be very proud and conceited. But the truth is that I have no knowledge of the kind.

Now perhaps someone might object, "Yes, Socrates, but what *do* you do? Where do these accusations that are brought against you come from? You must have been doing *something* exceptional. All these rumors and this talk about you would never have arisen if you were like other men. Tell us, then, what is the cause of them, for we don't want

d to judge you too hastily." Now I regard this as a fair challenge, and I will try to explain to you what has conferred upon me the name "wise" and incurred the slander against me. Please listen. And although some of you may think that I am joking, I assure you that I will tell you nothing but the truth.

[8]At whose house the *Protagoras* takes place; again, see above on the Dramatis Personae of that work.

Men of Athens, this reputation of mine has resulted from nothing but a certain sort of wisdom that I possess. What kind of wisdom? The kind that may perhaps be attained by man, for in that I am inclined to believe that I really am wise; whereas the people of whom I was just speaking have a kind of superhuman wisdom, which I do ᵉ not know how to describe, because I don't have it myself; and anyone who says that I have is a liar, and says this to slander me. And now, men of Athens, I beg you not to cry out in protest at me, even if I should now say something that seems boastful. And so I will disown in advance the story that I am about to relate to you, and will refer it to its teller, a figure deserving of your credit. That witness will be the god of Delphi—he will tell you about my wisdom, if I actually have any, and what sort it is. For you all must have known Chaerephon; he was my friend from boyhood, 21 and also yours, for he shared in the recent exile of the people, and returned with you.[9] Well, Chaerephon, as you know, was very impetuous in all his doings, and he went to Delphi and actually had the nerve to ask the oracle to tell him whether—as I was saying, I must ask you not to interrupt—he actually asked the oracle to tell him whether anyone was wiser than me, and the Pythian prophetess answered that there was no man wiser. Chaerephon himself is dead, but his brother, who is in court, will confirm the truth of what I am saying.

Why do I mention this? Because I am trying to explain ᵇ to you the source of my bad reputation. When I heard the oracle's answer, I said to myself, "What on earth can the

[9]For a short time during the period following Athens' defeat by Sparta in 404 B.C., a brutal oligarchy, called "The Thirty," ruled the city, and many of its democratic opponents ("the people" Socrates refers to here) went into exile. The exiles returned, and the democracy was restored in 403.

god mean? And what is the interpretation of his riddle? For I know that I have no wisdom, great or small. What then can he mean when he says that I am the wisest of men? For surely he is not lying—that is not an option available to a god." For a long time I puzzled over what he meant. Finally, with great reluctance, I brought myself to look into the matter in the following way: I approached one of those people who had a reputation for wisdom, thinking that

c here, if anywhere, I would refute the oracle and prove to it that "Here is a man who is wiser than I am, but you said that I was the wisest." So I went and started examining this man—I don't need to mention his name, but it was one of the politicians, men of Athens, who made this impression on me when I was examining him—and while talking with him, I could not help thinking that he was not really wise, although he was thought wise by many, and by himself still wiser; and thereupon I tried to explain to him that he thought himself wise, but in fact was not; and the conse-

d quence was that he hated me, and his enmity was shared by many who were present and heard me. So I left, saying to myself as I went away: "Well, although I do not suppose that either of us knows anything really worth knowing, I am at least wiser than this fellow—for he knows nothing, and thinks that he knows; I neither know nor think that I know. In this one little point, then, I seem to have the advantage over him." Then I went to another who had even higher pretensions to wisdom, and my conclusion was exactly the same. Whereupon I became hateful to him, and to

e many others besides him.

Then I started approaching one man after another, being not unconscious of the enmity I provoked, and I lamented and feared this; but nevertheless it seemed to me absolutely necessary that I make the business of the god my first priority. And I said to myself, "I must approach everyone who appears to possess knowledge of anything, and find out the meaning of the oracle." And by the dog[10]   22 I swear to you, Athenians—for I must tell you the truth— the result of my mission, instigated by the god, was this: I found that the men with the highest reputations were just about the most foolish; and that others of far humbler status were, by the standard of intelligence, in fact superior. I will tell you the tale of my wanderings and of the "Herculean" labors, as I may call them, which I endured only to find the oracle, at last, irrefutable. After the politicians, I went to the poets; tragic, dithyrambic, and all sorts. "And   b there," I said to myself, "you will be instantly detected; now you will find out that you are more ignorant than they are." Accordingly, I took them some of what seemed to me the most painstakingly wrought passages in their own writings, and asked what was the meaning of them—thinking that I would at the same time learn something from them. Would you believe it? I am ashamed to confess the truth, but it must be told. There was hardly a person present who would not have talked better about their poetry than they did themselves—the very people who composed it. So I soon learned this in turn about poets, namely, that they do not write poetry through wisdom, but by a sort of genius and inspiration; they are like diviners or soothsayers who   c also say many admirable things, but don't understand a word of what they say; it became clear to me that poets had just that kind of thing happen to them, too. I further observed that on the strength of their poetry they believed themselves to be the wisest of men in other things in which they were not wise. So I went away, conceiving myself to

[10]See note 6 to the *Phaedrus* above.

be superior to them in the same respect that I was superior to the politicians.

d At last I went to the artisans,[11] for I was conscious that I knew nothing at all, as I may say, and I was sure that they knew many admirable things; and here I was not mistaken, for they did know many things that I was ignorant of, and in this they certainly were wiser than I was. But I observed that even the good artisans fell into the same error as the poets—namely, that because they were expert workmen in their own crafts, they thought that they also knew all sorts of high matters, and this defect in them overshadowed e their wisdom; and therefore, I asked myself on behalf of the oracle whether I would prefer to be as I was, neither having their knowledge nor their ignorance, or to be like them in both; and I answered to myself and to the oracle that I was better off as I was.

23 This investigation has led to my having many enemies of the worst and most dangerous kind, and has given rise also to many slanders, including the name of "wise"; for my hearers always imagine that I myself possess whatever wisdom I prove others *not* to have. But the truth is, men of Athens, that the god alone is wise; and by his oracular response he intends to show that the wisdom of men is worth little or nothing; although speaking of this Socrates, he is b only using my name by way of illustration, as if he said, "That person, O mankind, is the wisest, who, like Socrates, knows that his wisdom is in truth worth nothing." And this is why I wander around, obedient to the god, and search and make inquiry into the wisdom of anyone, whether citizen or stranger, who appears to be wise; and if he is not

---

[11]Literally "handworkers," which in Greek would comprise everything from a ditchdigger to a sculptor or painter.

wise, then in vindication of the god I show him that he is not wise; and my occupation completely absorbs me, and I have had no time to do anything useful in either public affairs or any concern of my own, but I am in utter poverty by reason of my servitude to the god.   c

There is another thing. Young men of the richer classes, who do not have much to do, follow me around of their own accord; they like to hear people cross-examined, and they often imitate me, and proceed to do some cross-examining themselves; there are plenty of people, as they quickly discover, who think that they know something, but really know little or nothing; and then those who are examined by them, instead of being angry with themselves, are angry with me: "This damned Socrates," they say; "this d villainous misleader of youth!" And then, if somebody asks them, "Why, how does he mislead them? What evil does he practice or teach?" they do not know and cannot tell; but in order that they not appear to be at a loss, they repeat the ready-made charges that are used against all philosophers, about how they teach things up in the clouds and under the earth, and have no gods, and make the worse argument appear the better; for these people do not like to admit the truth, that they have been exposed as pretending to possess knowledge, while knowing nothing in fact. And because they are prideful, and vehement, and numerous, they talk e about me energetically and persuasively, and they have filled your ears with their loud and inveterate calumnies. And it is on the strength of this that my three accusers, Meletus and Anytus and Lycon, have set upon me: Meletus has a quarrel with me on behalf of the poets; Anytus, on behalf of the craftsmen and politicians; Lycon, on behalf of the speakers in the assembly: and as I said at the be- 24 ginning, I cannot expect to get rid of such a mass of slander all in one moment. And this, men of Athens, is the truth and the whole truth; I have concealed nothing. I have dissembled nothing. And yet, I feel sure that my plainness of speech is fanning their hatred of me, and what is their hatred but a proof that I am speaking the truth? Here is the source of the prejudice against me; and this is the reason b for it, as you will find out in either this or any future inquiry.

I have said enough in my defense against the first class of my accusers; I turn to the second class. They are headed by Meletus, that good man and true lover of his country, as he himself tells us. Against these, too, I must try to make a defense. So again, as if this were an entirely new prosecution, let us take up their affadavit, as we took up the earlier one. It contains something of this kind: it says that Socrates is guilty of corrupting the young, and of not worshiping c the gods whom the state worships, but religious novelties instead. Such is the charge; and now let us examine the particular counts. He says that I am guilty of corrupting the young; but I say, men of Athens, that Meletus is the guilty one, in that he is making a game out of a serious matter, frivolously bringing people to trial from an affected zeal and interest about matters in which he never really had the slightest interest. And the truth of this I will try to prove to you.[12]

Come, Meletus, and be so kind as to speak. Is it not the case that you attach great importance to the improvement d of youth?

Yes, I do.

---

[12]Athenian law permitted the parties to a case to cross-examine each other, and demanded that the examinee respond, as Socrates will point out later on when Meletus resists answering.

Tell the jurors, then, who is their improver; for you must know, since you take such interest in the subject, and have discovered their corrupter, as you say, and are citing and accusing me in this court. Speak, then, and tell the judges who is the improver of youth. .... Observe, Meletus, that you are silent, and have nothing to say. But isn't this disgraceful in your view, and a sufficient proof of what I was saying, that you have no interest in the matter? Speak up, friend, and tell us who their improver is.

The laws.

But that, my good sir, is not my question: Can't you e name some person—whose first qualification will be that he knows the laws?

The jurors, Socrates, who are present here in court.

What do you mean, Meletus—that these men here are able to instruct and improve youth?

Certainly they are.

What, all of them, or only some and not others?

All of them.

Truly, that is good news, by Hera! There are plenty of improvers, then. And what do you say of the audience—do they improve them?   25

Yes, they do.

And the members of the Council?[13]

Yes, the members of the Council.

But perhaps the members of the Assembly corrupt them? Or do they too improve them?

They improve them.

Then every Athenian improves and elevates them, all

[13]In Athens a body of five hundred citizens, chosen annually by lot, charged with general administration of the state and specifically with preparing matters for consideration by the sovereign Assembly (comprising all adult male citizens).

with the exception of me; and I alone am their corrupter? Is that what you claim?

That is what I strongly claim.

I am very unfortunate if you are right. But suppose I ask you a question: Is it the same with horses? Does one man
b do them harm and all the world good? Isn't the exact opposite the case? One man is able to do them good, or at least very few—the trainer of the horses, that is to say, does them good, but the ordinary man does them harm if he has anything to do with them? Isn't that true, Meletus, of horses, or of any other animals? Most certainly it is; whether you and Anytus say so or not. Bléssed indeed must be the condition of the young if they have only one corrupter, and all the rest of mankind are their benefactors.
c But you, Meletus, have adequately shown that you never gave one thought to the young: your indifference is seen plainly in your not caring about the very matters on which you bring me to court.

And now, Meletus, by god, I adjure you to answer me another question: Which is better, to live among bad citizens, or among good ones? Answer, my good sir, I say; the question I am asking is not a hard one. Don't the good do their neighbors good, and the bad do them evil?

Certainly.

d And is there anyone who would rather be injured than benefited by those who live with him? Answer, my good friend, the law requires you to answer—does anyone like to be injured?

Certainly not.

And when you accuse me of corrupting and deteriorating the youth, do you allege that I corrupt them intentionally or unintentionally?

Intentionally, I say.

Well *really*, Meletus. Are you at your age so much wiser than I am at mine, that while you have come to see that the evil always do evil to those closest to them, and the good, good, I, on the other hand, have fallen into such an abyss of e ignorance that I don't even know, if a man with whom I have to live is corrupted by me, I am very likely to be harmed by him—so that, since I don't know this, I go ahead and corrupt him, and do it intentionally, too?—at least, that's what you say, although neither I nor any other human being is ever likely to be convinced by you. But in fact either I do not corrupt them, or I corrupt them unin- 26 tentionally; and on either view of the case you lie. If my offense is unintentional, the law has no cognizance of un- intentional offenses: you ought to have taken me privately, and warned and admonished me; for clearly if I had had instruction, I would have left off doing what I did only un- intentionally; but you would have nothing to do with me and refused to teach me. And now you bring me up in this court, which is a place not of instruction, but of punish- ment.

It will be very clear to you, Athenians, as I was saying, that Meletus has never had any concern, great or small, b about the matter. But still I would like to know, Meletus, in what way I am claimed by you to corrupt the young. I sup- pose you mean, as I infer from your indictment, that I teach them not to worship the gods which the state wor- ships, but some religious novelties instead. These are the teachings by which I corrupt the young, according to you?

Yes, I say that emphatically.

Then, by the gods, Meletus, of whom we are speaking, tell me and the court, in somewhat clearer terms, what you mean. For I do not as yet understand whether you claim c that I teach them to worship some gods, and therefore that

I do believe in gods, and am not a complete atheist (and am therefore not guilty of this, at least)—but you say that they are not the same gods that the city recognizes—the charge is that they are different gods. Or do you mean that I simply do not worship gods at all, and teach this to the rest?

I mean the latter—that you are a complete atheist.

d   What an amazing statement! Why do you think so, Meletus? Do you mean that I do not believe that even the sun or moon are gods, as the rest of mankind does?

I assure you, judges, that he does not: for he says that the sun is stone and the moon earth.

My dear Meletus, do you think you are prosecuting Anaxagoras? Have you such a low opinion of the judges—do you think them so illiterate as not to know that these doctrines are found in the book of Anaxagoras the Clazomenian, which is bursting with them?[14] And so, indeed, the youth are said to be taught them by Socrates, when they can sometimes be bought in the book-market for one

e   drachma at most; and they can pay their money, and laugh at Socrates if he pretends that these extraordinary views are his own. But for god's sake, Meletus, do you really think that I do not believe in any god at all?

I swear by Zeus that you really believe in none at all.

Nobody will believe you, Meletus, and I am pretty sure that you do not even believe yourself. I cannot help thinking, men of Athens, that Meletus is reckless and lacking in self-control, and that he has brought this indictment in a

---

[14]Anaxagoras was an Ionian philosopher who came to Athens in the mid-fifth century B.C.; he enjoyed the friendship of Pericles, among others. He is said to have been prosecuted, like Socrates, on a charge of impiety, and driven out of Athens. (But some recent scholars have doubted the evidence for this.) He died around 428, almost thirty years before Socrates' trial. He did indeed propose that the sun was a red-hot stone, the size of the Peloponnese.

spirit of pure wantonness and youthful bravado. Doesn't he seem like someone who has composed a riddle, hoping to test me? He said to himself: "I will see whether the wise Socrates will discover my amusing paradox, or whether I will be able to deceive him and the rest of them." For he certainly does appear to me to contradict himself in the indictment as much as if he said that "Socrates violates the law by *not* believing in the gods, but by *believing* in them"— but this is not the work of a person who is serious.

I would like you, men of Athens, to join me in examining what I conceive to be his inconsistency; and you, Meletus, please answer. I must remind the audience of my request that they not make a disturbance if I speak in my accustomed manner:

Did any human being, Meletus, ever believe in the existence of human things, and not of human beings? . . . I wish, men of Athens, that he would answer, and not always be trying to make these random and sundry objections. Did anyone ever believe in horsemanship, and not in horses? Or in flute-playing, and not in flute players? My noble friend, no one ever did; I answer to you and to the court, since you refuse to answer for yourself. But now please answer the next question: Can a man believe in the existence of spiritual and divine things, and not in spirits or demigods?[15]

<hr>

[15]"Spiritual and divine things"—this translates the Greek word *daimonia*, a form of the adjective derived from the noun *daimon*, from which comes the English "demon." Greek *daimon* designates a supernatural being, and can be applied to even the great Olympian gods, though it is used more typically of various entities approximately intermediate between gods and mortals. But the related adjective, which we have in the text here, is of very broad application, at times meaning something like (1) "having to do with religion," in which sense it seems to have been used in Meletus' indictment of Socrates in the phrase *daimonia kaina* (*kaina* = "new, novel"), translated earlier as "religious novelties." In other uses the

He cannot.

What a kindness you have done me in answering!—albeit reluctantly, and under the compulsion of the court. But then you swear in the indictment that I teach and believe in divine or spiritual things (novelties or not—it doesn't matter); at any rate, I believe in spiritual things— so you say and swear in the affidavit; and yet if I believe in them, it is entirely necessary that I believe there to be spirits or demigods—isn't that so? ... I assume you agree, since you don't answer. Now what are spirits or demigods? Are they not either gods or the sons of gods?

Certainly they are.

Then if I believe in spirits and demigods, as you say I do, granting that spirits and demigods are in fact gods of a kind, then this would be precisely what I am calling that amusing paradox dreamed up by you—that you say that I,

---

adjective *daimonios* means (2) "divine" in contrast to "human." Jowett's translation formula, "spiritual and divine," which I have here (but not everywhere) preserved, is designed to represent the argument Socrates is now making against Meletus, which assumes, or pretends to assume, that Meletus used the word in the indictment in meaning (2); Socrates argues now that belief in the existence of "spiritual and divine things" (the plural adjective *daimonia*) implies belief in the existence of "spirits and demigods," which is Jowett's translation for the plural of the noun *daimon*. This whole matter is dramatically complicated by the use in this work and elsewhere of the adjective *daimonios* to specify the so-called divine sign, or voice that Socrates was privileged to hear throughout his life, as he relates later in the text. Was Meletus aiming at this specific "daimonic thing" *(daimonion)* in his indictment? It seems more likely that he was not, but meant to say that the tendency of Socrates' intellectual activity was to put into doubt, disrupt, and supersede the traditional religious assumptions and practices of the city; the innovatory aspect of this supersession he specified as "religious novelties." But his use in this last phrase of the adjective *daimonios* opened up the possibility that he had the "divine sign" in mind, or had it in mind *also*. Given the complexity of the word and the issues surrounding it, I have sometimes indicated its occurrences with a parenthetical "*(daimon)*" or "*(daimonion)*," etc., placed after the English word used to translate it.

while not believing in gods, in turn believe in gods, that is, if I believe in demigods (*daimons*). For if the demigods are the illegitimate sons of gods, whether by Nymphs, or by other mothers, as some are said to be—what human being will ever believe that there are no gods when there are sons of gods? You might as well affirm the existence of mules, e and deny that of horses and asses. Such nonsense, Meletus, could only have been intended by you to make trial of us. Or else you put this into the indictment because you could think of nothing real to accuse me of. But no one who has a particle of understanding will ever be convinced by you that a man can believe in the existence of things divine and superhuman, and at the same time refuse to believe in gods 28 and demigods and heroes.

I have said enough in answer to the charge of Meletus: any elaborate defense is unnecessary. You know well the truth of my earlier statement that I have incurred many violent enmities; and this is what will be my destruction if I am destroyed—not Meletus, nor yet Anytus, but the envy and slander of the multitude, which has been the death of many good men, and will probably be the death of many b more; there is no danger of my being the last of them.

Perhaps someone will say: "Then aren't you ashamed, Socrates, of a course of life that is likely to bring you to an untimely end?" To him I may fairly answer: "There you are mistaken, fellow: a man who is good for anything ought not to calculate the chance of living or dying; he ought only to consider whether in doing anything he is doing right or wrong—acting the part of a good man or of a bad. Whereas, on your view, the heroes who fell at Troy were men of no account, and the son of Thetis above all,[16] who c

---

[16]I.e., Achilles.

altogether despised danger in comparison with disgrace; and when he was so eager to slay Hector, his goddess mother spoke to him somewhat as follows, I believe: "Child," she said, "if you go ahead and avenge the death of your friend Patroclus by killing Hector, you yourself will die; for Fate waits for you next after Hector." He, receiving this warning, utterly despised danger and death and, instead of fearing them, feared rather to live in dishonor, and

d not to avenge his friend. "Let me die forthwith," he replies, "And be avenged of my enemy, rather than abide here by the beaked ships, a laughing-stock and a burden on the earth."[17] Did Achilles have any thought of death and danger?

This is the truth of the matter, men of Athens: wherever a man's station is, whether he has chosen it himself in the belief that it is for the best, or he has been placed in it by a commander, there he must remain in the hour of danger, taking no account of death or of anything else in comparison with disgrace. And so my conduct would be strange indeed, men of Athens, if I who, when I was ordered by the

e generals whom you chose to command me at Potidaea and Amphipolis and Delium,[18] remained where they placed me, like any other man, and faced death—if now, when, as I have conceived it and imagined, the god is the one giving the orders, bidding me to fulfill the philosopher's mission of searching into myself and other men, I were to desert

29 my post through fear of death, or any other fear—that would indeed be strange, and I might justly be arraigned in court for denying the existence of the gods, if I disobeyed

[17]The conversation between Achilles and Thetis begins at *Iliad* 18. 94.

[18]Important Athenian battles, occurring in 432, 422, and 424 B.C., respectively. For a memorable and highly laudatory account of Socrates' comportment in battle and on campaign generally, see *Symposium* 219e–221c.

the oracle because I was afraid of death, thinking that I was wise when I was not wise. For to fear death is indeed to pretend to be wise when not, since it is to pretend to know what is unknown; and no one knows whether death, of which men are afraid because they consider it to be the greatest evil for a person, may not indeed be the greatest good. And yet is this not an ignorance of the most contemptible kind, the ignorance of thinking yourself to know what you don't know? And in this respect only do I believe myself to differ from men in general, and may perhaps claim to be wiser than they are: that whereas I know little of the world below, I do not suppose that I know; but I do know that injustice and disobedience to a better, whether a god or a man, is evil and dishonorable, and I will never fear or avoid a potential good rather than a guaranteed evil. And therefore if you let me go now, and are not convinced by Anytus, who said that since I had been prosecuted I must be put to death (or if not that, I ought never to have been prosecuted at all); and that if I am acquitted now, your sons will all be utterly ruined by practicing what I teach— if in response to that you should say to me, "Socrates, this time we will not obey Anytus, and you shall be let off, but on one condition, that you are not to engage in this quest, nor yet in philosophy, and that if you are caught doing so again you shall die"—if this were to be the condition on which you let me go, I would reply: Men of Athens, I care for and love you, but I shall obey the god rather than you, and while I have life and strength I shall *never* cease from the practice and teaching of philosophy, exhorting and expostulating with any one of you whom I meet and saying to him in my usual manner: "You, my friend—a citizen of the great city of Athens, famous for its culture and power—are you not ashamed of heaping up the largest

amount of money and status and reputation, and caring so
e little about wisdom and truth and improving as much as
possible your soul, which you never regard nor heed at all?"
And if some one of you disagrees and says that he does
care, then I will not leave him nor let him go at once, but
will interrogate and examine and cross-examine him, and
30 if I think that he has no virtue in him but only says that he
has, I shall reproach him with undervaluing what is most
precious, and overvaluing what is less. And I shall repeat
the same words to everyone whom I meet, young and old,
citizen and foreigner, but especially to you citizens, inasmuch as you are my brothers. For this is the command of
the god—know it well. And I believe that no greater good
has ever happened to you in this city than my service to the
god. For I do nothing but go about persuading you all, old
b and young alike, not to take thought for your person or
your property, but first and foremost to take care of your
soul, that it be as good as possible, saying, "Virtue is not
given by money, but from virtue comes money and every
other human good, public as well as private." This is my
teaching, and if it corrupts the young, it is pernicious; but
if anyone says that this is not my teaching, he is talking
rubbish. Wherefore, men of Athens, I say to you, do as
Anytus bids or don't do as Anytus bids, and either acquit
c me or not; but whichever you do, understand that I shall
never alter my ways, not even if I have to die many times.

Men of Athens, please abide by my earlier request that
you not cry out and interrupt what I say, but listen to it; for
in my opinion, you will profit from hearing it. I ask this because I am now going to say something else to you at which
you may be inclined to cry out; but don't do it.

And what I say is this: Know it well, that if you kill such
a one as I say I am, you will injure yourselves more than

you will injure me. Nothing will injure me, not Meletus nor yet Anytus—they cannot, for it is not given to a bad d man to be able to injure a man better than himself. I do not deny that Anytus may, perhaps, kill him, or drive him into exile, or deprive him of his civil rights; and he may imagine, and others may imagine, that he is inflicting a great injury upon him: but there I do not agree. For the evil of doing as he is doing—the evil of seeking unjustly to take the life of another—is greater by far.

And now, Athenians, I am not going to argue for my own sake, as you may think, but for yours, that you may not sin against the gift of the god by condemning me. For if you e kill me you will not easily find a successor to me, who, if I may use such a ludicrous figure of speech, am a sort of gadfly, settled on the city by the god; and the city is a great and noble steed who is sluggish in his movements, owing to his great size, and needs to be stirred into life. I am that gadfly which the god has attached to the city, and all day long and in all places I never stop landing on you, arousing and persuading and reproaching each one. You will not 31 easily find another like me, and therefore I would advise you to spare me. I daresay that you may feel angry (like a person who is suddenly awakened from sleep) and think that you might easily swat me dead, as Anytus advises, and then you could sleep on for the remainder of your lives, unless the god in his care for you sent you another gadfly. When I say that I am given to you by the god, the proof is this: if I had been like other men, I would not have ne- b glected all my own concerns or tolerated the neglect of them during all these years, and been looking after your interests constantly, coming to you individually like a father or elder brother, exhorting you to concern yourselves with virtue; such behavior, I say, would be not characteristic of human nature. If I gained anything from it, or if my exhortations were paid, there would be some sense in my doing so; but now, as you see for yourselves, not even the unfailing impudence of my accusers dares to say that I

c have ever exacted or sought pay from anyone; of that they can produce no witnesses. And I have a sufficient witness to the truth of what I say—my poverty.

Now perhaps it might strike someone as strange that I go about in private giving advice and concerning myself with other people's business, but do not dare in the public interest to come forward in the Assembly and advise the state. I will tell you why I don't. The reason is that which you have often heard me mention in many circumstances, namely, that something divine and supernatural (*daimo-*

d *nion*) happens to me—precisely the phenomenon that Meletus makes a joke of in the indictment. This sign, which comes as a kind of voice, first began for me when I was a child; whenever it comes, it always forbids me to do whatever I am about to do, but never makes any positive commands. This is what prevents me from being a politician. And, as I think, it does so altogether rightly. For I am certain, men of Athens, that if I had engaged in politics, I would have perished long ago, and done no good either for

e you or for myself. And do not be offended at my telling you the truth: for the truth is that no man who sets himself firmly against you or any other multitude, honestly striving to keep the state from many lawless and unrighteous deeds, will survive; rather, it is obligatory for the person

32 who truly fights for the right, if he hopes to survive for even a brief space, to operate in private, and not occupy a public station.

I can give you convincing evidence of what I say, not words only, but what you value far more—actions. Let me relate to you a passage of my own life which will prove to you that I would not from a fear of death yield to any man if that meant contravening justice—even though for not yielding I should perish on the spot. The story I have to tell you is a commonplace sort of courtroom boast, but it happens in my case to be true. The only office of state that I ever held, men of Athens, was that of councilman: the tribe b Antiochis, which is my tribe, happened to have the prytany[19] at the time when you[20] wanted to try the generals who had not recovered the bodies of the slain after the battle of Arginusae,[21] and wanted to try them as a group, contrary to law, as you all decided afterward;[22] but at the time I was the only one of the presiding officers who opposed your illegality, and I voted against you; and when the political leaders threatened to impeach and arrest me on the spot, and you were urging them with shouts and cries to do so, I made up my mind that I preferred to be on the side of law and justice and run this risk, rather than to align myself c with you, because I feared imprisonment and death, when you were urging injustice.

[19]The Athenian citizenry was organized into ten "tribes"; the five-hundred-member Council (see note 13) was constituted of ten groups of fifty men chosen by lot from each tribe; each of these ten tribal groups of councilmen held the prytany or presidency of the Council for one of the Athenian year's ten months.

[20]Socrates addresses the jury as representative members of the Assembly.

[21]The site (off the northwestern Asia Minor coast) of an enormous naval battle between Athens and Sparta in 406 B.C. The Athenians won the battle, but some of their dead were not picked up after it, when a storm arose. The outrage this failure incurred led to the illegal mass trial of the commanding officers Socrates discusses here.

[22]That is, the Assembly shortly afterward repented of its decision (but too late for those of the generals who had come to trial and been put to death) and demanded that the men who had "misled" it, i.e., led the move to try the generals en masse, be themselves brought to trial. The impetuosity and fickleness of the direct (i.e., nonrepresentative) popular democratic government led people like Plato to despise it.

This happened in the days of the democracy. But when the oligarchy of The Thirty was in power, they summoned me and four others into the rotunda,[23] and ordered us to bring Leon the Salaminian from Salamis, as they wanted to put him to death.[24] This command was a specimen of the sort that they were always giving with the view of implicating as many as possible in their crimes; and then I showed again, not only in word but in deed, that, if I may be allowed to use such an expression, I don't give a damn about death, and that my great and sole concern is that I not commit any unrighteous or impious deed. For that regime, though it was so brutal and harsh, did not frighten me into doing wrong; and when we came out of the rotunda, the other four went to Salamis and fetched Leon, but I went home.[25] For which I might have lost my life, had not the power of The Thirty shortly afterward come to an end. And many will bear witness to my words.

Now do you really imagine that I could have survived all these years if I had led a public life, and, conducting it in a manner worthy of a good man, I had always sought to defend justice from attack and had made it, as I ought, my first concern? No indeed, men of Athens, neither I nor any other man. But I will be found to have been always the

[23]The so-called *tholos*, or beehive-shaped building, in Athens, which served as, in effect, the seat of government under the democracy, and was appropriated by The Thirty during their regime.

[24]Not much else is known of Leon, but this episode was quite notorious, and seems to have contributed significantly to the regime's downfall.

[25]Other evidence we have about this event raises the possibility that one of "the other four" was none other than Meletus, the chief prosecutor of Socrates, examined by Socrates earlier in the speech. If that was so, Socrates' failure to mention the fact here is extraordinary. On the other hand, if Meletus' involvement was common knowledge, the impact of Socrates' forebearance, while all eyes in the courtroom bored in on Meletus, and of the implicit contrast with Socrates' own behavior, must have been overwhelming.

same in all my actions, public as well as private, and never
to have made any concession against justice, either to those
whom my slanderers call my disciples, or to any other. In
point of fact I have never been anybody's teacher. But if
anyone desires to come and listen to me while I am pursuing my mission, whether young or old, I have never be-
grudged it. Nor do I converse with people who pay me and
not with those who don't, but I make myself available for   b
questioning to anyone, rich or poor, and likewise if someone wishes to be the answerer and let me do the questioning. And whether he turns out to be a bad man or a good
one, neither result can be justly imputed to me; for I never
taught nor professed to teach anything. And if anyone says
that he has ever learned or heard anything from me in private which all the world has not heard also, let me tell you
that he is lying.

But I shall be asked, "Why on earth do these people
enjoy conversing with you so much?" You have already
heard the answer, Athenians; I told the whole truth about   c
this matter: they like to hear the cross-examination of
people who pretend to be wise, but aren't. After all, it's
amusing. But for my part, I assure you, this duty of cross-
examining other men has been imposed upon me by the
god; and has been signified to me by oracles, dreams, and
in any way in which divine providence has ever imposed
on a human a task to perform. This is true, Athenians; and
if it is not true, it can easily be disproved. For if I really am
or have been corrupting the young, those of them who are   d
now grown up and have come to realize that I gave them
bad advice in the days of their youth should of course
come forward as accusers, and take their revenge; or if they
do not want to come themselves, then some of their relatives, fathers, brothers, or other kinsmen should call to

mind the evil their families have suffered at my hands. At any rate, I see that many of them are here in my support. There is Crito,[26] who is of the same age and of the same
e deme with myself, and father of Critobulus here. Then again there is Lysanias of Sphettus, who is the father of Aeschines[27]—he is present; and also there is Antiphon of Cephisus, who is the father of Epigenes;[28] and there are the brothers of several who have associated with me in my mission. There is Nicostratus the son of Theozotides, and the brother of Theodotus (Theodotus himself is dead, and therefore he, at any rate, will not try to stop him);[29] and here is Paralus the son of Demodocus, who had a brother,
34 Theages;[30] and Adeimantus the son of Ariston, whose brother Plato is present;[31] and Aeantodorus, who is the brother of Apollodorus,[32] whom I also see. I might mention a great many others, at least one of whom Meletus should have produced as a witness, preferably in the course of his speech; but let him still produce them, if he simply forgot to—I will yield the floor to him. And let him say if he has

[26]After whom the dialogue *Crito* is named. His son Critobulus was something of a ne'er-do-well.

[27]Like Plato, this Aeschines wrote Socratic dialogues, some fragments of which survive.

[28]Little is known of this pair.

[29]Theozotides was an eminent leader of the democratic, i.e., anti-oligarchical faction.

[30]Another prominent family; the dialogue *Theages*, which may or may not have been written by Plato, shows Demodocus introducing his son to Socrates, and their conversation about education.

[31]Plato depicted his two brothers, Adeimantus and Glaucon, in extended conversation with Socrates in the *Republic.* It would appear that Plato was considerably younger than Adeimantus.

[32]This Apollodorus, who was present at the death of Socrates (as described in Plato's *Phaedo*), on which occasion his extravagant lamentation and weeping won disapproving notice, is the narrator of the *Symposium.*

any testimony of this sort that he can produce. But you will find, Athenians, that the very opposite is the truth. For all these are ready to bear witness on behalf of me, their corrupter, the injurer of their kindred, as Meletus and Anytus call me; not the corrupted youth only—there b might have been a motive for that—but their uncorrupted older relatives. Why should they come to defend me with their testimony? Why, indeed, except for the sake of truth and justice, and because they know that I am speaking the truth, and that Meletus is a liar.

Well, Athenians, this and the like of this is all the defense which I have to offer. Yet a word more. Perhaps there may be someone who is offended at me, when he calls to mind how he himself on a similar, or even a less serious oc- c casion, begged and entreated the judges with many tears, and how he brought his children up to the stand to excite as much pity as possible, together with a mass of relations and friends, whereas I, who am in danger of my life, as it might appear to him, will do none of these things. The contrast may occur to his mind, and he may take against me and vote in anger because he is displeased with me on this account. Now if there is such a person among you— d mind you, I doubt that there is, but just in case—to him I offer a suitable reply: My friend, I *do* have a family, and that saying of Homer's applies to me, also—I too am not made "of wood or stone,"[33] but was born of human stock, so that, yes, I have a family, and sons, O Athenians, three of them, one a young man, and two who are little children. But nevertheless, I will not bring any of them in here to beg you to acquit me. And why will I not do any of these things? Not out of arrogance or lack of respect for you, Athenians. And

[33] *Odyssey* 19. 163.

e whether I am or am not afraid of death is another question, of which I will not now speak; but when I think of my own good name, and yours, and that of the whole city, I feel that such conduct would be discreditable. A person who has reached my years, and has the name I have, ought not to demean himself. Whether this opinion of me is deserved

35 or not—at any rate the world has decided that Socrates surpasses the rest of mankind in some respect. And if those among you who are said to be exceptional for your wisdom, or courage, or any other virtue, are going to demean themselves in this way, it would be disgraceful. I have seen certain men behaving in this way while they were being tried, men who seemed to be of some substance, but there they were, doing the strangest things, as if they thought they were going to suffer something outrageous if they had to die, and that they would live forever if you spared them; and I think that such people bring dishonor to the city, and

b that any stranger coming in would have said of them that the most eminent men of Athens, whom the Athenians place before themselves in offices and honors, are no better than women. And I say this because these things ought not to be done by those of us who have a reputation in any walk of life; and if we try to do them, you ought not to permit it; you ought rather to show that you are far more disposed to condemn the man who enacts these piteous dramas, and makes the city contemptible, than him who maintains his dignity.

But, setting aside the question of honor, there seems to

c be something wrong in asking a favor of a judge, and thus procuring an acquittal, instead of informing and convincing him. For his duty is not to make a present of justice, but to give judgment; and he has sworn that he will judge according to the laws, and not grant favors to whomever it appeals to him to; and we ought not to encourage you, nor should you allow yourselves to be encouraged, in this habit of departing from your oath—for otherwise neither of us would be righteous. Do not then expect me to do what I consider dishonorable and impious and wrong, especially d now, when it is on a charge of impiety that I am being prosecuted by Meletus. For if, by force of persuasion and entreaty, I tried to overpower your oaths, then I would be teaching you to believe that there are no gods, and in making my defense would literally prove myself to be guilty of not believing in them. But that is not so—far from it. For I do believe that there are gods, and in a sense higher than that in which any of my accusers believe in them. And to you and to the god I commit my case, to be determined as is best for you and me.

SECOND SPEECH

By Athenian legal procedure, the jury voted immediately, and the votes were immediately tallied. Socrates was found guilty by a vote of, as it would appear, 280 to 220. No penalty was prescribed by law; rather, the two parties to the suit were next called upon to propose penalties, and the jury then to choose between them. Meletus proposed a penalty of death; Socrates is now called upon to make a counterproposal. A prudent defendant in Socrates' position would probably propose exile, since, as Socrates himself points out, the jury might well accept that in place of the death sentence.

35e   There are many reasons why I am not aggrieved, men of Athens, at the vote of condemnation. I expected it, and am
36 only surprised that the votes are so nearly equal; for I had thought that the majority against me would have been far larger; but now, as it seems, had thirty votes gone over to the other side, I would have been acquitted. And I may say, I think, that I have escaped Meletus. I may say more; for without the assistance of Anytus and Lycon, anyone can see that he would not have had a fifth of the votes, as the

law requires, in which case he would have incurred a fine b
of a thousand drachmas.[34]

And so he proposes death as the penalty. Well. And what
shall I propose on my part, men of Athens? Clearly something I deserve. And what would that be? What ought I to
have done to me, or to pay—a man who has never had the
wit to keep quiet during his whole life, but has been careless of what the majority cares for—commerce, and tend-
ing to their properties, and military offices, and speaking in
the assembly, and magistracies, and conspiracies, and party
factions. Reflecting that I was really too honest a man to be c
a politician and live, I did not go where I could do no good
to you or to myself; but where I could do privately the
greatest good (as I affirm it to be) to every one of you,
there I went, and sought to persuade every man among you
that he must attend to no business before he attends to
himself, seeing to it that he become as virtuous and wise as
possible, nor yet attend to the business of the city before he
had attended to the city itself; and that this should be the
order which he observes in all his actions. What, then, does d
such a one as I am deserve to have done to him? Something
good, men of Athens, if he is to get his due reward; and the
good should be tailored to be suitable to him. What would
be a reward suitable to a poor man who is your benefactor,
and who needs leisure to devote to instructing you? There
could be no reward more fitting for such a man than to be
given free meals in the Prytaneum for life, men of Athens,
a reward that he deserves far more than the citizen who has

---

[34]Socrates' reasoning here is not entirely perspicuous. It would appear that he
is affecting to regard the votes as constituting in effect the takings of the two
sides, with himself taking 220, and the three prosecutors divvying up 280 among
themselves; that would leave each with fewer than the 100 required by the law if
a fine is to be avoided (a requirement designed to discourage frivolous lawsuits).

won the prize at Olympia in the horse or chariot race, whether the chariots were drawn by two horses or by many. For I am in need of support, and the chariot racer already e has enough; and he only gives you the appearance of hap-37 piness, and I give you the reality.[35] And if I am to estimate the penalty fairly, I should say that meals in the Prytaneum is the just return.

Perhaps you think that I am displaying arrogance in what I am saying now, as in what I said before about the tears and the entreaties. But this is not so. Rather, I speak this way because I am convinced that I have never intentionally wronged anyone, although I cannot convince you—the time for our conversation has been too short; if there were a law at Athens, as there is in other cities, that a capital case should not be decided in one day, then I beb lieve that I would have convinced you. But as it is, it is not easy to clear my name of great slanders in a brief time. Still, since I am convinced that I never wronged another, I will assuredly not wrong myself, nor say of myself that I deserve any evil, nor propose any penalty. Why should I? Because I am afraid of the penalty of death which Meletus proposes? When I do not know whether death is a good or an evil, why should I propose a penalty that would certainly be an evil? Shall I say imprisonment? And why c should I live in prison, and be the slave of the magistrates of the year—of The Eleven?[36] Or shall the penalty be a fine, and imprisonment until the fine is paid? There is the same objection, since I have no money with which to pay. But should I propose exile? For you might actually vote for

[35]Athenian citizens who won Olympic victories were rewarded by the city with meals for life. Chariot-racing was of course a pastime limited to the very rich.

[36]A board in charge of prisons, among other things.

that. But that would bespeak a great love of life in me, if I am so irrational as to expect that when you, who are my own fellow citizens, cannot endure my conversation and arguments, and have found them so unbearable and odious d that you are now seeking to be rid of them, others are likely to endure them. No indeed, men of Athens, that is not very likely. And what a life would I lead, at my age, wandering from city to city, constantly changing my place of exile, and always being driven out! For I am quite sure that wherever I go, there, as here, the young men will flock to listen to me; and if I drive them away, their elders will drive me out at their request; and if I let them come, their e fathers and friends will drive me out for their sakes.

Perhaps someone will say: "Yes, Socrates, but if you kept quietly to yourself—then wouldn't it be possible for you to go away and live in exile, with our blessing?" This is the hardest thing to get you to understand. For if I tell you that to do as you say would be disobedience to the god, and therefore that I cannot keep silent, you will not believe that 38 I am serious; and if I say again that to converse every day on the subject of virtue, and on those other things about which you hear me examining myself and others, is in fact the greatest good there can be for mortal man, and that the life without examination is no life for a human being, you are still less likely to believe me. But what I say is true, although it is hard for me to persuade you of it. What is more, I have never been accustomed to think that I deserve to suffer any harm. If I had money I would have proposed b a fine to the amount of whatever I was able to pay, since that would have done me no harm. But I have none, and therefore I must ask you to proportion the fine to my means. Well, perhaps I could afford a mina, and therefore I propose that penalty.

But look, men of Athens, Plato, and Crito, and Critobulus, and Apollodorus, my friends here, are telling me to propose thirty minas, and they will be the sureties. So let thirty minas be the penalty; for which sum they will be ample security to you.[37]

---

[37]A mina is slightly less than a pound of silver. Thirty minas would appear to have been a substantial sum of money, enough to pay a full-time unskilled laborer for about ten years, or to buy ten good horses.

THIRD SPEECH

The jury voted—reportedly by a larger majority than that with which it had rendered its original verdict—in favor of the death penalty proposed by Meletus. Socrates now makes some informal remarks to the jury before being led off to prison to await execution.

For the sake of not much time, Athenians, you will suffer ill repute and blame at the hands of those who wish to malign the city, who will say that you killed Socrates, a wise man; for they will call me wise, even though I am not wise, when they want to insult you. If you had waited a little while, your desire would have been fulfilled in the course of nature. For you can see that I am far advanced in years and not far from death. I am speaking now not to all of you, but only to those who have condemned me to death. And I have another thing to say to them: perhaps you think that I was convicted for lack of arguments of the sort that would have persuaded you—I mean, if I had thought fit to leave nothing undone or unsaid. Not so. I was indeed convicted by a lack, but not of arguments—rather, of brazen temerity, and impudence, and the inclination to address to you the kind of thing that would have been sweetest for you to hear from me, as I wept and wailed and lamented, and said and did many things of the kind that

e you have become accustomed to hear from others, but I maintain to be unworthy of myself. I thought at the time that I ought not to do anything illiberal or undignified when in danger; nor do I now repent of the style of my defense; I would rather die having spoken in my manner than live in the manner you like. For neither in war nor yet at law ought I or any man to try to bring it about that he es-

39 cape death at the price of consenting to do *anything*. Often in battle there can be no doubt that if a man will throw away his arms, and fall on his knees before his pursuers, he may escape death; and in other dangers there are other ways of escaping death, if a man has the shamelessness to say and do anything. The difficulty, my friends, is not to avoid death; it is much harder to avoid unrighteousness, for

b that runs faster than death. I am old and move slowly, and the slower runner has overtaken me; my accusers are keen and quick, and the faster runner, who is wickedness, has overtaken them. And now I depart from here condemned by you to suffer the penalty of death—they too go their ways condemned by the truth to suffer the penalty of villainy and wrong; and I must abide by my award—let them abide by theirs. I suppose that these things may be regarded as fated—and I think that they are fair.

c And now, O you who have condemned me, I wish to prophesy to you; for I am about to die, and in the hour of death, men are most endowed with prophetic power. And I prophesy to you who are my murderers that immediately after my departure, punishment far heavier than you have inflicted on me surely awaits you. Me, you have killed in the belief that you would thereby escape from giving an account of your lives. But just the opposite will happen, as I affirm: there will be more accusers of you than there are now; accusers whom hitherto I have restrained, but you did d not perceive it. And as they are younger, they will be more severe with you, and you will be more troubled by them. If you think that by killing men you will stop all censure of your evil lives, you are mistaken; that is not a way of escape which is either very possible or honorable; the easiest and the noblest way is not by disabling others, but by improving yourselves. This is the prophecy that I utter before my departure to the judges who have condemned me.

Friends, you who would have acquitted me, I would like e also to talk with you about the thing that has come to pass, while the magistrates are busy, and before I go to the place where I must die. Stay then a little, for we may as well talk with one another while there is time. You are my friends, 40 and I would like to show you the meaning of this event which has happened to me. I would like to tell you, my judges—for you I may truly call judges—about something amazing that has befallen me. Hitherto the warning sign which habitually comes to me from the divinity (*daimonion*) has throughout the past been very frequent, and opposed me even about trifles, if I was going to make a slip or error in any matter; and now, as you see, there has come upon me that which may plausibly be thought, and is generally believed to be, the last and worst evil. But the oracle made b no signs of opposition, either when I was leaving my house in the morning, or when I appeared in court, or while I was speaking, at anything that I was going to say; and yet it has often stopped me in the middle of saying something, but now in nothing I either said or did, touching the matter in hand, has the oracle opposed me. What do I take to be the explanation of this silence? I will tell you. It is an intimation that what has happened to me is a good, and therefore

c those of us who think that death is an evil must be in error. I have a powerful piece of evidence for this: the customary sign surely would have opposed me unless I had been embarking on something good to do.

Let us reflect in another way on the suggestion that there is great reason to hope that death is a good; for it is one of two things—either death is a state of nothingness and the dead man suffers utter unconsciousness, or, as men say, there is a change and migration of the soul from this world to another. Now if you suppose that in death there is no consciousness, but a sleep like the sleep of someone

d who is undisturbed even by dreams, death must be a marvelous improvement. For if a person were to select the night in which his sleep was undisturbed even by dreams, and were to compare with this the other days and nights of his life, and then were to tell us how many days and nights he had passed in the course of his life better and more pleasantly than this one, I think that any man, I will not say just a private man, but even the great king himself[38] will

e not find many such days or nights when compared with the others. Now if death is like that, then I say that to die is a gain; for eternity seems, then, to be no more than a single night. But if death is a journey from here to another place, and, as men say, all the dead are gathered there, what good,

---

[38]I.e., of Persia.

my friends and judges, could be greater than this? If indeed when the pilgrim arrives in the world below, delivered 41 from these men here who claim to be judges, and finds the true judges who are said to give judgment there, Minos and Rhadamanthys and Aeacus and Triptolemus,[39] and other demigods who were righteous in their own life, that pilgrimage would be worth making. What would a man not give to converse with Orpheus and Musaeus and Hesiod and Homer? No, if this is true, let me die again and again—since for me, especially, the entertainment there b would be particularly wonderful, meeting and conversing with Palamedes,[40] and Ajax the son of Telamon,[41] and any other ancient hero who suffered death through an unjust judgment; I would compare my experiences with theirs— which would be, as I imagine, quite enjoyable—and what is most important, I would be able to continue with my investigations, now scrutinizing the men there as I have those here, trying to find out who of them is wise, and who

[39]The first three are all sons of Zeus, the first two both by Europa, Aeacus by Aegina. Triptolemus would seem to be more of an Athenian figure, a legendary prince of Eleusis, the Attic town in which the Eleusinian Mysteries were based. All four were paradigms of the good king, and were famed for their justice and piety. Thus they were rewarded with judgeships in the afterlife.

[40]A legendarily clever and creative hero who was credited with inventing such useful things as writing and dice-playing as antidotes to boredom during the Trojan War; he was ultimately framed by Odysseus on a charge of treachery and stoned to death. Odysseus thereby acceded to the title of cleverest.

[41]The second greatest warrior of the Greek army at Troy, after Achilles. He too was done in by Odysseus: after Achilles' death it was decided to award his armor, made for him by the god Hephaestus, to the most valuable soldier, to be determined by vote. Odysseus, though inferior on the battlefield to Ajax, was able to argue that his contributions overall outweighed those of Ajax, and was awarded the armor. Ajax killed himself.

pretends to be wise, and is not. What would a man not give,
c judges, to be able to examine the leader of the great Trojan
expedition,[42] or Odysseus or Sisyphus,[43] or countless others, men and women whom it would be an overwhelming
happiness to converse with and question. In the other
world they do not put a man to death for asking questions—certainly not. For besides being happier than we
are, they are also immortal, if what is said is true.

Wherefore, judges, be optimistic about death, and con-
centrate all your thought on this one single truth, that no
d evil can happen to a good man, either in life or after death,
and that he and his are not neglected by the gods. Nor has
my own approaching end happened by mere chance; I see
clearly that the time had arrived when it was better for me
to die and be released from trouble; that is why the divine
sign did not deflect me, and for that reason also I am not at
all angry with my condemners, or with my accusers. But
although they have done me no harm, they intended to;
e and for this I may properly blame them.

Still, I have a favor to ask of them. When my sons are
grown up, I would ask you, gentlemen, to punish them;
please trouble them, as I have troubled you, if they seem to
care about riches, or anything, more than about virtue, or if
they pretend to be something when they are really nothing—then chastise them, as I have chastised you, for not

---

[42]I.e., Agamemnon—a curious choice, in that being, in Homer's rendering, a
rather coarse, brutal, and unreflective man, he does not seem to be Socrates'
type.

[43]Another legendarily clever figure of myth, said to have outwitted death itself—for a while, at any rate. His punishment, of having to roll up to the top of
a hill a great boulder, which always rolls back down just as the summit is approached, is observed by Odysseus in Hades in *Odyssey* 11. 593–600.

caring about what they ought to care about, and for thinking that they are something when they are really nothing.
And if you do this, I shall have received justice at your 42
hands, and so will my sons.

The hour of departure has arrived, and we go our
ways—I to die, and you to live. Which is the better the god
only knows.

A Note on the Type

The principal text of this Modern Library edition
was set in a digitized version of Janson,
a typeface that dates from about 1690 and was cut
by Nicholas Kis, a Hungarian working in Amsterdam.
The original matrices have survived and are held by the
Stempel foundry in Germany. Hermann Zapf redesigned
some of the weights and sizes for Stempel, basing his revisions
on the original design.

MODERN LIBRARY IS ONLINE AT
WWW.MODERNLIBRARY.COM

MODERN LIBRARY ONLINE IS YOUR GUIDE TO CLASSIC LITERATURE ON THE WEB

THE MODERN LIBRARY E-NEWSLETTER

Our free e-mail newsletter is sent to subscribers, and features sample chapters, interviews with and essays by our authors, upcoming books, special promotions, announcements, and news.

To subscribe to the Modern Library e-newsletter, send a blank e-mail to: **sub_modernlibrary@info.randomhouse.com** or visit **www.modernlibrary.com**

THE MODERN LIBRARY WEBSITE

Check out the Modern Library website at
www.modernlibrary.com for:

- The Modern Library e-newsletter
- A list of our current and upcoming titles and series
- Reading Group Guides and exclusive author spotlights
- Special features with information on the classics and other paperback series
- Excerpts from new releases and other titles
- A list of our e-books and information on where to buy them
- The Modern Library Editorial Board's 100 Best Novels and 100 Best Nonfiction Books of the Twentieth Century written in the English language
- News and announcements

Questions? E-mail us at **modernlibrary@randomhouse.com**.
For questions about examination or desk copies, please visit
the Random House Academic Resources site at
www.randomhouse.com/academic